The Compassionate Court?

Corey S. Shdaimah, Chrysanthi S. Leon,
and Shelly A. Wiechelt

The Compassionate Court?

Support, Surveillance, and Survival
in Prostitution Diversion Programs

TEMPLE UNIVERSITY PRESS
Philadelphia • *Rome* • *Tokyo*

TEMPLE UNIVERSITY PRESS
Philadelphia, Pennsylvania 19122
tupress.temple.edu

Library of Congress Cataloging-in-Publication Data

Names: Shdaimah, Corey S., author. | Leon, Chrysanthi S., author. |
  Wiechelt, Shelly A., author.
Title: The compassionate court? : support, surveillance, and survival in
  prostitution diversion programs / Corey S. Shdaimah, Chrysanthi S. Leon,
  and Shelly A. Wiechelt.
Description: Philadelphia : Temple University Press, 2023. | Includes
  bibliographical references and index. | Summary: "This book draws on
  interviews and observations from two court-affiliated prostitution
  diversion programs and a nonprofit agency following participants through
  court, prison, probation, programming, and returns to their lives. They
  compare the forces coercing women towards and away from sex work"—
  Provided by publisher.
Identifiers: LCCN 2022053639 (print) | LCCN 2022053640 (ebook) | ISBN
  9781439922002 (cloth) | ISBN 9781439922019 (paperback) | ISBN
  9781439922026 (pdf)
Subjects: LCSH: Prostitutes—Rehabilitation—United States. |
  Prostitutes—Services for—United States. | Social work with
  prostitutes—United States. | Prostitutes—United States—Case studies.
  | Prostitutes—Legal status, laws, etc.—United States. | Courts of
  special jurisdiction—United States.
Classification: LCC HQ314 .S533 2023 (print) | LCC HQ314 (ebook) | DDC
  306.740973—dc23/eng/20230321
LC record available at https://lccn.loc.gov/2022053639
LC ebook record available at https://lccn.loc.gov/2022053640

Printed in the United States of America

9 8 7 6 5 4 3 2 1

*We dedicate this book to all of the people
in Project Dawn Court and the Specialized Prostitution
Diversion Program who shared with us their stories,
their humor, and their recommendations.
We think of you often.*

Contents

Acknowledgments

We thank all the people in the study who shared their experiences and perspectives with us. We appreciate the individuals who contributed research assistance: Jonas Rosen, Mia Shelton, and Deborah Svoboda.

There are many ways to express truths. Francisca Moreno immediately understood what we wanted to convey in the "Sea of Coercion" and brought it beautifully to life in Figure 3.1. From our transcripts, Maggie Buckridge crafted I-poems and we-poems that respect the authority of our participants. Karen Hartman wrote the original play *Project Dawn* (2017), commissioned by the nationally renowned New Play Frontiers Residency at People's Light.

We thank all the people we've been in dialogue with from our first introduction to this area of research, including Michelle Bloothoofd and Sid Ford, as well all of those who have graciously provided feedback through reviews and conference proceedings, with special thanks to Theresa Anasti, Joan Blakey, Kate D'Adamo, Tali Gal, Daria Mueller, Jennifer Musto, and Hadar Dancig-Rosenberg, and to the Law & Society Association Collaborative Research Network on Sex, Work, Law and Society and organizers Menaka Raguparan, Angela Jones, Alex Nelson, Kathryn Hausbeck Korgan, and Raven Bowen.

Our thinking was challenged and enriched by the people with whom we have collaborated over more than a decade on various aspects of sex work and diversion: Marie Bailey-Kloch, Todd Becker, Aneesa Baboolal, Anne Bowler, Inbar Cohen, Eileen Corcoran, Nancy Franke, Nili Gesser, Katie Hail-Jares, James Highberger, Terry Glenn Lilley, Lauren Myers, Erin O'Brien, Kevin Ralston, and Corinne Schwarz.

The Compassionate Court?

Introduction

Prostitution Diversion Programs—
A New Paradigm or Business as Usual?

P roblem-solving courts reflect larger trends in the justice system. Sex work as a site of intervention adds another layer to diversion programs, as they are part of historical and pervasive surveillance and control of women, bodies, and sex. While other scholars and advocates debate the virtues of criminalization, legalization, or regulation of people who sell or buy sex or facilitate the sale of sex, this book examines a court system that is predicated on a legal regime where the sale of sex is criminal. This book looks at how criminal justice personnel respond to perceived tensions between criminal responses to prostitution and the needs of those who are charged with prostitution offenses,[1] and it centers the lived experiences of those who are most affected. Drawing on a rich ethnographic dataset that features over two dozen follow-up interviews spanning a decade, we reveal how program participants perceive court-affiliated prostitution diversion programs (PDPs) and the professionals who work within them and how both of these groups shape these programs and respond to their limitations.

Situating Prostitution Diversion Programs within Sex Work Debates

We acknowledge the important debates surrounding terminology. Our respondents do not self-identify either as sex workers or as people who are trafficked. Grounded in the lived experience of our respondents, we choose to use the term *prostitution* to reflect that it is about people who engage in sex work that is criminalized in the U.S. jurisdictions where we conducted our study. This terminology also reflects our respondents' focus on actions rather than identity. When we draw on literature or other studies, we use the designations those authors specify.

Increasingly, system professionals recognize that existing criminal legal system responses to the exchange of sex for money ineffectively and unfairly punish people for behaviors they would prefer to avoid—PDPs represent one system response (Wolf, 2001). Like the larger problem-solving justice movement of which they are a part, described in Chapter 1, PDPs are based on the notion that rehabilitation, through intensive services and supervision, changes offenders' behaviors and attitudes and reduces crimes. Reformers view prostitution as a particularly appropriate site for diversion programs because the perceived victimization experienced by those engaged in prostitution brings out many of the contradictions in traditional criminal justice models (Corrigan & Shdaimah, 2016). People selling sex in outdoor markets who are caught up in street sweeps or arrested in undercover sting operations, the chief targets of criminal prosecution, are likely to suffer from physical and mental health concerns, addiction, trauma, and violence both as a precursor to engagement in prostitution and on the job (Lewis, 2010; Weitzer, 2009; Wiechelt & Shdaimah, 2011). Legal system actors, who view them as victims as much as perpetrators, simultaneously use lenses of stigma and empathy. This perception may be enhanced by the lack of specific victims resulting from prostitution, which is usually viewed as harming the community rather than individuals (Shdaimah et al., 2014).

Sex work, trafficking, and prostitution are subjects that involve contested ideas about gender and sexuality, and therefore have been the subject of feminist analysis. Debates about sex work, trafficking, and prostitution are far too often characterized by approaches that deny a range of voices and that question the agency of those who are arguably most affected by policy and programs. Many feminist perspectives are polarized, such as the early "abolitionist" and "pro-sex" camps. Abolitionist feminism focuses on what it considers to be inherent harms of sexual exploitation, including pornography, as well as all forms of sex work (MacKinnon, 2004). Pro-sex feminism emphasizes the pleasures of sexuality free from coercion, as well as its economic potential when it is treated as legitimate work or a business enterprise (Vance, 1984). While many feminist researchers challenge polarized perspectives, polarization persists in current policy and advocacy debates around prostitution, trafficking, and sex work.

The framing of people charged with prostitution as victims is also influenced by narratives of sex trafficking, which pervade U.S. and global discussion about all forms of sexual labor in multiple ways. One way is the seemingly unreflective conflation of sex work and sex trafficking, which rejects an understanding of sex work as a legal and moral choice, or even as a form of what Showden (2011) refers to as "bounded agency" when it stems from constrained circumstances like other forms of stigmatized and risky labor (O'Brien, 2013; Parmanand, 2022). Those who see sex work as akin to, or a form of, trafficking or exploitation construct their ideas of intervention within a rescue narrative that requires what Jennifer Musto (2016) describes as carceral protection. Abolitionist feminists, for example, consider sex work exploitative of individual women and of women as a group (Powell, 2021), although others have pointed out that such stances in fact reinforce patriarchal control of women's bodies (Bateman, 2021). While trafficking and sex work abolitionist discourses may give rise to empathy (Shdaimah & Wiechelt, 2012a) and may even prompt calls to decriminalize some forms of sex work, the framework also assumes that exploitation makes women in the sex trade coerced targets in need of rescue and redemption (Gruber et al., 2016; Musto, 2016). PDPs are perfect examples of these rescue-and-punish, punish-to-rescue, and be-rescued-or-be-punished programs.

U.S. Exceptionalism? Think Again

The United States is often justifiably viewed as exceptionally moralizing, punitive, and carceral—generally, and specifically in relation to gender, sexuality, and sex work. We challenge our international readers and those who believe that the decriminalization of U.S. street-based sex work is close on the horizon to think critically about historical and future echoes in the surveillance and regulation of women and their bodies and to question how radical any pending changes can be. Economic precarity and vulnerability are central to PDPs.

Neoliberalism, with core facets of mass incarceration and a rise in precarity, has been enthusiastically embraced globally (Garrett, 2019). Global feminist scholars highlight the ways that "women's responsibility for reproductive work . . . is a structural feature of neoliberalism" (Radhakrishnan & Solari, 2015, p. 785). PDPs and other interventions into sex work and trafficking are recognizable neoliberal practices through their tendency to individualize, psychologize, and control through bureaucratic rationales and "accountability." Neoliberal interventions that seek to influence through internalization of the state (Foucault biopower) use pervasive surveillance. Problem-solving "help" continues to be realized and adapted to international context. At the culmination of a multiyear pilot program in six sites, Israel passed legislation creating a national program of community courts (Knesset,

2022). Quirouette et al. (2016) have documented how problem-solving courts in Canada use housing to extend the reach of neoliberal criminal legal systems as a tool for surveillance.

The current wave of global efforts to combat trafficking, including its calls for interruption of digital financial flows (European Commission, 2021), should be closely watched. For example, the European Sex Workers' Rights Alliance's description of their work in the area of legal reform raises many of the fundamental concerns—especially salient for street-based sex workers—which cut across the variety of legal regimes and that we illuminate through our study of PDPs:

> Criminalisation of sex work through the criminalisation of sex workers, third parties or clients has been shown to increase violence and health risks and reduce effective access to justice and health care.
>
> Several countries such as Sweden, Norway, France and Ireland have implemented the "Swedish model" criminalising clients of sex workers. Since the implementation of this model sex workers have faced increased violence and stigma. Migrants and street-based sex workers are especially vulnerable to repressive laws. (European Sex Workers' Rights Alliance, n.d.)

The punish-to-rescue impulse is worldwide, and it impacts sex workers adversely. In response, sex worker advocates call for forefronting sex worker knowledge in order to create effective policy that protects sex workers and those who are trafficked and avoids harm (Berg et al., 2022; Berg et al., n.d.). Many researchers have documented how, similarly to the PDPs we study, measures taken to curb trafficking and help people who are trafficked outside the United States focus excessively on trafficking for purposes of sex work (Kinney, 2017; O'Brien, 2013) and usually result in harm to sex workers. Sharmila Parmanand (2022) recently showed how the stigma of sex work carries over into antitrafficking efforts in the Philippines, shutting out the voices of sex workers and resulting in continued harm. Antitrafficking efforts cannot succeed until they recognize the "slow violence" of trafficking, including "the gradual slide into financial precarity induced by tracking trafficking survivors into low-wage labour, the accretive layers of legal tenuousness for undocumented survivors or survivors with pre-existing felony charges . . . that is typically not viewed as violence at all" (Schwarz, 2022, p. 11). We explore how PDPs not only fail to disrupt this slow violence in the lives of street-based sex workers but contribute to it.

Beyond battles over criminality and legalization, the harms of stigma, paternalism, and maternalism continue to disadvantage sex workers and their loved ones. Reno and colleagues (2021) show how inclusion of sex worker perspectives would help researchers and policy-makers achieve the World Health Organization (WHO) goals—shared by sex workers themselves—of increasing breastfeeding among sex workers in Nepal for the health and safety of their children. Lynzi Armstrong (2021) makes a case that social harm, which includes not only physical and psychological harm but all forms of social exclusion and marginalization, continues to operate even in most decriminalization or end-demand policies. The experience of New Zealand's sex work policies in comparison to those of other well-meaning rescue-focused regimes provides evidence that treating sex work like any other work is most likely to allow sex workers to benefit from their labor and not be harmed by ineffective policies and shaming. Anasti's (2018) study of advocacy and helping organizations shows that engaging with sex worker–led organizations may be effectively incorporated into programming and policy advocacy.

Prostitution Diversion Programs

A small but growing body of literature exists about PDPs (Beaujolais & Dillard, 2020). The only comprehensive U.S. report found just over 20 such programs, some of which were no longer running (Mueller, 2012). Since then, there has been growing interest in creating such PDPs, and a number are in the planning stages or have come to fruition (see, for example, Blakey et al., 2017; Singh, 2017). The earliest PDPs were the night courts of Manhattan that began at the turn of the twentieth century; some researchers have noted similarities between these and the twenty-first-century PDPs as mechanisms of social control (Quinn, 2006) that focus on the individual as the locus of intervention, despite differences across time in how the PDPs were framed (Cohen, 2017).

Like other diversion programs, PDPs operate within the existing framework of criminalization and thus do not change the legal status of sex work. PDPs rest on the assumptions that prostitution is harmful and that it can best be addressed through some form of individualized rehabilitation of those who sell or purchase sex (Wahab, 2006). Some PDPs, like problem-solving courts and other diversion programs that require group interventions, have a public or performative aspect that is designed to foster connections and accountability among and between defendants. Defendants serve as role models (or cautionary tales) for others as they move through programs (Begun & Hammond, 2012; Singh, 2017; Shdaimah & Leon, 2016). Criminal justice personnel come to know defendants, and their interactions take on a paternal or mentoring dimension. In fact, PDPs take on a distinctly maternalist approach within a paternalistic criminal legal system and broader society. While some diversion programs are open to the general public, due to the stigma surrounding prostitution even those PDPs with collective elements are often closed to outsiders.

Like their counterparts in other areas, PDPs use multidisciplinary teams, which typically include case managers, public defenders, prosecutors, judges (for court programs), probation officers, and mental health providers (Franke & Shdaimah, 2022). Participants are referred to community agencies for services that can include substance use and/or trauma treatment, job training, education, and medical services (Beaujolais & Dillard, 2020; Leon & Shdaimah, 2019). Courts and decision-makers in the justice system usually view the agencies providing services as crucial collaborators and engage them in ongoing dialogue to provide special programming or set-asides. Indeed, criminal justice agencies such as the police or the courts are unable to provide the services that they mandate, so they rely on their community partners. This means that the quality and types of services vary widely and may not be appropriate or effective for all PDP participants. Ideally, PDPs do their best to ensure a match between defendants and services, as a mismatch can set participants up for failure that engenders criminal justice consequences and reflects poorly on PDPs (e.g., Bailey-Kloch et al., 2015).

PDPs vary widely. Key differences include who is being diverted, from what, and how. These factors shape the content and structure of the programs. Jurisdictions develop programs based on their own goals and available resources and are also the product of negotiation among different stakeholders who may support programs for different reasons. A few programs target consumers, the most famous of which is San Francisco's "John School" (Shively et al., 2008). However, the majority of PDPs target sellers of sex (Global Health Justice Partnership, 2018). Most of these focus on cisgender women, although there are programs such as Baltimore City's Specialized Pretrial Diversion (SPD) program that accept defendants of any gender (Bailey-Kloch et al., 2015). As we show in Chapter 2, eligibility criteria vary, often excluding people who have been charged with violent felony offenses. While some PDPs target first-time offenders, others require a minimum number of prostitution convictions or charges, with some programs targeting individuals with long histories of prostitution convictions that are seen as costly to the criminal legal system (Mueller, 2012). Still others target anyone arrested for prostitution, regardless of pre-existing records. PDPs do not specify types of prostitution offenses but de facto serve primarily street-based sex workers, who are the most likely to be arrested. This group is also the most likely to experience stigma, victimization, and poverty; programs often therefore assume that defendants have experienced trauma and have high levels of addiction and mental illness (Begun & Hammond, 2012; Shdaimah & Bailey-Kloch, 2014; Murasesku, 2017). For this reason, key components of most PDPs are addiction and mental health treatment, including trauma treatment.

PDPs do not fundamentally change the legal status of prostitution but, as the name suggests, divert individuals from consequences at different stages of the criminal legal process. At the earliest stage are programs that divert individuals at point-of-arrest by police officers. Eligible individuals arrested for prostitution who opt for participation in a diversion program are diverted from the charging process. Successful graduates of this kind of program often have their charges dropped and are eligible for expungement. Unsuccessful participants will see their charges move forward. But programs that require a guilty plea are more common. In these, defendants waive their legal right to challenge the charges in court. Defendants are then diverted from punishment while they remain in the program. If they complete the program successfully, their charges are dismissed. Defendants may be able to have their charges expunged as well. It is important to note that expungement processes vary and generally require a fee. Some programs also have additional criteria for expungement, such as remaining free of charges for a year upon completion of a program.

PDP requirements also vary. Like their traditional criminal legal system counterparts in most locations, PDPs for those who sell sex are much more onerous than programs for buyers; programs for buyers typically utilize "scared straight" tactics and may require no more than one day of education. The longest documented PDP duration is the minimum-2-year Cook County Women in Need of Gender Specific Services (WINGS) Court, which was replaced by a Law Enforcement Assisted Diversion (LEAD) program when Illinois eliminated prostitution as a felony offense in 2013 (Chicago Appleseed Center for Fair Courts, 2023).[2] Longer programs often have phases. As the literature on PDPs cited here describes, most programs combine standardized requirements that apply to all participants (such as drug testing, weekly probation meetings, monthly court hearings, or a particular kind of treatment or therapy) with customized programming, such as education or employment programs appropriate to the participants' backgrounds, or specialized drug treatment. Participation is mandatory, including compliance with the rules of any program to which defendants are referred. Some PDPs also offer defendants voluntary enrichment, which can include cycling, yoga, art programs, or assistance reconnecting with children or adult family members. As part of the PDP philosophy of incentives and deterrence, progress is met by rewards while program breaches result in sanctions. Rewards can be in the form of praise in open court, receipt of certificates, and decrease in supervision. Most programs subscribe to a philosophy by which sanctions are graduated and customized so as to provide an opportunity for reflection and learning (National Drug Court Resource Center, 2016). These sanctions typically start as more rehabilitative in focus and can include essays that are read in open court and community service, with incarceration as the threat on the severe end of the spectrum of available sanctions. In phased programs, sanctions are usually accompanied by a restart of the current program phase, lengthening the overall program duration. Continued breaches or certain kinds of program violations may lead to termination of the defendants' participation, thus triggering the original criminal legal consequences from which defendants were diverted.

The small but growing body of literature on PDPs indicates that some programs show better outcomes than their traditional counterparts, largely in the form of cost savings (Begun & Hammond, 2012; Roe-Sepowitz et al., 2012; Shively et al., 2008), program satisfaction (Shdaimah & Bailey-Kloch, 2014), and the increased understanding that criminal justice stakeholders gain about the lived realities that people engaged in sex work face (Wahab, 2005; Leon & Shdaimah, 2012). It is less clear whether prostitution defendants are better off participating in diversion programs in the long run (Shdaimah & Bailey-Kloch, 2014), or if such programs are universally appropriate (Bailey-Kloch et al., 2015). Concerns have also been raised about the appropriateness and quality of treatment and the tension that arises from the provision of rehabilitative services, particularly therapy, within the criminal legal system requiring public disclosure and the threat of punishment (Singh, 2017). Equally important, diversion programs rarely address systemic conditions that contribute to people's motivation for engaging in prostitution, such as lack of affordable housing, discrimination, and the dearth of adequate and appropriate treatment and living wage employment (Blakey et al., 2017; Leon & Shdaimah, 2012; Shdaimah & Bailey-Kloch, 2014).

PDPs' incorporation of rehabilitative services within the criminal legal system presents both opportunities and challenges. With growing empirical evidence and critical attention to how programs operate on the ground, policy-makers and those impacted by PDPs are able to make more informed choices as they shape new and existing programs and balance the interests and goals of stakeholders. PDPs are also best understood and evaluated in light of the existing legal treatment of criminalized sex work in a given jurisdiction to which they serve as an alternative.

Chapter 1 contextualizes PDPs more thoroughly within problem-solving justice and provides what academic audiences will recognize as a literature review. Chapter 2 then describes the two programs featured in this book. The following chapters use vignettes drawn from multiple interviews with program participants and stakeholders. Chapters 3 through 7 each foreground the stories of one or two people, followed by discussion of the salient themes and supported by data from multiple sources. Readers wishing to move directly into accounts of participant and stakeholder perspectives could therefore skip ahead to Chapter 3, which uses Maria's story to demonstrate the coercion built into the fabric of PDPs. In Chapter 4 we explain trauma as a clinical concept and then contrast this with its usage in PDPs, through Tootles's story. In Ava's story in Chapter 5, we examine the impact of stigmatization and constructions of shame and how the court contributes to harmful narratives of shame. Chapter 6, using Amy's story, provides a nuanced and critical analysis of how relationships are built, rebuilt, and surveilled as part of the ongoing court efforts to support, rescue, and control program participants. In Chapter 7, Lily's reflections on her evolution in her role as a court coordinator are the basis for a discussion of the motivations, vision, and goals of PDP staff and the potential for inequity and disempowerment of program participants in light of these. We draw on the insights and perspectives of other court personnel, including judges, social workers, public defenders, probation officers, and prosecutors as well as therapists and agency administrators, to better consider the court and its impacts from stakeholders' perspectives. Chapter 8 provides a summary that brings together the concepts and experiences that we have shared throughout the book. Our three vignettes about our own changing perspectives on prostitution courts and programs, as well as updates on participants whose stories were used in our analyses throughout the book, help contextualize our findings.

We present our findings in a number of different ways. In keeping with an ethic of inquiry informed by feminist and decolonizing practices, we use many quotes to center the words of our respondents. This imperative also influenced our use of extended vignettes in Chapters 3 through 7. We also cite our observations (primarily in court), many of which contain verbatim snippets of conversation. Finally, we draw on I-poem techniques where we believe they can convey a feeling or sense of the person better than a more didactic presentation or framing of respondents' words (Bailey-Kloch, 2017; Buckridge et al., 2022). Readers who wish for greater detail on our methods, including data collection and analysis, rigor, and ethical concerns, can turn to Appendixes A and B.

1

Prostitution Diversion

Criminalization, Individual Responsibility,
and Rescue

Prostitution diversion programs (PDPs) are nested within policies that criminalize the sale of sex. PDPs are also situated within popular discourses that ostensibly softened some of the harsh consequences of oppressive criminal systems in the name of rescue and rehabilitation (Dewey & St. Germain, 2016; Leon & Shdaimah, 2019, 2021). These narratives include the popularization of trauma as a key cause of a host of problems. They also include the framing of all forms of commercial sex transactions through the lens of sex trafficking and its justification for rescue and surveillance (Corrigan & Shdaimah, 2016; Hill, 2014). When unchallenged, these assumptions and ways of talking about sex work rely on and (re)produce neoliberal governance that individualizes both the sources of social ills and the locus of change, and they also single out sex work for unique treatment different from other forms of labor (O'Brien, 2013). In this chapter, we provide a description of the legal and policy backdrop for PDPs. This is followed by a discussion of the problem-solving framework generally and its specific fit for prostitution as it is currently viewed by those who create and implement policy and programming, that is, as behavior that traumatized people suffering from addiction resort to because they do not have "better" coping mechanisms. We end this chapter with a brief description of the theoretical frameworks that informed our study and the critical analysis we present here.

Legal and Policy Backdrop

In the United States, commercial sex is governed by state law. It is criminalized, meaning that prostitution is illegal and, if detected, violation of the law prompts criminal legal system involvement, everywhere except in Nevada, where the determination of legality is left up to each individual county. Recently, a handful of jurisdictions, including Washington, D.C., have considered legislation that would decriminalize commercial sex (North, 2019). This would make sex work no longer a crime, instead making it subject to other forms of legal regulation. In the United States, prostitution is generally classified as a misdemeanor with possible punishments of fines or imprisonment that vary by state or county jurisdictions. The criminalization of prostitution in the United States is rooted in both public health and morality concerns (Weitzer, 2010). As some of the most marginalized members of our society, persons who engage in illegal sex work are vulnerable to attacks, physical and otherwise, by clients, community members, and sometimes law enforcement (Sanders, 2004; Wiechelt & Shdaimah, 2011).

Whether sexual commerce is regarded as work or as exploitation, laws that repress sex work are associated with negative health and safety concerns for sex workers (Platt et al., 2018). Punishments fall more heavily on sex workers, who are disproportionately women and gender minorities, than on their predominantly cisgender male clients, and African American women are disproportionately targeted for prostitution arrest (Pfeffer et al., 2018). Relations between police and sex workers can be fraught, often reflecting gender bias and discrimination, and police frequently ignore claims of sexual assault and coerced sex (Dank et al., 2017). Street-based sex work is often overlooked except when neighborhoods begin to gentrify, when street-based sex workers may become more vulnerable to displacement and heightened safety concerns (Lyons et al., 2017; Oselin et al., 2022). Prostitution and sex workers are flashpoints for neighborhood conflicts, particularly around economic change and gentrification (Hail-Jares et al., 2017; Cheng, 2013) and policing (Steele & Terruso, 2021).

Many scholars consider those who engage in street-level prostitution to be the most vulnerable to harm, lowest paid, and most easily targeted for arrest and prosecution (Weitzer, 2009). They may also be among the most vulnerable to stigmatization, for their work in this area is public (Oselin, 2014). Due to public exposure that makes them both more vulnerable and more likely to be perceived as a nuisance by host communities, people in street-based sex work make up the majority of those targeted for arrest and prosecution.

The goal of U.S. prostitution policy in most locations is primarily to deter individuals from selling sex. However, for more than 20 years, it has been a common complaint that arrest and prosecution of prostitution *as implemented* are ineffective (Shdaimah, 2010; Wolf, 2001). One reason for this may be that current policy does not satisfactorily take into account the reasons why people sell sex or the context in which they do, including the availability of acceptable alternatives. It is also clear that legal regimes structure the experience of prostitution and adversely impact women's safety (Scoular, 2010). Criminalization and policing practices themselves contribute to the vulnerability and harm experienced by street-based sex workers. These include the impact of prostitution arrest records that make it harder to find legal employment and the (re)traumatization of incarceration. They also include attitudes of indifference or hostility that deter women from seeking assistance from law enforcement and reporting crime (Corrigan & Shdaimah, 2016; Mueller, 2022) and practices that may compromise women's health and safety such as the seizure of condoms and use of condoms as evidence of sex work (Footer et al., 2016; Human Rights Watch, 2012; Sherman et al., 2015).

Social science literature has paid some attention to pathways into sexual exchange, largely focusing on experiences such as trauma or drug use (Verona et al., 2016) that typically take a damage-centered or pathologizing approach to the individuals (Shdaimah & Leon, 2018; Cheng, 2013). The harm experienced by women in prostitution may be rooted in or influenced by experiences they had prior to entering prostitution, such as childhood physical or sexual abuse, domestic violence, homelessness, and poverty (Wiechelt & Shdaimah, 2011). Regardless, once women enter sex work, they are at increased risk of additional violence and victimization (Dalla et al., 2003; El-Bassel et al., 2001; Millan-Alanis et al., 2021). Stigmatization and shame, sometimes coupled with the effects of harmful substance use and trauma, may make it difficult for women in prostitution to maintain intimate relationships, thereby increasing women's sense of isolation and loneliness (Sanders, 2005). Fukushima et al. (2018) describe a multiplicity of stigma that occurs at micro, meso, and macro levels in regard to responses to trafficking for sexual labor. The literature on sex work also shows a multiplicity of stigma around sex work, where policy and programs often address stigma and other harms at one level but not others. For example, Lynzi Armstrong (2019) finds residual stigma among service providers in New Zealand, where sex work is legal and thus officially destigmatized at the macro level. Raven Bowen's (2021) examination of duality reveals that some people who engage in both sex work and square work compartmentalize their labor due to stigma, giving rise to the need to address the social context for sex work. Blakey and Gunn (2018) also examine how micro-level interventions can be undermined by persistent meso and macro stigma.

The creation of the diversion programs that we describe in this book came at a time when a growing number of scholars began to examine systemic factors that influence prostitution, such as poverty, limited employment opportunities, and cultural understandings of women's roles and opportunities that may make prostitution the best of extremely circumscribed options that women have to survive (O'Connell Davidson, 1998; Phoenix, 1999; Lutnick & Cohan, 2009; Shdaimah & Wiechelt, 2012b). However, the exploitation and harm experienced by many women in prostitution remain largely invisible in both legal and treatment processes, as these are often designed to encourage desistance without recognizing or addressing the poverty and trauma that is so often prevalent and intertwined with prostitution. Not only does criminalization generally take no account of systemic or individual motivations to enter into or continue engaging in prostitution, it can also increase harm. Criminalization often reduces the power and leverage of women engaged in prostitution, making sex work even more dangerous (Brewis & Linstead, 2000; Human Rights Watch, 2019; Sanders, 2005).

Many sex workers' rights organizations identify harms from the criminal status of prostitution that limit sex workers' recourse when they are injured due to lack of employment rights and their inability to call for legal protection if and when they are threatened or harmed, or to safeguard their health (Global Network of Sex Work Projects, 2017). Those who do report assaults to the police often find themselves dismissed and humiliated, as was documented in a U.S. Department of Justice (2016) report on gender-biased policing in Baltimore and in research on sexual assault reporting across the country (Corrigan, 2013; Stolberg & Bidgood, 2016). The case of police officer Daniel Holtzclaw is one of the more publicized incidents of exploitation of this vulnerability to coerce sexual acts from sex workers (Diaz et al., 2016). There is also widespread anecdotal evidence that police exploit the vulnerability of sex workers in order to coerce them into cooperating in investigations, which may endanger them on the streets. Criminalization reduces their leverage with customers, exposing sex workers to unsafe sexual practices and violent encounters (Footer et al., 2016).

Scholars and advocates debate whether decriminalization or legalization of sex work leads to an increase in human trafficking. Weitzer (2021) contends that most assessments rely on incorrect interpretation and analysis of existing data and lack of attention to details among widely varying legal regimes. Even those who claim that legalization may lead to an increase in trafficking, however, acknowledge that criminalization has a negative impact on sex workers who are not trafficked (Cho et al., 2013). Harms against sex workers may persist even when sexual commerce is decriminalized or legalized. Armstrong (2019), reporting on sex workers in New Zealand, indicates that stigma and the harm it causes may remain even after legalization, indicating that decriminalization or legalization may be insufficient to reduce harms to sex workers. Abolitionists who do not want to cause further harm to women engaged in prostitution advocate policies that criminalize only purchasers of sex, such as the models in Scandinavian countries (Skilbrei & Holmström, 2014). One study in Canada found that criminalization of clients did not enhance the safety of street-based sex workers (Krüsi et al., 2014). Other attempts to further decriminalize commercial sex are civil sanctions or the use of criminal sanctions that do not target prostitution per se but instead the related activities such as "kerb-crawling" or soliciting in public spaces (Melrose, 2006). These efforts have been motivated by a desire to remove sex work from public spaces, rather than concern for those engaging in sex work who have little say in official policies, even if some are adept at learning to work within and around policy changes (Blunt & Wolf, 2020; Sanders, 2005; Red Umbrella Fund, n.d.).

In 2016, Amnesty International issued a highly publicized report calling "for the decriminalization of all aspects of adult consensual sex work due to the foreseeable barriers that criminalization creates to the realization of the human rights of sex workers" (Amnesty International, 2016, p. 2). Their report, based on research from around the globe, notes the vulnerability caused by criminalization of sex work in the forms of stigma, barriers to human rights, a need to operate clandestinely, and abuses of power (often without recourse) at the hands of clients, communities, and agents of the state. Careful to distinguish between consensual sex work and human trafficking, Amnesty International (2016) rejects policies that conflate the two as creating adverse consequences to vulnerable sex workers and denying their basic human rights. Similar concerns have been raised about PDPs (Gruber et al., 2016; Red Umbrella Fund, 2014).

While the prevailing policy response to prostitution in the United States remains criminal sanction, in the first decade of the 2000s some jurisdictions began experimenting with punitive responses that include a supportive or therapeutic component. These hybrid responses are part of the broader problem-solving court efforts across the country (Porter et al., 2010). Like their mental health and drug court counterparts, prostitution problem-solving efforts are premised on the belief that the current criminal justice responses that Wolf (2001) refers to as "revolving door justice" are insufficient. This is because they do not address underlying problems such as addiction, inadequate education or employment opportunities, and lack of affordable housing, which may contribute to continued engagement in prostitution. The goal of these court-related programs is to decrease prostitution by providing services and attempting to rehabilitate offenders (Shively et al., 2008). The programs represent the profound ambivalence that society has toward women who engage in prostitution and other forms of sex work. On the one hand, those engaged in prostitution are prosecuted as criminals; on the other hand, proponents of these efforts seek alternatives to the dominant criminal justice framework that defines them exclusively as perpetrators (Leon & Shdaimah, 2019, 2021). This tension may remain entrenched in court-based programs, even as some try to resolve it through the provision of desperately needed services, because criminal justice attempts remain individually focused and do not interrogate or challenge underlying societal factors that motivate women to engage in prostitution.

Problem-Solving Justice

Problem-solving courts are arguably among the most prolific contemporary judicial and criminal legal system innovations in the United States. They involve target populations that are credited with the ability to change and reform. These populations, however, are also viewed as lacking in agency due to their characterization as people suffering from conditions or circumstances that may mitigate responsibility, such as mental health problems or substance use disorders (Baylson, 2017; Corrigan & Shdaimah, 2016; Paik, 2009). Problem-solving courts are grounded in the therapeutic justice movement that has been optimistically embraced by policy-makers, judges, lawyers, and case managers (Nolan, 2001; Winick & Wexler, 2003). Most accounts of the problem-solving court movement tell of a grassroots response by judges, lawyers, and treatment personnel to the failure of traditional criminal legal system responses to crime. As the first and most prevalent form of problem-solving courts, drug courts were ostensibly created from the bottom up by charismatic local judges due to the increasing number of cases overwhelming court dockets and high rates of repeat offenders (Berman & Feinblatt, 2005), which many believe to be the result of mandatory sentencing and increased criminalization of drug offenses (Boldt & Singer, 2006; McCoy, 2003; Nolan, 2001).

Problem-solving programs work within existing criminal justice frameworks, and they do not seek to change the underlying criminalization of the behaviors that they address. Indeed, problem-solving justice views the power of the criminal justice system as a valuable tool for fostering behavioral changes where voluntary efforts may not succeed. They wield the sticks of jail time, fines, and criminal records to encourage participants to engage in various tasks and behaviors that may otherwise be optional, such as drug treatment, medication compliance, and therapy. Simultaneously, they offer the carrots of facilitating access to coveted services and removal of a variety of criminal consequences. This means that such programs designed to address prostitution do not contest the criminal status of selling sex but rather see it as an undesirable (and illegal) behavior to be eradicated. Once inside the diversion program, the question of prostitution as a legal offense is irrelevant. However, personal beliefs may motivate some of the criminal justice professionals to create or participate in these programs (Leon & Shdaimah, 2019, 2021).

Judges, lawyers, social workers, and probation officers who embrace problem-solving efforts often do so for personal reasons, as an opportunity to engage in meaningful work that "makes a difference" by changing people's lives (McCoy, 2003; Nolan, 2001; Leon & Shdaimah, 2019, 2021). Others describe professional reasons, such as resisting the bureaucratization and routinization that mandatory sentencing and high caseloads necessitate (Nolan, 2001; see also Heydebrand & Seron, 1990, on this phenomenon in federal courts). Still others assert crime control rationales based on a desire for more effective responses to criminal behavior in order to stem the flow of cases to court (Berman & Feinblatt, 2005). Problem-solving courts are touted as an attempt at managing crime through effective treatment of the underlying circumstances that gave rise to offenses (Hora et al., 1999). Drug courts in particular have also been viewed as a reassertion of prosecutorial and judicial discretion that had been circumscribed by the policies that were part of the get-tough-on-crime and war-on-drugs agendas of the 1980s (Boldt & Singer, 2006; see also Singer et al., 2000, on a similar phenomenon in the juvenile courts).

Problem-solving courts have increased in popularity across the country since the early 1990s (Casey & Rottman, 2005). Over 3,100 such courts exist nationwide (Haskins, 2019). The majority of these are drug courts, but there are also mental health courts, veterans' courts, prostitution courts, and domestic violence courts. Significant federal resources have been devoted to problem-solving courts (e.g., SAMHSA Awards, 2009). They have been endorsed by the Conference of the Chief Justices/Conference of State Court Administrators Courts Committee (2004) and are reported to be popular with judges (Farole, 2009). Problem-solving courts are largely based on the notion that rehabilitation will prevent first-time offenders from reoffending (McCoy, 2003) or represent an effort to change the habits of repeat offenders (Wolf, 2001) to eventually reduce the prevalence of the targeted crimes (McCoy, 2003; Mirchandani, 2005). Studies that examine the development of court-based intervention programs focus primarily on impediments to the successful implementation of programs, such as lack of resources for defendants and sustainability (Farole et al., 2004; O'Keefe, 2006; Shively et al., 2008).

A growing number of academics and practitioners have voiced concerns with problem-solving courts. The most vocal critics are public defenders, who are concerned about defendants' rights, unequal distribution of opportunities, and net-widening effects that result in increasing arrests and surveillance (O'Hear, 2009; Quinn, 2000; Strangio, 2017). Many question whether in fact defendants are better off participating in problem-solving courts in the long run (Orr et al., 2009). Defendants may be required to plead guilty in order to participate in problem-solving courts; because the courts provide access to much-needed resources, this raises concerns about coercion of defendants as well as the diversion of scarce community resources, such as treatment beds or housing slots, into the criminal legal system (Shdaimah, 2010). Critics see problem-solving courts as an extension of the power of the criminal justice apparatus over a broader swath of people and into more minute details of their clients' lives for a longer duration (Mirchandani, 2005; Nolan, 2001; Orr et al., 2009). However, very few consider the perspectives of program participants in the creation and implementation of this bureaucratic innovation that is designed to influence their behavior.

Concerns have also been raised about the appropriateness and quality of treatment (Taxman & Bouffard, 2002; Franke & Shdaimah, 2022) and the way in which the public shaming that is part of many court programs reflects stigmatizing beliefs and practices that may interfere with therapeutic goals (Ma et al., 2018). In fact, Nolan (2001) reports that judges often pride themselves and "sell" programs to the public and legislatures based on the *more* stringent demands that drug courts place on participants in comparison to traditional models. In an overview of recent evaluations of court-affiliated PDPs, Beaujolais and Dillard (2020) reported some modest improvements in short-time outcomes in comparison to criminal legal processing as usual, although risks and concerns persist in other reports (Global Health Justice Partnership, 2018). Problem-solving courts can have worse outcomes for participants who do not succeed, such as increased surveillance, longer incarcerations, or the effectual waiver of a trial with the activation of guilty pleas that are tendered as a prerequisite for program participation (Boldt, 2010; Orr et al., 2009). All of these should be serious considerations for policy-makers, advocates, and researchers in weighing the risks and benefits to vulnerable populations who are offered participation. Their marginal status and circumscribed options compound concerns about coercion and obstacles to successful completion of prostitution problem-solving programs. It is therefore particularly important to understand how those who are offered court-based interventions make decisions about whether to participate, how their participation impacts their goals, and any hardships they face. Given the goals of reducing recidivism and addressing what are viewed by many as root causes for offending, it is also important to understand the impact that their participation has on their future engagement with prostitution and more general health and well-being.

Negotiated Decision-Making Within
Problem-Solving Justice

In order to achieve their stated goals of addressing underlying factors that cause people to (re)offend, problem-solving courts mix social control with the delivery of services. It should be no surprise, then, that the small but growing number of studies focus on what happens in the "black box" of problem-solving courts. Most of these studies examine how criminal justice professionals use their discretion in the intensive and ongoing interactions between themselves and program participants to shape the programs and individual case trajectories and outcomes (Castellano, 2017; Portillo & Rudes, 2014). These studies are helpful in understanding the decisions of criminal legal system personnel and point to the importance of examining the interplay of social norms, court culture, and client attitudes and behaviors that influence their decisions.

Criminal justice personnel in problem-solving programs are what Michael Lipsky (1980) famously called "street level bureaucrats" (SLBs): government employees who work directly with (in)voluntary service recipients. Their work is characterized by tensions, including conflicting mandates (such as penal and therapeutic mandates) and limited resources in the face of great need. Early research on SLBs focused on how they manage and make sense of their work, for example, by rationing resources. While SLBs often perceive themselves as powerless to change policies mandated from above, they wield great power over the people they serve, who may be dependent on their discretionary authority for crucial goods and services. In problem-solving programs, this can include the ability to mete out sanctions within the criminal justice system, from writing an essay to paying fines and serving jail time. Discretionary influence on policy implementation persists even in highly rule-bound bureaucracies (Lens, 2005) and in fact may play an even more important role in rigid institutional environments (Simon, 1983).

More recent work, including our own research with lawyers, judges, and social workers in the context of child welfare (Shdaimah, 2020; Shdaimah, 2010), focuses on how SLBs act in the face of dissonance between their own professional and personal norms and workplace constraints. A study of "cops, teachers, and counselors" by Maynard-Moody and Musheno (2003) describes decision-making by SLBs when legal and bureaucratic rules ("law abidance") conflict with SLBs' personal and professional perspectives ("moral abidance"). The study found that SLBs typically resolve the tensions between the two by working within and around rules to further the dictates of moral abidance (at the expense of legal abidance), with varying degrees of success. Maynard-Moody and Musheno also found that SLBs were often motivated to respond directly to the needs of specific clients (see also Hasenfeld, 1992), underscoring the importance of clients in the formulation of their responses. The professionals we spoke with involved in PDPs similarly strove to resolve the tensions between law abidance and moral abidance (see particularly Chapter 7, which focuses on professional stakeholders).

Similar to the moral typification employed in other bureaucratic settings (Hasenfeld, 1983, 2000), which SLBs use to make decisions based on their interpretation of client "deservingness," problem-solving court professionals' decisions are often based upon their moral judgments of client behavior. Mackinem and Higgins (2007) found that judges' and treatment personnel's responses to drug court clients' perceived illicit drug use hinged not so much on whether clients were able to convince the court that they had not, in fact, used illicit drugs. Instead, they depended upon whether clients admitted to drug use and showed contrition, responses that drug court SLBs believed were conducive to the therapeutic treatment model. Assessment of client behavior centered on the perception of clients' embrace of treatment, which was evidenced by (1) acceptance of a stigmatized identity (i.e., drug addict), (2) acceptance of responsibility for their behaviors, and (3) commitment to change. In examining these factors, judges, lawyers, and treatment personnel often employed cultural scripts or existing "knowledge" about drug use, clients, and treatment methods to assess client credibility. They then decided whether (and how) to sanction clients in the face of substantiated or suspected violations of court rules (Burns & Peyrot, 2003; Mackinem & Higgins, 2007; Paik, 2006).

Leslie Paik (2006), in her study of a juvenile drug court, describes a more complex balancing of pre-existing "knowledge" with information regarding specific cases. Criminal justice stakeholders consider a wide variety of factors, including information about particular drugs (i.e., how long a drug stays in the body, what behavior it might cause) and familiarity with addiction and treatment, as well as the history of particular drug court clients and their current state, as evidenced by their actions in multiple areas (are they attending school and being respectful of their parents) and the possibility of mental illness (Paik, 2006, 2009). While there may be fewer cultural scripts specific to prostitution, Stefanie Wahab (2006, p. 214) found that prostitution problem-solving court professionals' decisions were influenced by their assessment of the degree to which clients were engaged in prostitution as a result of victimization and these professionals were both harsher on and had less empathy for clients who chose prostitution when they were perceived to have other options.

As we have reported elsewhere, criminal justice personnel may come to see PDP participants as victims, and thus may reward them with legal and material benefits, if (and for as long as) they exhibit certain behaviors (Corrigan & Shdaimah, 2016). These behaviors include performances of contrition and trauma, what is considered appropriate demeanor and attire, and an expressed desire to change themselves and their relationships. PDPs are designed to motivate through positive rewards and sanctions, and participants may respond to either or both (Shdaimah, 2019). Similar to what Jill McCorkel (2013) describes in her ethnography of incarcerated women, some diversion program participants conform with such behaviors and programming requirements through genuine or internalized motivations and goals. Others may comply in order to gain the benefits offered for compliance (Shdaimah & Leon, 2015). Still others may decide that conforming to program standards and behaviors that assault their integrity, sense of self, or survival mechanisms is untenable or too high a price to pay (Dewey & St. Germain, 2016).

PDP personnel rely on their generalized knowledge about trauma to employ tools, such as trauma-informed court practices and behavior modeling, to mitigate some of the harsher criminal justice consequences and to provide assistance (Leon & Shdaimah, 2019, 2021). Such assistance also helps criminal justice professionals reconcile the disjuncture that they experience between current prostitution policy and their professional understanding of the largely coercive forces that impact women's illegal sex work. This understanding comes from prevalent trauma and trafficking discourses that construct women's engagement in prostitution as a choiceless choice influenced by cruel personal histories of abuse, trauma, and victimization largely disconnected from social forces that may shape them (Dewey & St. Germain, 2016; Leon & Shdaimah, 2019, 2021). These discourses are confirmed and reinforced by PDP personnel's encounters with women who come through the system; these are, overwhelmingly, women with long-term substance use disorders who engage in low-paid street-level survival sex work (Baylson, 2017; Muraresku, 2017). Structural critiques including those offered by academics like ourselves (see also Weitzer, 2013; Cohen, 2017) and sex worker activists (e.g., Red Umbrella Fund, 2014)—do not permeate the street level. Similarly, firsthand or academic portrayals of sex work as a rational and logical choice—even as a form of low-wage labor—are largely missing from program formulation and policy formulation as they are inconsistent with prevailing political and institutional interests and norms (Corrigan & Shdaimah, 2016; Majic, 2015).

Program Participants as Cocreators

Much of the literature notes the importance of interactions with "clients," or the beneficiaries of bureaucratic services. However, clients are often seen as objects to which SLBs react, rather than as co-constructors of SLB adaptations. This study takes seriously the importance of looking at what Sandfort et al. (1999) call the "two faces" of policy implementation that takes place in a dynamic and unpredictable context (Brodkin, 1986). These two faces are the different, and mutually influential, perspectives of SLBs and of their clients. It is generally presumed that service recipients wield less power than SLBs. Their personal agency has often gone understudied, as have the encounters between SLBs and clients as mutual dialogue. However, a number of studies show that clients can wield power over service providers regarding goals and practices (e.g., Linda Gordon's [1994] historic study of Progressive Era clients of social service agencies). Despite power imbalances and dependence, bureaucratic citizens are able to engage with SLBs to resist dominant narratives (White, 1990) and get what they need, including social services (Gordon, 1994), welfare benefits (Gilliom, 2001), and legal services (Sarat, 1990). In her account of what she calls "reformer judges" in fair hearings for public benefits, Lens (2009) shows that official actors, too, can join with "clients" to create counternarratives and to secure needed benefits (see also Shdaimah & McGarry, 2018). This book looks at how *clients* in court-affiliated PDPs serve as cocreators of the programs; their responses, experiences, and dialogue with criminal justice actors play a key role in shaping the program.

Client perspectives are critical because clients are an important partner in the court movement. Since they are the target of reform efforts, their actions and behaviors are what criminal legal system professionals must work with to promote problem-solving courts within the dictates of policy and institutional mandates. Mackinem and Higgins (2007, p. 425) explain, "Judges are committed to the success of the drug court program and want cases to succeed, not only for the good of the client, but also because their success validates the program." Paik (2009), for example, shows how clients' mental health concerns are used by juvenile drug court staff as a pressure valve to explain and find solutions to practical problems posed by clients who do not seem to be doing well in the drug courts. While problem-solving court studies consider negotiations between clients and SLBs (Burns & Peyrot, 2003; Mackinem & Higgins, 2007), they do not explore them, or the drug court experience, from the clients' perspective. Stefanie Wahab's (2005, 2006) study of a Salt Lake City prostitution court is the only one we've found that examines the perceptions of problem-solving court clients. Her study examines professional and client assessments of the program, which were largely positive. Client satisfaction hinged not only on the services they received but also on their perception of respectful and compassionate treatment by program staff (Wahab, 2005; see also Shdaimah & Bailey-Kloch, 2014, on Baltimore City's program). This indicates that the way clients are treated by criminal legal system personnel who implement problem-solving justice is crucial to clients' experiences of, and performance in, the program.

Drawing upon their respective research in criminal courts and county jails, Lara-Millán and Van Cleve (2017) argue that what they identify as "welfare stigma"

> changes how professionals view the criminal justice system, their role in it, and the defendants they are processing: Punishment is a type of privilege to be parsed out, defendants are not considered criminal elements but social burdens to be managed, and criminal justice professionals become more akin to welfare bureaucrats primarily tasked with seeking to disqualify people for purported benefits. (p. 77)

Although the process functions differently within the PDPs we study, PDP stakeholders make similar judgments about how to enact their values through their professional roles in ways that constitute particular kinds of people who are worthy of help (Leon & Shdaimah, 2021). Participation in specialized diversion programs may function as an expression of emotion for these professionals in a way analogous to how passing a tough-on-crime law functions for policy-makers as an expression of outrage—in our case, these function as an expression of systemic understanding (to a point) and compassion. As Williams et al. (2020) explain, "symbolic laws"

> seldom solve these issues once and for all. Instead, symbolic laws that address pressing social problems concentrate on the expressive, emotional, and moral aspects of crime, which often exaggerate the scope of the problems they intend to fix and detract from the real causes of those problems. The public may be more likely to support crime prevention policies that acknowledge the emotional and social aspects of crime-related problems. (p. 211)

Understanding the nuance involved in how and why frontline workers engage with problem-solving courts like PDPs also contributes to our understanding of the broader penal changes at work in the United States and beyond (Leon & Shdaimah, 2019; Lynch, 2017, p. 201).

2

Study Sites

Prostitution Diversion Programs in
Baltimore and Philadelphia

In this chapter, we provide an overview of the two prostitution diversion programs (PDPs) that are the subject of this book. This review is intended to provide our readers with the local context that informed how and why these PDPs came to be, as well as the specific contours of each program. We draw from media, academic literature, and our personal experience as close observers and peripheral members of different stakeholder groups. Both Baltimore and Philadelphia are urban areas with high rates of poverty and violent crime. Both cities have seen increased tension in relations between the police and the community, especially regarding racial inequities and police violence, and have been sites of widespread demonstrations and calls for accountability. Both are cities with a majority Black population (U.S. Census Bureau, n.d.a.; U.S. Census Bureau, n.d.b.), where Black people are overrepresented in the criminal legal system (Nelson et al., 2015; Office of the State's Attorney for Baltimore City, 2022). However, prostitution arrests tend to be made up of comparatively more White defendants than arrests for other criminal offenses, as corroborated by professional stakeholders. Those who offered explanations speculated that this may be an artifact of policing, which targets neighborhoods with specific strolls where those who sell sex are disproportionately White cisgender women. Between our initial data collection from 2011 to 2014 and the follow-up study in 2021, racial tensions increased, as did the attention paid to police violence. Both cities have seen a retreat from policing in general, particularly of low-level crimes, which was exacerbated by the COVID-19 pandemic (Westervelt, 2021; but see Li & Mahajan, 2021).

TABLE 2.1 PROGRAM OVERVIEW

Program	Participant Gender	Program Duration	Stage of Diversion	Program Sites/ Arenas	Program Content	Outcomes	Legal Status
Baltimore's Specialized Prostitution Diversion (SPD) program	Any	90 days	Pre-plea	Social work and pretrial offices; community	Individualized	Success: *Nolle prosequi*; can be expunged after completion Failure: Return to plea state	Maryland statute: Up to 1 year incarceration or $500 in fines Decriminalized by order of State Attorney's Office
Philadelphia's Project Dawn Court (PDC)	Cisgender women	Minimum 1 year (4 Phases)	No contest plea	Courts and probation offices; community	Individualized, with required sexual trauma treatment therapy	Success: Cases dismissed with prejudice; can be expunged after a year Failure: Guilty verdict entered and move to sentencing	Pennsylvania statute: For third offense (first-degree misdemeanor), up to 5 years incarceration and/or $10,000 As per State Attorney's order, currently not prosecuting

Table 2.1 provides an overview of the salient aspects of the two programs, followed by narrative descriptions.

Baltimore City's Specialized Prostitution Diversion Program

In the first decade of the 2000s, a great deal of attention focused on problems related to prostitution in Baltimore, Maryland. Residents' concerns in Baltimore and other urban centers saw prostitution as connected with problems of substance use, violence, solicitation of neighborhood residents, and a general public nuisance (see also Shively et al., 2008). In Baltimore, community associations concerned about the ongoing impact of prostitution on their neighborhoods complained to the Baltimore City State's Attorney's Office. In Maryland, prostitution is a third-degree misdemeanor, subject to fines of $500 and/or up to one year imprisonment. Law enforcement, prosecutors, and defense attorneys had limited options to address behavior that they viewed as symptomatic of more systemic mental health, substance abuse, trauma, and housing needs among individuals engaged in prostitution. Based on their common concerns, representatives from these groups convened a task force to explore how the criminal justice system might better combat prostitution (Shdaimah, 2010).

The stakeholder group and subsequent program was led by the Baltimore City State's Attorney's Office (SAO). Initially, the SAO contemplated a traditional problem-solving court with judicial oversight. During the course of the stakeholder meetings, however, the Office of the Public Defender (OPD) filed a constitutional lawsuit challenging the constitutionality of Maryland's drug courts, which according to the state's Public Defender denied defendants their rights to due process (*Brown v. Maryland*, 2009; Cauvin, 2009). Maryland's Office of Problem-Solving Courts placed a moratorium on new problem-solving courts until the lawsuit was eventually dismissed on technical grounds. The lawsuit was part of larger opposition in the OPD to problem-solving courts, which the OPD viewed as inimical to the interests of clients, with potentially disastrous outcomes. The OPD withdrew from the stakeholder committee, although negotiations continued. The resulting program, known as the Specialized Prostitution Diversion Program (SPD), was, at least in part, a product of these concerns: Participants are diverted entirely from the court process prior to the plea stage of their cases. This court-affiliated PDP is, therefore, decidedly and purposefully not a problem-solving court.

The SPD began operation in 2009. Although cases are generally routed to one of three Baltimore City district courts based upon place of arrest, upon inauguration of the SPD all prostitution cases were routed to the Eastside District Court's Monday morning Part 7 docket. Part 7 is the Early Resolution (ER) Court that refers cases to a number of diversionary programs. For the first six years of the SPD's operation, the presiding judge for this docket rotated every three months. Beginning in 2016, the docket began to operate under one presiding judge. The SPD was initially open to prostitution defendants who do not have felony charges and who are not currently on probation. Despite this exclusion criterion, the SPD employs discretion in accepting participants who have felony charges. Due to logistic concerns, the SPD is not similarly flexible regarding the probation criterion. With the decrease in prostitution arrests over time, the SPD expanded eligibility to defendants who had a history of prostitution convictions and was renamed Specialized Pretrial Prostitution Diversion Program. Prospective participants are identified by the SAO, which provides the OPD with their offers for defendants on the ER docket. At various points in the program, OPD attorneys and SPD social workers could also recommend defendants for the program. However, room for negotiation and input on referrals varies depending on the working relationships among these SPD stakeholders, as well as the presiding judge. These working relationships are driven, in large part, by the personalities, philosophical orientations, and working styles of those involved, and by the knowledge and investment of these individuals in the program.

The cases of those who successfully complete the 90-day program are *null processed*. Defendants may ask for the charges to be expunged immediately upon completion. The $35 expungement fees are waived for clients with no prior records. Successful participants who come to court are awarded a certificate and a rose. Those who are unsuccessful find themselves back in court at the plea stage; defendants therefore lose none of their legal rights for trying the program, even if they are unsuccessful. The pre-plea timing of diversion is a key feature of the program and makes it an exception to other court-affiliated PDPs (Mueller, 2012). In July 2016, however, we witnessed the presiding judge offer admittance to the program to an incarcerated defendant in exchange for her guilty plea. The plea was to be held under advisement while the defendant participated in the program, with charges dismissed upon successful completion or entered upon failure. There was some debate whether guilty pleas had been required prior to this listing; if so, they were rare and had occurred only under that judge. It is unclear whether this will become a more regular feature of the program. If it does, the requirement of a guilty plea represents a significant departure from the initial program philosophy, which was to hold participants legally harmless for having tried the program and failed.

The Eastside District Court is located on a part of Baltimore's North Avenue surrounded by blocks that contain many boarded-up houses, often alongside occupied homes. There is a bus stop at the courthouse, and along the corner vendors sell water and food as well as various services—for example, what people refer to as "Obama phones," government-sponsored cell phones for those who are income-eligible, and a mobile dental unit housed in a refurbished bus. Depending on the hour, people are eating, smoking, and wait- ing for family members around all the court's entrances and exits. Visitors pass through a metal detector, and no food or drink is permitted in the court- room. Part 7 is located in the basement. Before the daily docket begins, a pub- lic defender seeks out each defendant among the people in the waiting area outside the courtroom. They do this in order to ascertain who is present and to review their cases, including sharing offers with defendants whom the SAO has identified as eligible for the SPD. This is the first time a defendant will meet a public defender, who may or may not have had the opportunity to review their case before that morning. The public defender explains the program, answers questions, and provides a recommendation to the client, which gen- erally includes the public defender's assessment of the likely case trajectory if the client chooses to plead rather than enter the program.

The docket lists all early resolution cases; thus, the courtroom may be full of people with a variety of charges. Once in court, defendants who choose to enter the SPD appear before the judge, who asks whether the defendants understand their options and have any questions and, sometimes, whether the defendants are ready to make life changes. Upon receiving papers from the bailiff, defendants proceed directly from the courtroom to an intake pro- cess. Whenever possible, the program social worker walks with the new pro- gram entrants to make sure that they do not leave or get lost on the way to their next stops for intake. This includes an initial meeting with three staff members. A program social worker records self-reported information regard- ing what the participants wants to accomplish while in the program, as well as demographic information that may impact program goals and participa- tion, such as gender identity, educational attainment, family information, and living situation. A pretrial agent records information required for contact and supervision. Participants are also screened by a mental health and substance use assessor for evaluation.

The participant must sign an agreement upon entrance to the program; although the agreement is also signed by a representative of the SPD, all of the obligations listed in the document are the defendants' responsibility. The agreement lists the program requirements and attests that the participant understands that violation of any requirement may result in termination of their participation in the SPD and a return of their case to "court for trial." Program participants are also required to maintain weekly contact with a designated pretrial agent to check in, provide updated contact information, and, on occasion, submit to a urinalysis. Participants meet weekly with one of the three part-time program social workers. These meetings are primar- ily designed for case management personnel to review whether current ser- vices are meeting the needs of a participant and to identify any other areas the participant might want to work on, such as obtaining government identification; signing up for health insurance, mental health treatment, or addiction treatment; or pursuing a GED or employment. In addition to these program requirements, SPD participants are to be assessed, evaluated, and treated and to comply with the rules of any programs to which they are referred:

> I agree that I will cooperate in any physical and mental examinations or tests, or any treatment and counseling recommended by the SPD Case Manager to maintain a satisfactory standard of health and conduct. Specifically: random urinalysis and drug treatment upon referral. (State of Maryland Department of Public Safety and Correctional Services Division of Pretrial Detention and Services, n.d., §7)

They also waive their rights to confidentiality so that the SPD social workers can monitor their participation in mandated services and can assess how they are faring. While legal protections of this information are officially removed through defendant waivers, this information remains with the social workers and is not shared with prosecutors, pretrial agents, or judges, so that it will not be considered if program participants fail and face charges. While the program is not necessarily designed to go beyond 90 days, some struggling defendants have been allowed to extend the program rather than being returned to court to face their charges. These extensions were a product of negotiation between program social workers, pretrial agents, and the attorneys involved in the case. During our study, most participants who breached the program but reengaged and wanted to continue were allowed to do so, although we were unable to obtain detailed information on this and it appears to be a matter of discretion.

Although not officially designed for therapy, social workers and participants report that meetings with their designated social workers often take this turn. Social workers see part of their role as providing program participants with support and encouragement and are keenly aware of (and critical of) arresting and charging as a gateway to provision of their services. The interactions between the program participants and their designated social worker are the core of the SPD, and these are the most stable ongoing relationships that are formed over the course of the three-month program.

There are no comprehensive figures available on the program, but a number of reports provide snapshots of various information regarding program participants and program uptake and completion rates at different points in time. One of our prior studies (Shdaimah & Bailey-Kloch, 2014) drew on SPD administrative data obtained from staff members. The data involved 616 people arrested for street-level prostitution in Baltimore City between January and December of 2010. Of those arrested, 90 percent were cisgender women, 9 percent were transgender women, and 1 percent were cisgender men. The defendants' mean age was 34 years old (SD 1.3). The data indicated that 61 percent had not received a high school diploma or GED, 28 percent had graduated from high school, and 11 percent had at least some college. The sample had a mean of 1.3 (SD 1.6) minor children, 56 percent of whom lived with them. Of the group, 13 percent were homeless, and concerns that they identified included ill health (48 percent), substance use problems (64 percent), and mental health problems (59 percent).

The SPD is a popular program, with most people accepting the offer, although in its busiest times some were "capped out" due to space limitations.[1] About half of those who do not enter the program formally reject it; the remainder simply do not appear in court.[2] These numbers indicate that the program was popular and participants in the qualitative portion of the study indicated that "word on the street" was positive. When there is a waiting list and the number of defendants exceeds the capacity, some of the "capped out" defendants are given deferred court dates, at the discretion of the prosecutor in consultation with the program social workers and public defender, in order to wait for an opening. Similar to the findings of other SPD studies, SPD participants during this period identified a variety of needs, including mental health and addiction treatment, housing, employment, transportation, and physical health concerns. Of the participants, 31 percent reported bipolar disorder, 14 percent reported depression, and 80 percent reported substance abuse problems. Cisgender program participants were statistically significantly more likely to report mental health and substance abuse problems than transgender participants were. While no administrative data is available on housing or employment, qualitative data suggest that transgender participants identify job and housing discrimination as the primary focus of their service needs (Bailey-Kloch et al., 2015). Fifty-four of the 2010 SPD participants (58 percent) successfully graduated from the SPD; 15 (16 percent) never appeared for their first appointment or received services; and 24 (26 percent) engaged with the program, at least initially, and failed or were rearrested.

Another study was conducted by SPD social workers and TurnAround, Inc.,[3] with 99 women charged with prostitution at the Eastside Courthouse between September 2012 and February 2013. Of the 47 SPD-eligible participants, 11 "traded sexual activity before the age of 18 and/or had to give their money from sexual activity to someone else," which was the study definition for trafficking (TurnAround, Inc. & Specialized Prostitution Diversion Program, n.d., p. 1). Women were most commonly introduced to prostitution through peers or friends (20), or on their own (26). Less common was introduction by men[4] (8) or family members (11) and social situations (9). Most traded sex not only for money but also for drugs, shelter, or something else. One woman reported someone preventing her from leaving prostitution. Others identified a range of barriers, including drug habits, lack of job skills or job training, or basic needs such as housing, food, cigarettes, and medication, or indicated that they had already left. Of the participants, 67 and 66, respectively, were receiving mental health treatment and substance abuse treatment currently or had in the past; some of these women were in both categories. One other study (Koelger, 2014; Koegler et al., 2020) examined recidivism (for first arrest) over a 30-month period following prostitution for defendants arrested during 2010. There were no statistically significant differences between those who completed the SPD and those who rejected it. However, those who completed the program were 53 percent less likely to be arrested for prostitution and 51 percent less likely to be arrested for anything within two years of beginning the 90-day program (Koegler, n.d.). This suggests the importance of understanding what factors might contribute to program completion or failure. Program participants in our qualitative study reported satisfaction with this program, mainly citing the offer of material, social, and health support as well as the relationships they developed with staff; many were also left in the same rather precarious financial, housing, and employment situations that they entered the program with (Shdaimah & Bailey-Kloch, 2014). In sum, the SPD appears to address individual concerns, but has little impact on the structural and resource constraints that shape the lives of many of the program participants.

Prostitution arrests in Baltimore have long been declining, despite ongoing public concern with sex work, resulting in a near elimination of the pool of potential SPD participants. This decline has been accompanied by a shift in public and nonprofit efforts. For example, Police Commissioner Michael Harrison sought to reduce sex work by targeting clients in response to citizen complaints, reflecting a characterization of sex workers as vulnerable people in need of rescue *rather* than punishment (Barron, 2019). Sex workers and sex work organizations in Baltimore, such as Sex Workers Outreach Project (SWOP), Power Inside, and the Gay, Lesbian, Bisexual, and Transgender Community Center of Baltimore have attempted to address stigma, marginalization, and heightened vulnerability due to gentrifications through mutual aid and advocacy (Weigel, 2017).

In March 2020, as a response to the COVID-19 epidemic, Baltimore City temporarily decriminalized sex work—a policy change made permanent by the State's Attorney's Office a year later, citing interests of justice, efficient use of limited law enforcement resources, and public health. Evidence from an ongoing study in a Baltimore community suggests that there is mixed support for this policy. Bordered by a county that has not decriminalized sex work, residents have voiced concerns that decriminalization has become a welcome mat for the sex work industry, increasing incidents in their community; at the same time, residents have shared a growing frustration with a seeming lack of enforcement in response to their sex work–related calls for service. Similar concerns have been reported in the popular press, coming from neighborhood residents across Baltimore who seek limitations on sex work and what they view as attendant quality of life and safety concerns (Schwartzman, 2021). Baltimore City State's Attorney Ivan Bates, who took office in January 2023, ran on a campaign to roll back decriminalization and "pledged to use low-level offenses such as drug possession and prostitution to divert people into addiction treatment and other services" (Gessler, 2023).

Project Dawn Court

Philadelphia's Project Dawn Court (Baylson, 2017) was the first prostitution problem-solving court in the country, modeled on the city's highly touted drug court. It was designed to improve on the traditional criminal justice system's response to prostitution, which was perceived as ineffective and unfair. The year before Project Dawn Court launched, in 2009, Philadelphia police arrested 837 women for prostitution, many of whom had been arrested previously (Murtha, 2010). The pilot version of Project Dawn Court (PDC) was launched in 2010 and enrolled 28 women. Unlike many other problem-solving courts, PDC was not for first-time offenders.

Project Dawn Court is part of the Philadelphia Municipal Court. Like other problem-solving courts, the PDC comprises a team of dedicated agency representatives. Specifically designed to avoid the traditional adversarial relationships, the team, led by the judge, includes a probation officer, a prosecutor, a public defender, and the PDC coordinator, who is a master's degree–level social worker. The team meets monthly to discuss cases, and in the interim it communicates as necessary regarding clients. PDC also has an Oversight Committee that includes members of key partners such as the Adult Probation and Parole Department, the Joseph J. Peters Institute, the Office of the District Attorney, and the Defenders' Association of Philadelphia, the Philadelphia Department of Behavioral Health and Intellectual Disability Services, service provider representatives, the Forensic Intensive Recovery Program, and experts such as the first author of this book and a former PDC prosecutor who runs the Villanova Law Institute to Address Commercial Sexual Exploitation. The Oversight Committee serves as a sounding board for the PDC and helps troubleshoot any concerns raised by the program. These concerns may include trends or patterns identified by program participants and staff, identification of useful resources, and concerns such as unsuitable programs, long waiting lists for services, or the need to provide better trauma training to organizations that work with program participants.

In order to be considered for the PDC, which serves only adult cisgender women, prospective participants must have an open prostitution case and at least three prior prostitution or prostitution-related charges or convictions (Muraresku, 2017). The PDC will not accept women with violent felony charges. Although the PDC generally does not accept women who do not reside in Philadelphia, some exceptions have been made for women who were arrested in and had been living in Philadelphia. Potential participants can be identified by public defenders, prosecutors, and judges; defendants can also self-refer. If the PDC stakeholder team agrees, these potential participants will be offered the program. The majority of these defendants are incarcerated because they cannot afford bail when the public defender meets with them to discuss the offer. Entering the program often shortens the participant's jail time, which can be a powerful incentive. The public defender therefore is careful to lay out which rights the defendant gives up, what the program obligations are, and the maximum potential penalty for program failure. The legal rights a participant surrenders upon entering the program are pretrial rights, the participant's right to a trial, and most of her rights to appeal, in addition to the prostitution conviction that will be triggered by program failure. These are again reviewed by the judge at the defendant's first hearing as part of the colloquy that is signed by the defendant, her lawyer, the prosecutor, and the judge.

Women must enter a *nolo contendere* plea to participate in the program, which means that they do not contest the facts of the case.[5] Their plea is held in abeyance until they leave the program through completion or failure. Successful graduates of the program have their charges dismissed with prejudice, meaning that the charges cannot be filed again. In the PDC pilot, all prostitution-related convictions as well as charges were dismissed. The current PDC, however, dismisses only those charges with which the defendant enters the program. After a year of no new arrests, convictions, or evidence that the woman used drugs or engaged in prostitution, she may ask to have those charges expunged by the PDC judge.

When women are terminated from the program due to noncompliance, their *nolo contendere* pleas are entered and they are sentenced (Leon & Shdaimah, 2012). Sentences vary and are at the discretion of the presiding judge, except that the sentence cannot exceed the maximum penalty and the judge must give credit for any time served in relation to the case. The penalties for prostitution in Pennsylvania vary with the number of offenses. Those who have three or more offenses can be charged with a first-degree misdemeanor, imposing the harshest level of penalty of up to 5 years' incarceration and up to $10,000 in fines for each charge. In addition, convictions might result in violations of probation or parole, which carry their own jail time and do not run concurrently so they would be added onto any jail time for the prostitution offense. PDC requires participants to engage with the court for a minimum of one year, comprising of four phases (Philadelphia District Attorney's Office, n.d.). The phase lengths gradually increase (30, 90, 120, and 120 days, respectively). Program requirements, level of supervision, and independence change in response to the PDC participants' progress, emerging needs, and goals. As participants enter their final phases, the PDC focuses attention on their future after graduation, planning for housing, education, employment, and continued recovery.

Entering participants undergo a Forensic Intensive Recovery (FIR) evaluation to determine the appropriate level and type of care. Philadelphia's Department of Behavioral Health and Intellectual Disability Services (DBHIDS) confirms the level of care and funding and refers participants to specific programs for substance abuse or behavioral health concerns. All PDC participants must undergo individual and group trauma treatment. A representative of the Joseph J. Peters Institute (JJPI), which provides the mandated trauma treatment for all PDC participants, reported that a randomly chosen sample of 10 of the 40 women then enrolled in the program indicated that 50 percent had experienced childhood sexual abuse, 100 percent had suffered trauma from sexual violence, 85 percent started substance abuse in adolescence, 50 percent suffered trauma from physical abuse as adults, 30 percent disclosed a life-threatening illness, 90 percent suffered from severe mental illness, and 80 percent had a history of homelessness. This is consistent with what program participants report in open court, as well as what program staff report based on their individual interactions with participants.

Participants may move through several programs throughout the course of their PDC participation, often decreasingly intensive and less supervised as they progress. Programs include detoxification, long- or short-term inpatient care, halfway houses, intensive outpatient care, and outpatient care. Programs are identified through collaboration between FIR and the participants' insurance provider. While the PDC cannot choose which programs participants are referred to, they do provide input. Since quality and appropriateness can vary, the PDC also follows up on concerns voiced by participants or PDC team members. PDC provides feedback for improvement or to request that participants be referred to appropriate programs where the level of quality is more consistently satisfactory. The PDC also offers training to providers so that they can better serve PDC clients. All PDC participants receive mandatory sexual trauma treatment at JJPI, which created specialized programming for PDC participants; treatment includes individual and group therapy.

PDC holds mandatory monthly court meetings, although the court holds an additional monthly listing for incoming participants or for participants whom they deem to be in need of additional supervision or assistance. Like other problem-solving courts, the PDC requires all participants to remain throughout the listing so that they can observe their peers. Admonitions, praise, and advice are always meant for the entire court, even when they are directed at specific individuals. As is the case with most problem-solving courts, the monthly courtroom meetings are a key component of the program. The meetings are set up in a regular courtroom, and the judge sits above the other team members and the court. The public defender, prosecutor, and probation officer sit inside the gated area facing the judge; PDC participants, guests, and staff from allied programs waiting to report to the court sit on the other side of the gate, seated in rows. The court is careful to ask who is present; any unidentified people will be approached, questioned, and often asked to leave. Men are the target of heightened suspicion. This is due to the court's recognition that prostitution is a stigmatized offense, and women may not feel as free to be candid if outsiders are present. It is also because many of the women have been abused by male clients and other men in their lives, and professional stakeholders worried that that "pimps" or traffickers might pressure women although little evidence of such activity has been found.

As each woman is called up, she goes through the swinging gate to stand next to the public defender. If present, her JJPI therapist will come forward to provide an update to the court. The judge greets the participant; there is often a brief and cordial exchange between the two. The judge listens to the probation officer's report, which includes praise for progress and concerns. The therapist then reports generally on attendance and engagement, without providing specific detail of the content of therapeutic encounters. These formal reports are always accompanied by direct conversation between the judge and the participant. Sometimes the reports are brief. The judge always inquires whether the participant would like to share or ask anything. In instances of phase completion or other progress, good news is shared and praise is given, with the judge often asking the participant how it feels to accomplish her goal. Similarly, program breaches, personal struggles and concerns, and special requests (e.g., to visit a family member out of state) are discussed. Most of these are shared in open court, and the prosecutor and the public defender may weigh in. If matters are sensitive and not to be shared with the full court, or if there is disagreement, one of the PDC team members may call for a sidebar conference. In these instances, the judge generally explains to the room what they are discussing or the outcome of the discussion without revealing the more confidential information, asking the room to wait quietly. As noted in Chapter 1, problem-solving courts are public venues, and the exchanges are watched carefully by the spectators, who often make running commentary and compare their own and others' situations to the participant who is at the bar. At no time is this clearer than when a participant enters from the side door inside the bar: the door leading from lockup where women transported from the municipal correctional facility enter. Intakes of breath, shouts of encouragement and empathy, and expression of frustration, sadness, or disgust are all part of the repertoire.

Court time is also a time for socializing; many of the women know each other from the streets, treatment programs, and jail and are often happy to see friends, exchange stories, and support each other (Shdaimah & Leon, 2016). The following We-poem,[6] crafted by Maggie Buckridge from a focus group for PDC participants that was held just before a monthly court hearing, captures some of the importance of PDC as a space for coming together (Gesser, 2022).

"We've Seen Each Other"

We have a understanding because we know the struggle
We don't have to say anything to each other
We can just look at each other
We just know, 'cause
We know that struggle
We know what it's like
We've been out there
We know what goes on
We do have that understanding
We do love each other for that.
We know
We know we have that understanding
We all, us going through this together it's like our emotions are all attached
We feel that inside
'cause we know that
We cheer for each other
We keep each other strong
We've come across each other's paths
We were running too much
We did
maybe We didn't
We talked sitting in a sheriff's van or something or shackled together somewhere.
We seen each other
We've seen each other
We've gotten to know each other intimately; you know what I mean?

Another core feature of the PDC is the regular (usually weekly) meeting with participants and their probation officer. In what might seem like a counterintuitive plan, the PDC's dedicated probation officer is a female officer from the sex offender unit. This was a conscious decision based on the initially assigned officer's special expertise in working with women and on her ability to build rapport. Her unit supervisor, who sits on the PDC Oversight Committee, was also supportive of the program. From working for many years with perpetrators of sexual crimes, the PDC team and the probation department felt that an officer from this unit would be more likely to believe and be empathetic to PDC participants' experiences as victims of sexual assault, which they presumed would be part of the professional and personal histories of all PDC participants. A disadvantage of this arrangement, however, is that the waiting room is filled primarily with male perpetrators, which can be stressful for PDC participants. The probation officer's role is supervisory; she conducts home visits to inspect suitability of programs and living arrangements and remains in touch with therapists and treatment programs. There is a balance of care and authority. Her job is to ensure compliance, but rapport-building is a key component of the weekly visits, and she encourages and offers assistance to those who struggle. PDC participants often inform the probation officer if they are worried about their peers. Meetings take place "in booth," a small cubicle where the probation officer enters through one door and the probationer through the other. There is a button under the desk on the probation officer's side that she uses to call security when a woman is to be taken into custody. The stance of the probation office,[7] like the stance of the PDC team in general, is clear: They are empathetic but firm, and they consider transparency an important component of fairness so that participants know what to expect in good times and bad.

PDC participants who breach program requirements, including participation in mandatory treatment programs or housing placements, must restart their current phase. They also receive an additional sanction. In accordance with problem-solving justice principles of holding defendants accountable and of rehabilitation, sanctions are graduated and designed to serve not only as punishment but also as a tool for reflection and learning. These can include the participants writing essays that they must read aloud in court, spending time in a jury box observing court, performing community service, and being incarcerated for up to 10 days in a treatment unit of the city prison. The majority of participants face at least one sanction, and thus are in the program for more than a year. Program breach, while met with punishment, is normalized by the PDC as part of the recovery process—not just from addiction to drugs but as part of the process of exiting prostitution, given the complex and multiple problems that many of the participants face. These include sometimes mediocre treatment facilities, difficult economic circumstances, and treatment that requires participants to confront histories of trauma. Problems also include the pull of friends and families who may themselves be using drugs or engaging in prostitution, as most of a participant's social circle are people with whom they attend programs or who also reside in the low-income areas where participants continue to live and work, as these are where most of the treatment programs and recovery houses are located. These difficult circumstances are acknowledged and discussed in open court, with the judge and other stakeholders empathetic to the difficulties. Sanctions are thus generally meted out (and perceived) as a requirement of the program and an expression of concern, rather than a condemnation of the defendant. While there is no set limit to instances of noncompliance, the prosecutor can call for a "show cause" hearing, in which both sides present evidence as to whether the defendant's continued participation is warranted.

In addition to mandatory supervision and treatment, the PDC provides assistance in other areas as appropriate—provided these services are available. These include securing documentation (Social Security cards and identification); health insurance; medical treatment; dental care; and education (Adult Basic Education, General Education Diploma, Community College of Philadelphia). The PDC and partner agencies also work with clients to identify housing and job training or placement services, although these are clearly more difficult to obtain. The PDC has helped participants reunite with family members, supporting some through child welfare involvement or reaching out to siblings, parents, or adult children. A variety of enrichment programs, often designed for women in recovery, are offered through partnerships between nonprofit agencies and the PDC, including Gearing Up (a bicycle program) and the People's Paper Co-op (a nonprofit entrepreneurship venture). Programs are vetted by the PDC before they are offered to participants, and they are not mandatory.

As of April 2016, 99 women had participated in the PDC; an additional 28 women participated in its first incarnation, which PDC staff now refer to as "the pilot." Participants ranged in age from 22 to 55. Of these 99 women, 68 were identified as White, 24 as African American, and 7 as Hispanic/Latina. Data on race/ethnicity are recorded sometimes by self-report, and sometimes by others based on observation or assumptions, so there is likely some level of error in these figures. As of April 2016, 40 women were in the program. The most recent review conducted by the Philadelphia District Attorney's Office, in November 2015, showed that 6 of the then-39 successful graduates had been rearrested, although the program did not have information about whether these rearrests resulted in convictions. Of the 58 women no longer in the program, 44 graduated. Of those who had not graduated, five were placed in an alternative program due to mental health concerns, five were terminated for noncompliance, three were deceased, and one withdrew voluntarily (Lesha Sanders, personal communication, April 22, 2016). The number of active program participants has steadily declined, with the latest available figures indicating that in the year 2019, "Project Dawn admitted 4 individuals, 5 cases, 11 probation matters and recognized 7 individuals for successfully completing the program" (First Judicial District, 2020, p. 99). The decline in participants has likely been hastened by a moratorium on the prosecution of sex workers, although not their clients nor those accused of sex trafficking, declared by Philadelphia's self-described progressive prosecutor (Steele & Terruso, 2021; Vella, 2022).

3

"That Foot on Their Neck"

Coercion and Choice

C oercion operates in all facets of the prostitution diversion programs (PDPs). Here we place it at the center of our analysis. The nesting of PDPs within the criminal legal system is fundamental to their design: These programs cannot be viewed as simply rehabilitative opportunities. PDPs extend the criminal legal system into the lives of program participants and into agency and community contexts. Defendants' motivations for participating in criminal legal system–affiliated PDPs cannot be separated from the coercion present in respondents' pressing material needs and their fear of traditional consequences such as incarceration. Many PDP participants told us they "chose" a diversion program as an alternative to jail—not because of particular interest in the programs and what they had to offer. PDC participant Maria illustrates coercion as a larger force within and outside of the criminal legal system. It is present in the self-identified factors that led PDP participants to sell or exchange sex, such as the need for food, housing, love, and drugs. Illegal sex work was (or still is) the preferred option for some, despite the accompanying stigma and system involvement. Similarly, some professional stakeholders also support PDPs, despite their own concerns, due to lack of alternatives.

The controversial marriage of rehabilitative and penal practices is at the heart of problem-solving courts. The complex interplay between different forms of coercion and rehabilitation is focused on producing what the court (and sometimes participants) view as normative, law-abiding women. This chapter attempts to do justice to this complexity by providing a nuanced, emic (insider) perspective that is often absent from ideological debates, while retaining a critical stance (Karandikar, 2022b). For example, we take seriously that many program staff and participants articulated the need for coerced treatment and personal readiness, alongside the seemingly contradictory narratives of epiphany and change. These narratives raise more questions than answers: What is the appropriate balance of coercive power and therapeutic services? Is any form of coercion acceptable? In what circumstances can coercion reinforce individual readiness and therapeutic services? In what circumstances does it interfere? Even if coercion might be effective in some cases, is any amount of coercion ethically acceptable? How do PDP professionals reconcile their ethical discomfort with punishing in order to rescue, or with the criminalization of what they view as undesirable or coerced behaviors?

After the opening vignette, this chapter draws on interviews with criminal legal professionals (lawyers, judges, social workers, probation and pretrial workers, and therapists) to examine how they view their appropriate role and the ways they interact with others. We discuss how coercion and motivation bear on the allocation of scarce resources in programs that serve only a small percentage of those who are eligible. The difficulty of allocation is compounded by our respondents' declared inability to predict who is most likely to engage and succeed. However, focusing on coercion at only the individual level or program level further obscures the system-level coercive forces that often structure these individual choices and are reinforced through the red herring of PDPs, which become ends in themselves rather than a means to broader systemic change.

"I Have Them on My Back" (*Maria*)

Maria was in Project Dawn Court for about two years. In her late 20s, Maria is the only self-identified Hispanic woman in our sample. She started selling sex about five years before then, because of what she referred to as her "drug addiction." Maria steadily used drugs and sold sex to support her addiction, except when arrested and, for one six-month period, when she "had a boyfriend and [she] wanted to be with him, so [she] just stopped getting high, stopped prostituting." For Maria, as it is for nearly all participants, selling sex is inextricably entwined with drug use, and Maria "went back to prostituting" when she began "using again [as that] was the only way I knew how to get quick money."

Maria first learned about PDC while she was incarcerated. "One of the girls in jail enticed me to get into the program," and she reached out to Lily, the court coordinator. Maria's primary motivation to join was to get her charges expunged: "They help you get in school, into programs, and what interested me [more] was to get the prostitution off of my record. So they clear your record after a year." Maria also saw PDC as preferable to incarceration, which reinforced her addiction rather than serving as a break or deterrent from it. She had this to say:

[PDC]'s more fair because sometimes the jail won't help us, it just hinders us. 'Cause you could get high in jail. . . . So it's better to put you in a program and get you help for your addiction instead of just sending you to jail to make your addiction worse.

Following Maria's request to enter PDC, the public defender verified her eligibility and petitioned Maria's "back judge."[1] Maria learned more about PDC during a hearing to discuss her request to transfer into the program. It was then that she heard that PDC had four phases and that "if I run or I don't complete the program, I'm looking at my back time. It's like two years for each one of my cases. So that's like six years upstate." Maria was dismayed that entering the program might place her at risk for a more serious punishment than she already faced if she failed—in terms of both length of sentence and location (it would be served in state prison, rather than county jail). However, she did not regret her decision. Instead, she framed the threat of punishment as a key benefit of the program: "If I was just on probation by myself, I would have been locked up like four hot urines ago." In another interview, Maria explained:

I need to know when I gotta be . . . I got an hour travel time from here to going home. I gotta be home by 5:30; I get outta here at 4. And as soon as I come in they do a swab. 'Cause I need that structure and that stability. If I don't have structure and stability, and knew I could come and go as I please, then it'd be a problem. . . . Knowing that I have them on my back and that I'm looking at upstate time if I run or leave from the program, that's what kept me going.

While Maria described structure and stability as being what she "needed" from the program, she was also frustrated when the structure was *too* limiting or intrusive. For example, she compared two different inpatient programs that she attended during her early PDC phases. She preferred the program that balanced restrictions with limited freedoms, such as "just doing 2 weeks of blackout,[2] but you still could smoke cigarettes, you still could use the phone, still could have visits and stuff." Having some liberties made it easier to comply with program strictures, which included engaging with therapy, abstaining from alcohol or drugs, and remaining on the premises. Maria relapsed while in this program when she "tried to get my kids back all at one time and it was too much. And I left [First Inpatient Program] and I was just left to my own devices."

On her own and struggling, Maria followed probation officer Ronny Landis's advice to stay connected in order to mitigate sanctions. Maria's breach of the inpatient program's rules by leaving was, by definition, also a breach of PDC regulations, which require compliance with any mandated program rules. In both PDC and SPD we were told and we observed that remaining engaged with PDP staff through transgressions can stave off termination due to serious or continued noncompliance, and is an important demonstration of commitment that fosters goodwill among system professionals (Corrigan & Shdaimah, 2016). As Maria told us,

> She was like, "Just call me every day just to let me know you alive, you ain't get locked up, 'cause you don't wanna catch a new case in Dawn's Court. 'Cause then, that'll really make the judge mad." So I would call her every day, let her know, like, "I'm struggling."

Maria contrasted Judge Kahan's actual response to her relapse with the punitive response that she had expected. "I thought she was gonna say, 'Bailiff, take her back [to jail].' So I was like, 'Pshhhh [relief], thank God; she gave me a second chance at this and I'm gonna make it worth it.'" The threat of incarceration motivated Maria to stay in touch with Ronny, comply with program requirements while she waited for her insurance authorization, and get into a program as quickly as she could.

However, PDC restarted Maria's program phase after her relapse and sent her to a stricter program, where she struggled:

> It's hard, you can't smoke for 2 weeks, you go on a 30-day blackout, your boyfriend can't come see you. So it's like, just this is my last time going into a program cause it's . . . god, I thought it would get easier and it didn't: it got harder.

Maria believes that what probation officer Ronny and Judge Kahan know about her life makes them empathetic despite her noncompliance and struggles. They know her difficult personal history of abuse; they know how hard she has been trying and how well she is doing relative to her past; and they believe in her potential for success. For example, Maria explained why she believed that she was not incarcerated or removed from the program after a relapse:

> 'Cause I had 11 months clean . . . so [Judge Kahan] knew something was wrong. She knows my whole [story], with my children and stuff

and everything and what I went through as a child and everything. So she knows. She sees something in me that I didn't see.

This quote repeats a common refrain among program participants. Most were not uncomfortable when compelled to reveal details of their lives within the context of PDC. With some exceptions, most interpreted such requirements as opportunities to share information so that criminal legal system professionals would use their power with empathy for them as individuals, rather than as anonymous cases.

Participants knew the courts had the power to incarcerate, and appreciated when they refrained from using it. Maria said,

[PDC is] a whole different manner than regular court. Like they know we have a problem and they try to help us with it. They're not quick to send us right back to jail; they try to find a way around stuff.

When asked what "regular court" is like, Maria explained: "It's hell. . . . If I would've relapsed in regular court, they would've sent me back to jail. Thanks to Project Dawn, I'm still on the street, in a program, and can see my kids and stuff." Maria initially welcomed weekly probation meetings and monthly court hearings because they kept her motivated.

At first I was like, "Oh god; gotta go to the program. Gotta do this. Got this person on my back, [and] this person." But in honesty, that's what I needed; some people just need that foot on they neck to push 'em a little bit.

By our final interview, having been in PDC for nearly two years, Maria was fed up. In a hearing to *show cause*[3] as to why she should not be terminated from PDC and receive jail time, Maria accepted an alternative offer to move to the Mental Health Court, where she would stay under the auspices of the PDC judge.

During the *show cause* hearing, the prosecutor Erin voiced her frustration with Maria to Judge Kahan: "I have been angry, and disappointed, but at this point I'm just afraid that she's going to be her own undoing and I'll be going to her funeral" (PDC field notes, Summer 2012). Judge Kahan responded, reframing Erin's advice as a warning to Maria:

I understand [Ms. Archer's] concern. But we are outsiders looking in. [Turning to Maria, she says] My concern frankly is that you've had incredible support from a whole lot of people in PDC. And you have appreciated it sometimes but sometimes [you see these people as if]

they are in your way. At your age it just strikes me that you've been resistant and frankly I don't know why but you need to give some thought to that. Sometimes it feels like we're the only ones working for you and you're only working against yourself and the rest of us. (PDC field notes, Summer 2012)

Both Erin and Judge Kahan *know* Maria and invoke their personal investment to lend power to the wake-up call.

In the next quote, we see Judge Kahan evoking the limitations of her coercive power with Maria and, in doing so, ironically playing her proverbial last card in the form of a threat to coax Maria toward internal motivation. Both the prosecutor and the judge refer to adulthood as part of the expectation that Maria take responsibility for her actions, simultaneously raising the specter of "consequences." Judge Kahan told Maria this:

We do not really have favorites and are not supposed to have favorites, but you were everybody's project and even though PDC was not the right place, we really want to see you get it right. Not to force my hand to violate you. Not that it's going to do you any good, but it's not just a message to you but also to other people that there are rules and there are consequences. We can't plug away on our own. (PDC field notes, Summer 2012)

Regardless of whether her exhortation and concerns will do Maria "any good," Judge Kahan explicitly directs them as "a message" to all PDC participants present at the monthly court hearing.

Maria was relieved to exit PDC without further adverse consequences. Similarly, the PDC professionals were relieved to be able to offer a viable compromise so that Maria would not be viewed as a program failure. Their concern may have been driven by a desire to show policy-makers that PDC was a worthwhile investment of resources, but it also appeared to be driven by genuine concern. Maria explained that her current and former probation officers "got together and they decided that Dawn Court wasn't for me. They put me in mental health court instead of them sending me upstate for five years." Maria explained:

[Mental health court]'s actually better for me, 'cause they['re] dealing more with my mental status, and it ain't so much problems—I gotta do this, I gotta do that, I gotta be here, I gotta do this, and I ain't gotta worry about going back to jail. 'Cause Dawn Court, they want you to do it like this, like this, like this, like this, like that [says in a rigid voice]. And mental health court's more lenient 'cause they know you got mental issues.

During our last interview, Maria was in mental health court and living with her children and godsister. This living arrangement allowed her to "come and go as I please, eat when I want to, sleep when I want to. So it's like I got more freedom; I feel independent." The contrast between the much lower levels of risk, surveillance, and coercion in mental health court as compared to PDC raises many questions. As we have written elsewhere, the criminalization of sex work and the hypervigilance that it engenders is a theme that crosses geography and time (Lilley et al., 2020; Cohen, 2017; Shdaimah, 2018). It also raises the possibility that attitudes are at play that continue to view addiction as a poor choice to be addressed through regulation and willpower rather than a mental health condition (see Chapter 4).

Upon moving to mental health court, Maria was relieved to be done with PDC, which "was a struggle," while still able to remain under Judge Kahan's supervision:

> I like to continue with the one judge because . . . [Judge Kahan] has been in my case and everything, so she already knows what she's dealing with. To deal with somebody new, and for them not to know the rules, and gotta get to know the rules, and then they put Maria in jail not knowing the whole Maria [talking about herself in the third person], so I just rather deal with Kahan, 'cause she already knows the whole giddyup.

Change was a particular sticking point with Maria. She did not like to share her story with people she did not know, in case they would use information to harm her:

> It's so *nerve-racking* . . . Like why do *I* have to keep telling? I just hate it. . . . I get defensive over it, because I don't know you, so why should I be telling you what's going on with me? I never seen you before. I don't know if you [are] trying to hurt me or get me locked up or whatever or use what I say against me.

Maria also worried about having to manage new or confusing expectations. When her probation officer Ronny Landis was promoted, she was very upset. "I cried. . . . I was like, 'Hold it; who is you? Where's Landis at?' 'Oh, she got promoted.' I said, 'What!? No. I want Landis back.'" She was uncertain of her new probation officer's expectations:

> I had Landis for so many years, so I know Landis's dos and don'ts and wills and won'ts. [Now] I gotta learn Catherine's wills, won'ts, dos, and don'ts. Like, "What would she do if I do this?" . . . I try to keep the same people that I know in my circle because I'm already used to them. I know what's gonna happen, what ain't gonna happen, this, that, and the third.

In addition to the turmoil that having to navigate a new probation officer creates for people on probation, this fear is compounded for PDP participants like Maria by the fear of being abandoned by service providers, given Maria's tremendous distrust of people she does not know. Her willingness to accept coercive PDC rules often hinged on whether she perceived that they would come with support and care. Maria also found it easier to comply with the program when she knew its parameters (dos, don'ts, wills, won'ts) and felt she could predict which potential consequences she could live with. Maria's engagement with PDC unraveled when she found its unsustainably coercive and interfering mandates simply too much to bear.

"You Were Everybody's Project" (*Judge Kahan*)

In the previous section, Judge Kahan referenced the court's investment in Maria, which sometimes seemed even greater than Maria's investment in herself. Judge Kahan is channeling her own as well as other team members' frustration with, and fear for, Maria. The court is designed precisely to work with defendants to spur change that will become internalized, in order to effectively curtail future offending. Much of this change focuses on individual behaviors and attitudes, essentially making the individual a Pygmalion-like "project." However, PDPs also attempt to address some structural concerns—largely through case management, and in rare cases through meso-level interventions at the agency level. The PDP itself constitutes an agency-level intervention by providing a possible alternative within existing policy for a small subset of prostitution defendants. There are limitations to such change efforts: PDPs provide a meager bulwark against the powerful forces that constrain defendants and other PDP stakeholders.

After many conversations with respondents and among ourselves, we identified pervasive and powerful coercive factors that undermine participants in PDPs, such that they swim in a sea of coercion with the limited assistance provided by the "life buoy" of PDPs. To illustrate this, we commissioned artist Francisca Moreno to depict the multiple sources of coercion at the various levels of Dawn Court participants' ecosystem (see Figure 3.1). In the remainder of this chapter, we discuss the coercive context in which PDPs operate; then we examine how PDPs themselves understand the interplay of

Figure 3.1 Swimming in a Sea of Coercion

coercion stemming from PDPs, participants' prior criminal legal system involvement, and participants' own life circumstances more generally.

Swimming in a Sea of Coercion

It is abundantly clear from Maria's story, and from the participants in both the PDC and the SPD, that the women are immersed in a sea of coercive forces as illustrated in Figure 3.1. Nearly all respondents in both programs, and—according to professional stakeholders and as borne out in our observations—all of the PDC participants and the overwhelming majority of SPD participants grapple with severe, long-term, and often debilitating addiction. Such severe addictions give rise to the need to ensure an ongoing supply of illegal drugs, often in the moment. Sex work provides immediate access to what SPD participant CeeJay called "quick fast money." Many respondents were able to make enough money through sex trading to secure drugs for themselves, for significant others, and for friends who were "sick," that is, experiencing withdrawal.

PDP participants struggled to meet their most basic needs. One of the most frequent and pressing concerns, a pervasive problem in both Baltimore and Philadelphia, was the difficulty of finding shelter and remaining housed (Shdaimah et al., in press; Urban Displacement Project, 2021). PDC's Judge Kahan saw housing as "the biggest hurdle":

> So many of the mental health [stressors] people face is unstable housing to begin with. And even those who have more stable housing, they are going back to the same locations.... [pause] Was it AA [Alcoholics Anonymous] that started "person, places, things"? And NA [Narcotics Anonymous] has the same thing. And all the drug treatment programs—and I think that that is reality. And I think that it's really hard when you don't have a stable environment or you go back to where you have a comfort zone. We all have a comfort zone. You don't have to, you can be anyone of us, and you talk about the huge stressors in life and what do you have?—new marriage, new location, new job—you know, it's the big three. So housing transcends people who have issues with drugs and alcohol and people who have issues with prostitution and mental health—it's huge.

As Judge Kahan notes, housing is indicative of other struggles often associated with poverty and resource limitations, and it also can be a destabilizing force.

Housing struggles were one reason for high levels of precarity and other difficulties that accompany frequent moves, such as transportation challenges, difficulty staying connected to health care providers and therapists, and timely and steady compliance with required programming and criminal justice imperatives such as weekly meetings with probation officers and monthly court attendance. In 2021, the Philadelphia metro area and Baltimore metro area ranked 8th and 20th of 53 U.S. metropolitan areas of over 1 million people, respectively, on the 2021 Housing Precarity Risk Model. As Baltimore drug assessor George noted, "housing for women" is "the hardest resource to find." Similarly, PDC coordinator Maya explained the need for what she called "good housing." Despite the plethora of recovery housing in Philadelphia, "finding [recovery houses] that are supportive for [PDC participants], finding areas in which they can financially afford, and then also that transition into more stable housing past the recovery housing is a huge obstacle." The challenges facing those who run and rely on the recovery housing economy in Philadelphia have been well documented, showing that the availability and quality of recovery housing, as well as the suitability for different subpopulations, are both limited and variable (Fairbanks, 2009). As PDC participant Casey describes in the following quote, many respondents complained that the housing to which they were mandated did not adequately meet their needs. Casey, for example, cannot find a recovery house where she can live with her husband, nor one in an area that would help her avoid the seemingly incessant invitation to use drugs or sell sex, both of which would place her out of program compliance and make her subject to punishment.

> Me and my husband are getting along so much better [but] it's a little hard because I'm at the recovery house, at first it was a little hard for me and him. [Also because] I'm right there where I used to do my dirt. Which I think is totally [problematic] that they want us to go to a recovery house that's right there. That's one thing that I think can change. 'Cause some women aren't that strong, they're right there, they're going to want to make money, you know what I mean? And I can even say for myself it was a little hard. Like here I am, I see these tricks that I know, and they're like "Yeah, you wanna—?" They want a date and I'm broke like, I wouldn't, I haven't done it, but like who's to say on a bad day, when I don't have any cigarettes and money, when the phone bill needs to be paid, you know shit like that happens. And here I am, you know it kind of weighs on you. You know, I think the recovery house they really want you to go to should be somewhere else.

Like many women who have been incarcerated, PDP participants experienced what Smoyer et al. (2021) refer to as "ping-pong housing." This means that it was often temporary, with women soon having to rely on friends or family. The overwhelming majority of Project Dawn Court participants entered the program while incarcerated; indeed, one of the PDC selling points is that it allowed for earlier release. Many individuals went to inpatient drug treatment that provided housing, but these destinations were temporary and affordable and appropriate housing remained a concern throughout program participation and upon leaving. While some program participants experience absolute homelessness, ping-pong housing is more prevalent. As Baltimore social worker Brigit explains, many women in the programs are embedded in networks of support that provide both benefits and risks to PDP goals. For example, if participants needed to contribute to their households, and illegal sex work is the best means to do so:

> Homelessness is not where these folks are. For the most part, now that's not 100 percent true, but nothing is 100 percent true. They usually have a place to stay, or multiple places to stay. And family still, [where] many of them stay, and they are also contributing.

PDP participants not only receive support from diffuse networks but sex work may help them to contribute to mutual aid efforts and to support others. As we explore in Chapter 6, SPD participant Brown Sugar's decision to sell sex (and later to stop selling sex) was for her children. Once they were older, she saw the PDP as helping her avoid criminal sanctions that may have cruelly and ironically separated her from the children that she supported through sex work. Whether sex work is a "good" thing or a "bad" thing depends on one's vantage point and assessments of how best to navigate multiple coercive forces, including hunger, unemployment, addiction, and criminal sanctions. Sex work and the crucial networks in which women are embedded are important to everyday survival in precarious economic situations, but many criminal legal system professionals view them as only problematic. Coercive forces of poverty and choices limited by stigmatization and criminalization (Hankel et al., 2019) are *used to leverage compliance.*

Coercion as a Court Tool

Coercion is a central feature of court-affiliated programs. The carrot-and-stick approach uses both negative and positive forms of coercion, by which we mean a strong—possibly irrefusable—impetus to participate. The potential for punishment as a stick is predicated on the belief that defendants derive motivation from their desire to avoid the harsh realities of a punitive criminal legal system. In this sense, court-affiliated programs are no different than the reigning U.S. deterrence model of harsh and punitive criminal legal system responses to sex work. As Sofia, a program administrator, pointed out, "How supportive and trauma-informed is this whole operation that we're just dangling jail as a threat?"

Court-affiliated diversion programs differ from the predominant approach in their addition of rewards and resources that both entice and enable compliance. PDPs entice using praise, public recognition in the form of certificates and graduation ceremonies, dismissal of charges, or expungement. They provide resources in the form of support and services that give participants the *means* to comply with program requirements, such as drug treatment programs, bus tokens, or housing. Alongside the positive motivation and support, PDPs use mechanisms of surveillance and control. The following definition of *accountability* is one of the six core principles of problem-solving justice:

> An important goal of problem-solving justice is to demonstrate that criminal behavior—even minor, quality-of-life crime—has consequences. Thus problem-solving courts strive to enforce their sanctions and emphasize accountability. One of their primary tools for achiev-

ing this goal is compliance monitoring. By requiring offenders to check in regularly with the judge, clerk, or local partners, problem-solving courts can ensure that sanctions—even diversion programs and alternatives to incarceration—have real teeth. (Wolf, 2007, p. 8)

Accountability has two major components. First, it depends on ongoing communication among various program components, including service providers, to enhance the courts' ability to monitor behavior and detect noncompliance. The second component is swift, unequivocable responses to infractions: "Noncompliance must be communicated as soon as it is discovered and the court must make it clear that sanctions (e.g., letters of apology, curfews, increased frequency of reporting, even short-term jail) will be issued in response" (Wolf, 2007, p. 8).

Despite her support of therapeutic goals, probation officer Catherine Heathcliff believes that coercion is equally necessary. She described how many treatment professionals underestimate the role of coercion, and she provided an illustration of how she effectively threatened a PDC participant into compliance:

[Other professional stakeholders were] like, "Oh she did a turnaround." . . . And [in probation we] think differently. . . . I was getting *phone* call after *phone* call, one after another from the program [about a participant]: "She's doing this, she's not doing this, she's doing this— whatever." . . . So one day she comes in here and she sat across from me and I passed her a business card and I said "Read it." And she read it and she handed it back to me and I was like "One more phone call, one more whatever." Guess what it was? An immigration agent's [card]. After that? Not a peep. She went to everything [claps hands]. So what I'm saying is the judge doesn't know it, and the defender doesn't know it. It was my last resort; nothing else was working. We were going to have to lock her up. After that—fine, graduated, no problem.

Catherine relies on a flow of what is usually private information. Program participants are required to waive much of their privacy, which allows probation officers like Catherine to threaten to *share* incriminating information with other workgroup professionals. In all cases, the vulnerability of program participants is exploited for purposes of both rescue and public safety. Information is part of the workgroup members' toolkit, much as sanctions and resources are. In this case, Catherine believes that threatening deportation was justified, because it allowed her to avoid incarcerating this diversion program participant (considered the most severe sanction) and ultimately led to her successful graduation.

"If You've Got a Hot, Give a Hot" (*Nicole*): The Power of Symbols and Internalized Surveillance

The PDC courtroom space illustrates how support and coercion are leveraged by criminal legal system professionals and participants themselves to "motivate" the participants' exit from sex work and drug use. Most people enter the courtroom from the street. After screening at the ground-floor metal detectors, they ride the elevator up to the courtroom floor. They enter the dark, wood-paneled space through a thick door that shields the courtroom from outside noise, into a space with rows of benches for PDC participants and the general public. In front of these is a wooden bar with a swinging gate, beyond which are tables for the public defender and the prosecutor, each on their own side. In front of, and facing, them and the public, the judge presides on a raised platform. The robed judge enters and exits through the door to her chambers, behind her on the raised platform. There is no doubt from the physical layout that the judge holds the power of decision here, and that the prosecutor and public defender standing immediately before her are authorized to make claims and requests. To the prosecutor's right is a third door that leads to the lockup; when defendants are transported in shackles from the city jail, they are brought through this door from a holding area in the basement of the building.

Even when the lockup door is not in use, it signals the ever-present threat of incarceration. When PDC participants emerge through this door into the court wearing orange jumpsuits, the shift in attention is palpable. They elicit calls of sympathy as well as murmurings about how they look and speculation about what led them to engage in the prohibited activities that led to incarceration. More dramatic is when a PDC participant enters court freely and then exits through the lockup door. For example, when Angela left through the lockup door, the trauma was made more poignant by the confusion of her adult son, who had attended court with her, as she handed him her purse and was taken away. There is also a common refrain whereby PDC participants will actually point to the doors, indicating that they want to go out of "that door" (to the outside hallway) and not "the other door" (i.e., that leads to lockup). Similarly, the booth where PDC participants meet with probation officers (POs), separated by a glass divider, has a button under the table on the PO side. Everyone is aware of its presence, despite the fact that it is hidden, and everyone knows that at any point the PO can press the button to summon officers to take them away. The button need not be referenced or seen in order for it to exert its symbolic and actual power. These are some of the many reminders that the coercive power of the court is always nearby.

The uncertainty of whether and when the sanctions evoked by these symbols will be used only enhances their significance as a mechanism of internalized state power (Foucault, 1995). What PDC participant Ariella refers to as "a watchful eye" conjures up participants' sense of the omnipresent state. Participant Nicole, when asked what advice she would give other PDC participants, cautioned that they should always be forthcoming about prohibited drug use:

> Tell them, because then they already know that you're using. They're not gonna lock you up. They're gonna need your hot urines to get you [an assessment for treatment placement] or re-evaluate you. You know what I mean? So it's like, if you got a hot, give a hot.

Nicole frames the need to be forthcoming as a prerequisite for help. As Maria's vignette illustrates, it is also part of a strategy for retaining the sympathy and good will of the court, which is likely to discover and punish lapses of compliance.

Constant reminders of coercion and their harsh consequences belie the benign and celebratory approach that sees criminal legal tools as helping people address the individual problems that are presumed to underlie sex work. While the literature describes diversion programs as *alternatives* to traditional criminal legal responses, it often fails to sufficiently highlight that their existence is made possible only within a context of harsh punishment and the criminalization of the people and behaviors the programs target. Program participants choose PDPs not in a vacuum but as an alternative to unaffordable fines, dehumanizing and retraumatizing incarceration, and symbiotic harms that limit their financial, social, and employment opportunities (Condry & Minson, 2020; Leon & Kilmer, 2022). Such forced choices continue throughout program participation, as compliance decisions are always influenced by the consequences of noncompliance.

Is Coercion "Effective"?: What's Your Lens?

One of the strengths of qualitative research is its ability to test theories with particular on-the-ground realities, and one of the strengths of this study is our ability to follow emergent themes in subsequent interviews with the same participants. As the role of coercion emerged from the data and in our other work (Leon & Shdaimah, 2012; Leon & Shdaimah, 2021; Corrigan & Shdaimah, 2016), we asked about it explicitly. In many of our interviews we found evidence, initially implicitly and later in response to explicit questions, of both belief in and uncertainty or doubt regarding whether coercion was effective for SPD and PDC participants. We also identified a tension surrounding whether PDP participants were capable of making decisions about whether they should be engaging in sex work and, if not, whether and how participants could extricate themselves.

Maria's fear of incarceration and state time as a motivator to stay engaged and comply with program mandates is, in fact, built into the design of court-affiliated PDPs and other programs grounded in the principles of problem-solving justice (National Association of Drug Court Professionals, 2021; Shdaimah, 2020a; Leon & Shdaimah, 2019). Although few participants who did not successfully meet PDP requirements actually faced the full consequences of PDP failure, most respondents saw this as a frightening possibility. This fear was reinforced by court personnel, who often raised the specter of such punishment to motivate participants. Even the SPD, which took a far less heavy-handed pre-plea approach, saw arrest as a motivator to treatment. Such a function is espoused by those working within what Dewey and St. Germain (2016) define as the *criminal justice–social services alliance*. However, our study is rife with examples of the therapeutic-penal combination imploding under the weight of its own contradictions. This tension is heightened when the script of problem-solving courts comes up against the reality of peoples' lived experiences. In the following example, the imperatives pushed by so-called team members defied what Prosecutor Emily and the PDC participant she was supposedly prosecuting understood as what was most likely to help this participant on her own terms and to reach the program goals of reducing prostitution recidivism:

> I wanted to have more of a therapeutic, empathetic voice, rather than the voice of the law, because [PDC participants] were too vulnerable to need that. I don't think that [the voice of the law] was effective. And the one time that I really went in the back, and the judge insisted that I just ream someone out, she ended up going on the lam for several months before she was ultimately apprehended and came back to the program and that was the one time that I had been ordered to do this. Intuitively I knew that this was going to slap someone in the face. That it wasn't going to again help this lady. [pause] It wasn't going to edify her self-esteem. Her feelings of support; we were there to empower them [and] this was going to have the opposite effect.

Our analysis of coercion from those who wield it and those upon whom it is used reveals a divergence of understanding that varies depending on the individual, the resources available, and the perceived intent of the person who holds coercive power. These factors seem to influence whether coercion is experienced as a burden, as a promising way to regain self-control, or as an acceptable trade-off for material or emotional resources. In order to be acceptable as a tool, coercion must at minimum be accompanied by hope that something better will emerge from the risk—for example, Maria's ability to stay connected to the same stakeholders or to avoid incarceration. SPD social worker Brigit is keenly aware of this, in her desire not to sanction people for sex work until and unless there are viable financial alternatives. Losses of freedom, heightened and extended surveillance, and risk of criminal punishment may be worthwhile trade-offs for people who are, according to PDC participant Keisha's treatment-speak, "sick and tired of being sick and tired."

Conclusion

It is clear that PDPs that are nested within the shadow of a legal system that criminalizes sex work must be viewed in light of their coercive features, which further circumscribe the choices available to "participants." These programs sometimes come with enough benefits to make them provisionally acceptable, and for some, desirable. This may be especially true for participants who are able to use the PDPs as a source of social and material capital in the absence of access to robust medical, social, emotional, and financial resources. However, PDPs are limited by their insistence on individual choice, which means that most stakeholders (PDP participants and criminal legal system professionals alike) fail to consider alternatives that would reduce the coercive forces. Such a myopic, neoliberal understanding of these programs (Cohen & Shdaimah, under review; Fukushima et al., 2020; Leon & Shdaimah, 2012) is increasingly at odds with recent decriminalization efforts (Vella, 2022).

Whether Maria and other PDP participants welcome the "foot on [their] neck" is hard to say, even by stakeholders' own standards. Participants and court professionals assess the relative burdens and benefits using a calculus that varies with their beliefs, assumptions, fears, and hopes. Maria's struggle with whether to trust people, born of her experiences, makes her more willing to accept surveillance from familiars. Similarly, trauma treatment therapist Diane's willingness to consider coercion as part of her therapeutic practice exists in light of her fears for clients' lives.

Even if stakeholders deem PDPs to be provisionally acceptable, there are two noteworthy ways in which their calculus may not hold up . First, when they consider individual trajectories over time, most stakeholders see that PDP participants continue to face the same individual and structural hurdles, now possibly exacerbated by newly emphasized shame for meeting their needs through the sex trade or, if they give up the sex trade, in low-wage employment, with precarity in housing, caregiving arrangements, and other basic needs. Second, other stakeholders who reject the PDP calculus do so in light of a broader view that recognizes coercion as part of an ongoing historical practice of regulating women, including their bodies, their sexuality, and their economic freedom.

4

"I've Been Raped, I've Been Robbed, But I Could Have Been Killed"

Intersections of Trauma, Substance Use Problems, and Prostitution in the Eyes of the Court

C ourt coordinator Lily connected us to Toodles, the first PDC participant we interviewed. Lily felt that Toodles's experiences were similar
to those of other PDC participants and that she had insights we needed to hear. When we first spoke to Toodles in 2011, she was in her mid-40s
and living in Philadelphia. We met at the outpatient recovery program that
she attended, near the Community College of Philadelphia where she was
learning how to use a computer and struggling with her math classes. She
was both proud of herself, as someone who had completed the sixth grade
in school and earned a GED while incarcerated in state prison, and worried
that she would have to pay back student loans if she had to leave classes.

An African American cisgender woman, Toodles was the middle child
between older and younger brothers. When she was growing up, Toodles experienced multiple incidents of sexual abuse from several perpetrators within her emotionally neglectful environment. Her mother's partner sexually
abused her and introduced her to drugs when she was 12. When we asked
how she began engaging in prostitution, Toodles cited her experience of receiving compensation from her abuser for sexual acts. Toodles eventually
developed a substance use disorder and sold sex in the streets, for which she
was repeatedly arrested, experiencing the revolving door between street-based
sex work and incarceration for several years. After one of her later arrests,
she entered Project Dawn Court, where she felt cared about and supported.
Toodles stayed in touch with Lily for years after she graduated, sometimes
receiving emergency material support along with an empathetic ear. She also

continued to experience bouts of low-wage work, financial precarity, relationships with abusive partners, and incarceration.

What's the Problem? The Trauma and Addiction Explanation

Problem-solving programs such as Baltimore's SPD and Philadelphia's PDC are premised in part on the assumption that individuals engage in illegal behavior because of underlying problems, particularly experiences of childhood abuse, lifetime interpersonal violence, and addiction to drugs or alcohol. This assumption that women who engage in street-based sex work are victims of sexual assault and other forms of abuse is reinforced by much of the scholarly literature, as well as public discourse around trafficking for purposes of sexual exploitation (Lobasz, 2018; O'Brien, 2021). While many SPD and PDC participants in our study shared that childhood abuse and interpersonal trauma were in fact significant parts of both their history and their current situation, they viewed systemic factors such as poverty and housing instability as equally salient. Indeed, poverty is a chronic stressor that may contribute to traumatic impacts and limited choices (Collins et al., 2010).

Diversion program staff acknowledge that prostitution/sex work, intractable substance addiction, and chronic health problems are associated with poverty and limited employment opportunities, but staff are likely to view sexual exploitation as the underlying cause for all other problems and obstacles these women face. PDC Judge Hartwell made this observation:

> Most prostitutes have had hideous trauma from a really early age. And we have meetings where we talk to psychiatrists. . . . [the expert consultant] taught me things that I didn't know, because most people don't know what goes into making a woman a prostitute. I didn't realize that most women had been raped before they hit 10 or 9 years old, most times by mother's boyfriends. A lot of times by relatives. . . . So, I learned that. . . . And so when I looked at the women with the information of course I saw a different piece of their narrative; you know I really did. Just because then it became more than just a prostitution case; it became something that needs to be looked at a little deeper.

Judge Hartwell explains how her eyes were opened to new knowledge, as it was presented in the trainings that she received. These trainings are often designed for secondary or tertiary knowledge holders, who are not professional therapists, and therefore the trainings may lack nuance or avoid the presentation of critical or dissenting perspectives. Like other PDP professionals, Judge

Hartwell is sincere and firm in the newfound knowledge. It is striking that such knowledge is presented uncritically and without nuance, as it results in precisely the kind of framing that can do harm even as if it tries to do good. Prior to learning about trauma, many PDP professionals lacked a framework for understanding PDP participants. Judge Hartwell's new understanding links prostitution and child sexual abuse and makes prostitution explicable through the trauma lens provided by "psych experts" (Leon, 2011, pp. 125–143) such as psychiatrists and other mental health professionals (who have what we have described as primary expertise; Leon & Shdaimah, 2019).

Many respondents commented on the exceptionally awful circumstances that seem commonplace in the lives of PDP participants. For example, as Miss Anita Martin, a pretrial agent with the Baltimore SPD, said:

> Their parents were damaged goods. . . . I could never understand a parent that prostitutes a child, but that is what happens. But that's what they do to get the drugs. If their parents are on drugs and they can't get it, then that's what they do. They utilize their kids to get the drugs.

Regardless of the source, adverse experiences are assumed to leave deep psychological marks of trauma on diversion program participants. These signs reinforce the centering of psychological harm and associated problems and symptoms as the cause, effect, and treatment site for engaging in sex work. In PDPs, physical appearance is an outward manifestation of trauma that allows court staff to identify and classify participants. Women come into the programs in varying physical states.[1] New program participants commonly appear agitated, tapping their legs and arms, and looking around nervously in ways that may indicate drug addiction or withdrawal. Some have trouble getting through a long court day, waiting for hours until their case is called or to meet with staff. Some women appear to be under the influence of drugs, experiencing withdrawal symptoms, taking medication to aid in their recovery, nodding off, closing their eyes while talking, or sleeping through loud noises.

We once observed Baltimore SPD drug assessor George send home someone who was so soundly asleep in the waiting room that he practically shouted her name and touched her lightly before she opened her eyes, oriented herself with some difficulty, and responded. Consistent with the diversion programs' tolerance for "slips," George simply asked her to come back the following week to complete the assessment when she was more fully rested and able to answer questions. These physical manifestations of illness, trauma, and addiction are used as proxy indicators of victimization, and thus are intelligible in the context of PDPs aimed at addressing the perceived underlying causes that lead to offending.

As women move through the programs, PDC and SPD staff and participants interpret their "progress," as manifested through their appearance and health, through the lens of victimization. Criminal legal system personnel and program participants discuss withdrawal and recovery from addiction, improvements in physical and mental health, management of chronic illness, and signs of improved hygiene and self-care. Program staff and participants frequently make comments regarding appearance. Weight gain, improved hygiene, "appropriate" attire, and mental alertness are interpreted as signals of progress; appearing disheveled or "suggestive" is read as a lack of concern for self or for societal norms and may indicate relapses into problematic substance use and unaddressed trauma. Program staff commend the appearance of participants who are doing well, reminding them of what they looked like when they first entered the program. PDC program staff sometimes passed around arrest photographs, asking all those present in the courtroom to compare these images with the current appearance of successful participants. These photographs are also shown to participants, who are asked whether they see the changes that everyone present in the court is invited to see in their physical appearance. Insights about trauma and associated substance use problems and movement toward healing are hallmarks of progress and success.

PDPs assume that the women arrested for prostitution who come before them suffer[2] trauma-related issues and substance use problems. The court sees these as underlying conditions that contribute to engagement in criminalized sex work as well as a host of what the PDPs view as problematic relationships and behaviors (see also Chapter 6). Court personnel draw upon constructions of trauma and substance use disorders and their own perceived professional expertise to address these issues in their court-based roles to "do good" for the women (Leon & Shdaimah, 2019). Providing women engaged in prostitution with resources to address their needs appears beneficial when juxtaposed with cycling bouts of incarceration. However, the structures and processes of the court are fundamentally coercive and therefore cannot be fully trauma-informed, despite the court's best efforts.

Trauma and substance use disorders, as clinical phenomena, are very present in the lives of nearly all of the SPD and PDC defendants and are inseparable from their life trajectories and their experience of the court. As such, trauma and substance use disorders are also inseparable from the functioning of these programs and stakeholders' understandings and efforts. These phenomena exist in both the clinical realm and the personal realm and are also deployed as part of the court apparatus to surveil and shape the behaviors of participants. Here, we adopt a stance similar to that taken by Fassin and Rechtman (2009) by recognizing and describing the reality of trauma and substance use disorders, while also critically analyzing how they are used in PDPs. That is, we do not diminish the reality or impact of trauma and substance use disorders but we do call for critical attention to how those concepts are mobilized in PDPs, often without fidelity to their clinical meanings.

What Is Trauma?

Trauma is a frequently discussed cultural concept used colloquially, in the media, and in the press (Fassin & Rechtman, 2009). Courts, policy-makers, and program staff use it to describe, understand, and prescribe paths for women like Toodles who participate in PDPs (Corrigan & Shdaimah, 2016). These personnel draw on their training around trauma and trauma-informed responses to develop what we have elsewhere called secondary or tertiary expertise, that is, mediated knowledge gained from others who have clinical expertise (Leon & Shdaimah, 2019). However, trauma as a distinct clinical diagnostic concept is important to understand in order to examine tensions between how criminal legal responses correspond to and diverge from diagnostic criteria and what that means for the participants in these programs. In this section, we lay out the clinical definition of *trauma* as groundwork both for the court responses and to situate the experiences of the PDP participants.

The widely used conception of trauma in the United States is set forth in the posttraumatic stress disorder (PTSD) diagnostic criteria listed in the *Diagnostic and Statistical Manual of Mental Disorders*, 5th ed. (American Psychiatric Association, 2013, 2022).[3] Individuals who directly experience, witness in person, or learn that a loved one has experienced a qualifying traumatic event involving "actual or threatened death, serious injury, or sexual violence" or who experience "repeated or extreme exposure to aversive details of a traumatic event(s)" meet the threshold criterion for PTSD. They can then be considered for a PTSD diagnosis using additional evaluative criteria (American Psychiatric Association, 2013, p. 271). PTSD symptoms fall under four clusters: intrusion, avoidance, negative cognitions and mood, and arousal and reactivity.

Possible reactions to traumatic events are experiencing other psychiatric disorders (e.g., substance use disorders, major depressive disorder, and somatic symptom disorder) alone or co-occurring with PTSD, which can cause sleepiness, anxiety, agitation, or physical distress. People reacting to traumatic events may also have symptoms that either do not fully meet DSM criteria or exist entirely outside of DSM criteria. Definitions of complex-trauma syndromes such as *complex PTSD* (Herman, 1992) and *developmental trauma disorder* (van der Kolk, 2005) posit that individuals who experience prolonged and repeated traumatic stress, particularly of an interpersonal or purposeful nature, present with a complex constellation of problems or symptoms and have a variety of treatment needs. All of these can make it hard for people to be able to take care of their own needs, engage and communicate with others, and maintain employment or other social functions.

It is important to distinguish between the *experiencing* of a stressful or traumatic event, and the *response* to that event. Exposure to a stressful or traumatic event does not necessarily mean that a person will develop any or all of the specific PTSD or other trauma-related symptoms. Whether and how people respond to adverse events can depend on the person's pretrauma characteristics, perception of the event, experience of peritraumatic distress, and posttrauma experiences as well as the nature and severity of the traumatic event(s). These factors interact and influence the type and severity of trauma reactions that the person experiences (Briere & Scott, 2015). Such variation in individual experiences warrants careful consideration in diagnosis or treatment. However, PDPs are ill-equipped to address these critical nuances. Through a combination of assumptions about who engages in sex work and why, limited resources, and tertiary understanding of trauma, PDPs like the ones we study often require participants to engage with one-size-fits-all trauma treatment, with little regard for individual needs or circumstances.

Trauma Experience among Women Engaged in Street-Based Sex Work

Research shows that women engaged in street-based sex work report experiencing high rates of traumatic events such as childhood physical and sexual abuse, partner violence, and sexual assault (Millan-Alanis et al., 2021; Tschoeke et al., 2019). A meta-analysis that combined and examined the results of 15 studies conducted in various countries reported the rate of PTSD among female sex workers at 29 percent (Millan-Alanis et al., 2021). As a point of comparison, in the United States the lifetime prevalence of PTSD among women in the general population is just 9.7 percent, indicating that sex workers experience PTSD at nearly triple that rate (Kessler et al., 2005; see also Gradus, 2013). The cumulative impacts of multiple traumatic events across time likely result in complex-trauma syndromes among women engaged in street-based sex work.

We know from our interviews that the number of stressful and adverse life events that Toodles and most of our respondents experienced as children and as adults was much higher than average. These events set up our study participants for trauma-related problems such as PTSD and complex PTSD. Toodles's responses on the instruments used in our study—Stressful Life

Experiences Screening (Stamm et al., 1996), PTSD Checklist—Civilian Version (Weathers, Huska, & Keane, 1991; Weathers et al., 1993), and Trauma Symptom Checklist—40 (Briere, n.d.; Briere & Runtz, 1989)—indicate that she experienced nine stressful life events, met criteria for PTSD, and experienced problematic levels of trauma symptoms. Respondents in our study at YANA Place, a drop-in center for women in street-based sex work (Wiechelt & Shdaimah, 2011), reported experiencing 5–14 stressful life events, M = 10.4 (SD = 3.3), with most experiencing sexual and physical violence across the life span. They experienced high levels of PTSD symptoms, M = 56.8 (SD = 20.25), and trauma-related symptoms, M = 49.3 (SD = 30.43). The SPD and PDC participants in our study experienced 0–15 stressful life events, M = 7.3 (SD = 3.8), which are somewhat lower numbers, albeit still generally high. They also experienced more modest, yet still problematic, levels of PTSD symptoms, M = 43.1 (SD = 16.7), and trauma-related symptoms, M = 42.4 (SD = 25.7).

All of our participants' stories include experiences that would qualify as a traumatic event(s). For example, Jenn, an SPD participant who had engaged in sex work for less than a year, told us this:

> You don't know whose car you're getting into, you don't know if he's a serial killer, you don't know if he's a rapist. . . . I've been raped, I've been robbed, I've been chased with guns, I've been stabbed at, I've been shot with a BB gun, I've been tied to a tree on Route 40 and left for dead.

The high rates of traumatic events, PTSD, and other trauma-related symptoms among women engaged in sex work indicate that programs and services designed to address their needs should be, at a minimum, trauma-informed. Trauma-specific services should be made available to those who need and want them. Trauma-specific care includes a range of interventions specifically designed to remediate trauma-related symptoms and facilitate recovery from the effects of traumatic experiences, for example, PTSD and emotional dysregulation. Trauma-specific care is provided by professionally trained clinicians with specialized training in the etiology and treatment of trauma-associated problems and disorders. Prolonged Exposure (Foa et al., 2007) and Eye Movement Desensitization Reprocessing (EMDR) (Shapiro, 2018) are examples of trauma-specific interventions.

Standard trauma-informed care provides services in a manner that recognizes the likely impacts of trauma on the development of an array of problems, such as physical health, mental health, substance use, and criminal justice concerns. The guiding principle of trauma-informed care is to minimize the risk of exacerbating the effects of trauma or of retraumatizing individuals. This requires that all program processes be sensitive to trauma and be purposefully designed and implemented in a manner that reduces the likelihood of recapitulating or triggering trauma. Moses et al. (2003) delineate empowerment approaches that are necessary in trauma-informed care: respecting choice, utilizing relational collaboration, and building skills instead of managing symptoms. All program staff in every role and every part of the program should be trained in trauma-informed care and should operate from a trauma-informed perspective.

In practice, we have observed "trauma-informed" to rely on knowledge that is often a mixture of what program professionals have learned from experts and what they have picked up from media, including social media. Donisch and colleagues (2016) explored how social service professionals understood trauma and trauma-informed practices (TIP), and similarly they found significant departures from clinical understandings and "wide variations in the degree to which providers in different systems feel knowledgeable about TIP and possess the skills and strategies to respond to their traumatized clients" (p. 131). Trauma-informed practice is therefore not actually therapy or clinical care but rather program professionals' attempt to align criminal legal system practices with the understandings of trauma and trauma-informed care as best they can.

Intersection of Trauma and Substance Use

Substance use disorders are known to have a high concordance rate with PTSD and other trauma-related disorders (Bailey & Stewart, 2014; María-Ríos & Morrow, 2020). Substance use disorders are also commonly reported among women engaged in street-level sex work (Bachman et al., 2019; Smith, 2017). The women in our studies reported substance use problems as well. We used the Addiction Severity Index Lite version (ASI-L; McLellan et al., 1980) in our second interview to gather information on participants' substance use. Since many were in treatment at the time of our interviews, their use at the time (over the past 30 days) was not meaningful. The most frequently used substances reported by the women in our current study were cocaine (85 percent), cannabis (60 percent), alcohol to intoxication (50 percent), and heroin (40 percent). Approximately 70 percent used more than one substance per day. We also learned about study participant's substance use behaviors via the stories they shared with us during the interviews. Even though we did not gather data sufficient to make a substance use disorder diagnosis in accordance with DSM-5 criteria (American Psychiatric Association, 2013) for each participant, their stories reveal substance use behaviors and treatment histories indicating that they had serious substance use problems that likely were substance use disorders. The interviews and observations made it clear that problems with substance use impacted their lives and experiences in the court-based programs.

"I Just Felt So Alone" (*Toodles*)

Toodles's story illustrates how trauma and substance use problems might intersect in the lives of women engaged in street-level sex work and how formulaic criminal legal system responses, including diversion program "reforms," are inadequate and often harmful. Toodles experienced inattention and emotional neglect in her family and was sexually abused multiple times by multiple perpetrators during her childhood, including by an uncle when she was 7. She stated, "And I didn't know no better because no one ever paid any attention to me, and he was by doing little things like that." Toodles's mother left her family when Toodles was 12 years old. She came back for Toodles and she, her boyfriend, and Toodles moved into a rooming house where Toodles was frequently left alone. Toodles described how her mother treated her: "She never paid attention to me, she never told me I was pretty or praised me for anything. And I thought that being a little girl, you [are] supposed to be treated special; but I wasn't treated special. I was treated just like any other kid on the block." Toodles's vulnerability as a child was heightened by the feelings of embarrassment, loneliness, and low self-worth engendered by her relationship with her mother. Vulnerability and poor supervision increased her risk of being exploited. Indeed, the owner of the rooming house exploited Toodles by giving her money to engage in sexual acts with him. Toodles told us, "I continued to let him do it because it felt good and I never felt good before; I always was sad, a sad child."

Toodles subsequently moved into an apartment building with her mother and her mother's boyfriend. She experienced sexual abuse by her mother's boyfriend over several years and he provided her with drugs. Toodles's own words about her experiences help us understand the links between sexual abuse, substance use, and engagement in sex work from her perspective:

> One particular day my mom wasn't home and he, my mom's boyfriend, asked could he have sex with me; he said, "If you want the things that your mom have, you have to do what she do." And I said, "Okay." I was 12 years old. And my thing with that was, you know, somebody's paying attention to me and I didn't know that it was wrong for him to come on to me like that. And when he had propositioned me, he offered me money, jewelry, sex, and clothes; and I wanted those things 'cause my mom had 'em, to make me feel good about myself. And sure enough, I got a lot of attention from that. And by him molesting me, I say molestation because I was 12, 'til I was 19. I allowed it to happen

'cause by then he had already got me hooked [on] his drugs. He was a big drug dealer. That I didn't know. And how I knew that is because I went in the closet and it was large trash bags full of heroin, cocaine, and reefer, marijuana. And I tried to tell my mom what happened; she didn't believe me. So then again, I thought it was normal for him to do that. So, I continued to let it happen. And at the time of when I was 12 years old I thought that if a man wanted to sleep with me, he had to pay me like my stepfather did. And I began to be promiscuous with a lot of people and I got into the lifestyle of prostitution.

Toodles's vulnerability as a child was exploited by an uncle, by a landlord, and, from the age of 12 to 19, by her mother's partner, who used drugs to entice, control, and pay her. Toodles tells us that she learned from her interactions with him that sexual behavior should be compensated. Her drug use continued into adulthood and became intertwined with the impacts of trauma and her engagement in prostitution. Toodles smoked cocaine for 27 years and received addiction treatment five times. She identifies "tricking" as a factor leading her back to drugs when she tried to not use substances but still engaged in prostitution. She told us, "You know I remember being clean before from drugs and alcohol, but still was out there tricking, not knowing that dirty money led me to dirty things and I wound up smoking crack again." Toodles told us that the "disease of addiction" kept her out there.

Toodles first heard about Project Dawn when she was in court facing multiple legal challenges. Project Dawn staff were in the courtroom and worked to take on her case. She agreed to participate in the year-long program, starting with "rehab." Like all Project Dawn participants, Toodles was required to complete addiction treatment, have regular urine drug screens, attend Narcotics Anonymous, and remain drug-free. The court also required her to engage in one-to-one outpatient therapy for trauma at the Joseph J. Peters Institute (JJPI). Failure to comply with court requirements could result in dismissal from the program and incarceration. Toodles relapsed three times and was incarcerated after each relapse for approximately two months while the Forensic Intensive Recovery (FIR) staff located another publicly funded slot for her in a treatment program. She was required to restart her Project Dawn program phase after each relapse and was given opportunities/required to reengage in treatment.

Toodles reported that she felt cared about by the Project Dawn staff because they stuck by her and gave her another chance when she got into trouble using drugs again. Feeling cared about emerged in the interviews as very important to Toodles. She told us, "And that's what keeps me going now because I know I got people that care about me; and for a long time, I ain't think nobody ever cared about me. And that's my problem; I just felt so alone, and then crack just made me feel like I was on top of the world, you know what I mean? [tearful]" Toodles believed the judge cared for her: "And what I love about her is like she knows my name, it's like we have a personal relationship. If I see her on the streets, she speaks to me, she hugs me, she asks me how my son is doing, and stuff like that. And that means a lot to me." She indicated that the probation officer, social worker, and other women in the court are all there to help you. "It's beautiful; it's beautiful. It's so beautiful. I love Project Dawn."

At the point of our third interview, Toodles had 10 months "clean" post relapse, had just completed her intensive outpatient program for substance use treatment (she continued to go for optional outpatient groups), and continued to participate in one-to-one trauma therapy at JJPI. She was also attending community college but struggled to finance all the credits she needed to take and was employed in low-paying menial labor. Toodles had just completed probation and planned to attend her Project Dawn Graduation ceremony scheduled to occur in five days.

Toodles was discharged from Project Dawn in Fall 2011. She celebrated a year clean in January 2012 and soon thereafter resumed harmful substance use. As a result of her substance use she was required to leave the recovery house where she was living, so she moved in with her boyfriend. She continued to use substances for several months, and her boyfriend began hitting her. She also resumed engaging in sex work, was arrested, and was placed on probation for six months by the court. After nine months of active use, she was able to reengage in the recovery process. She enrolled in a treatment program, resumed attending 12-step meetings, obtained supportive housing, and got a housekeeping job. In her reflections on her "relapse," she indicated that she stopped going to meetings and stopped going to JJPI and was mentally in relapse before resuming drug use. Toodles remained positive about her experience with Project Dawn and used some of the skills and resources that she acquired in the program to reengage in recovery. In 2022, Toodles reconnected with the court coordinator Lily for the first time in several years.

The court-based program provided Toodles with an alternative to incarceration and an opportunity to address her trauma and addiction. Indeed, Toodles thought the program helped her. Despite her participation in the PDP and the feelings of support and caring engendered by that participation, Toodles repeatedly resumed using drugs and reengaged in prostitution. The complex interaction between trauma and substance use disorders is an important consideration in fostering successful treatment. Although the PDP did seem to recognize this complexity, mandating trauma treatment violates the principles of trauma-informed care. The substance use treatment programs, while perhaps trauma-informed, were not specifically designed to provide integrated trauma and substance use treatment. The treatment programs were selected based on available treatment slots coverable by public funds to place Toodles (as well as other women in Project Dawn). The compulsory trauma treatment was provided separately by JJPI, although evidence shows that integrated treatment for trauma and substance use disorders is more effective (Wiechelt, 2014). Separate programs of treatment typically involve separate treatment plans and a lack of communication or coordination, thereby not treating the "whole person" or complex intersecting problems. In some cases, parallel or sequential treatment for trauma and substance use disorders may be preferred. In any case, providers should carefully assess the individual's treatment needs and match the individual with the best evidence-based treatment approach and treatment provider(s) available to meet their needs. Toodles experienced challenges managing to live in "shelterlike" recovery houses with limited income from menial jobs. The social context and its potential impact on Toodles were not meaningfully addressed, that is, through vocational programming, educational support, or trauma-informed recovery housing. The well-meaning court is limited by its own design, personnel, and available treatment options.

The Well-Meaning Court

The well-meaning court intends to be trauma-informed and to provide a pathway out of prostitution and the criminal legal system. However, the court by design can never operate in full compliance with the tenets of standard trauma-informed care. The court determines what is acceptable behavior, what services are needed, what level of compliance with the court and treatment providers is expected, and what reward or consequence occurs when a defendant is viewed as compliant or not. In PDPs, court professionals become tertiary experts by drawing on the knowledge of trauma researchers and clinicians (Leon & Shdaimah, 2019).

Like many PDPs that target women in street-level sex work, both the SPD and the PDC view therapeutic exploration of trauma as a crucial step to develop coping mechanisms to replace the self-medication through drugs and alcohol or the low self-esteem that they believe underlie women's behavior. The following court observation reveals the persistent subtext that encourages women to disclose and "process" traumas:

> The judge acknowledges, but refuses to be persuaded by, Darlene's reticence to attend counseling. Darlene comes up. Sara, who graduated nearly a year before and now works at the house for women who are trafficked and in prostitution where Darlene lives, reports on Darlene's progress. Judge Kahan says, "You know what I'm going say. [Dar-

lene] needs a little push to go to [trauma counseling]." The judge then says to Darlene: "I see those eyes [rolling]."

Program staff cajole and, when necessary, force reluctant participants like Darlene to participate in required therapy. Judge Kahan uses the public court forum to contrast Darlene's resistance with the attitudes of participants like Jean who recognize their need for therapeutic interventions. After a program breach, Jean expressed to Judge Kahan in open court her desire to get into the therapy program:

> My need to use is stronger than my need for safety. I'm struggling. I need help. I get scared and I get caught up so quickly. Look at me, I'm emaciated. I don't know what to say. . . . I have no words. I don't know what to say. I'm going to die out there.

Denial of traumatic experiences is met with skepticism. The court usually construed denial as either a failure to recognize experiences as traumatic or a refusal to disclose such experiences. Most PDC and SPD criminal legal system professionals understand from their training that many of the people they supervise may deny or push down traumatic events; this may result from a combination of being injured, the ubiquity of traumatic experiences, and not being believed, or it may be a coping mechanism. PDP professionals understand their training as a mandate to recognize and respond to traumatic events. Such responses often include asking about these events and requiring that respondents address the events through treatment as a condition of their probation or participation in diversion programs.

John (a probation officer), talking with us in 2021, explained that the idea of trauma and its impact is "rampant in my division," where "[they]'re making trauma definitely a[n] issue here in probation." All of the officers undergo trauma training, and such training has changed the way John thinks of his work in the sex offender unit generally. This "40 hours of training a year by the state" includes lectures by treatment professionals as well as individuals who talk about the impact of trauma on their life trajectories and criminal legal system involvement. John says that these individuals see some of their experiences as ordinary traumas:

> Simply craziness where you're standing on a corner and the guy to the left of you and the guy to the right of you are shot and you're not. And they die and you don't. Like in a drive-by shooting.

PDC and SPD professionals see an additional layer of traumatic events and PTSD in their caseload of street-level sex workers, who are presumed to have had (and in fact often *have* had) experiences being trafficked, assaulted, and otherwise harmed. Probation officer Ronny Landis explained that one of the reasons the PDC cases were placed in the sex offender unit was precisely because many on the PDC caseload had experienced sexual abuse so extreme that other probation departments might not believe them or have the empathy that comes from their many years of hearing from offenders.

John explained that hearing from a former offender with firsthand experience of trauma was transformative:

> I went and saw this lady speak at Delaware County at a lecture hall. We were at the University of Delaware. It was for the surrounding county probation departments and this lady blew me away. She was arrested 88 times and she said, "Not one person ever asked me until the 88th time do I have sexual trauma in my background." It took 88 arrests and she's like, "That's talking to social workers, public defenders, district attorneys, judges. No one." Until one time this lady in the prison said to her, "Do you have sexual trauma?"

Described uniformly as a person with great empathy—as were the other probation officers—John uses his newly found and confirmed understanding to change his practices. Taking his cue from the lecturer, John said, "From that point on, I knew it and then . . . I would go into booths." Speaking specifically about "how we roll in probation" in working with Project Dawn Court participants, John explained "generally how it would work":

> I'd go in the booth with Catherine Heathcliff, I'd introduce myself, and I'd straight up say to them, "Listen, we know you have abuse in your background, sexual abuse." And they would look at you like [eyes wide]. I mean, I could tell you a lot of stories, but I would go in there and I'd be the bad cop, and I would jump on their asses and be like, "Da da da da da da [aggressive tone]. And if you da da da da da." But then I would end it by saying, "But we're here to help you, because we know you've had some trauma so I'm gonna leave the booth and I want you to talk to Catherine Heathcliff. And then you two figure this out and we're going to help you." . . . And then I would leave. I would go in there and be bad cop, let the PO be good cop. They would be like, "There's that fucking asshole" when I would walk by the booth. [laughs] But I didn't mind as long as it helped the ladies. And eventually once they get into treatment and start dealing with their trauma, we had success. We really did.

John and others often received accolades from PDC participants who ultimately credited coerced treatment and other forms of tough love, at least in part, for saving or transforming their lives. Vitality/Tranquility appreciated Catherine for being

> just a no-nonsense type of probation officer . . . she helped me out big time. Like, whew! Hats off to her. But you know, it's necessary. Those kinds of strong women are necessary. Very necessary.

Such feedback confirmed for these officers the value of these approaches, reinforcing the messages of trauma treatment that were conveyed in their training.

However, this tough love could also backfire. Ava shared what it was like to be on the receiving end of John's "bad cop" performance when John responded to her denial of trauma:

> He got very aggressive with me and because I wasn't—they termed it—"I was being evasive or dishonest," because I said I wasn't sexually traumatized. Well, I said to him, "You remind me of one of the guys who used to pick me up on the Avenue." . . . Then I spoke with [my probation officer] Catherine alone and I did self-disclose some things. But he was just standing over me and was very aggressive. So I was a little verbally abusive to him and said some things I shouldn't have. But I just felt like I was being abused all over again. So that was my introduction of my first time reporting. . . . It was horrible. I was in tears, I was crying hysterically 'cause I just felt like, "Why do they have this person in this position working with traumatized women if he's going to be like, [in an accusatory tone] 'Well, you have to have some sexual trauma in your history.'"

Trying to understand what she perceived as aggressive demands to acknowledge trauma, Ava speculated that it may have been prompted by other participants' dishonesty: "I was told maybe [others] in the program . . . lied or manipulated and maybe he was trying to weed me out." Although program staff expect trauma, they also expect denial, manipulation, and deceit from women even though they understand these as coping skills.

In a further conversation with John, we asked him to reflect on playing the bad cop, especially as it related to his own identity:

> Well, yeah, definitely gender and color of skin comes into play too. So a lot of times, if you come in and it'd be a Black female, she would think that like I'm The Man, like I'm a police or something. Sometimes they would think if I had my probation shirt on, they'd be like, "Are you a detective?" I'm like, "No, I'm not a detective." [laughs] So

all that came into play, but also too, [the] inflection in my voice. I would change it, be loud, soft, warming. I never left the booth thinking "You said the wrong stuff." But I have 30 years' experience too and I ran the sex offender unit for a lot of years and I saw treatment work, I saw men change. It's an amazing thing, so. I'm totally treatment oriented, and I could tell you this. My division, everyone has to do treatment, court ordered, and our arrests are always lower than the other divisions. Always. I mean, we get serious arrests, but we don't get a lot. And I have to attribute it to treatment.

John's statement reflected his care for vulnerable clients who he believes need treatment, which for him justified engaging in behavior that for others may be difficult to reconcile with trauma-informed approaches that are survivor-centered rather than manipulative.

As the court observation and report from John above illustrate, court personnel understand that trauma and associated substance use problems are concerns for the women in the court, and they believe that healing would facilitate success. However, the context of the court, lack of professional expertise, and lack of treatment resources (i.e., integrated treatment for trauma and substance use disorders) set participants up for a disempowering experience and possibly failure.

Courts vary on their expectations and consequences for those who participate in their programs. As noted in Chapter 2, we witnessed a judge in the SPD require a defendant to enter a guilty plea in order to participate in the SPD. This process was not how the program was originally designed. There may be variations in court processes depending on the particular judge or other court personnel, leading to a certain level of arbitrary decision-making. Unpredictability in processes and boundaries decreases one's sense of safety and increases retraumatization risks. The carrot-and-stick approach used by problem-solving courts is by definition coercive. Although individuals may choose to participate in the PDP or not, the alternative of incarceration may also be experienced as coercive. Individuals who have experienced interpersonal trauma in their lives have been coerced, have experienced loss of personal choice and power, and often have been harmed by a person who held power or authority over them. The court's processes could replicate these trauma dynamics and trigger or retraumatize individuals who are participating in their programs.

As we have written elsewhere, problem-solving justice and prostitution diversion programs in particular derive their legitimacy from integration of clinical and popular understandings of what many of our respondents refer to as "causes and conditions" of offending. In this case, trauma and substance use disorders are the causes and conditions considered by the court. Court professionals in PDPs become tertiary experts[4] by drawing on the knowledge of researchers and clinicians who specialize in trauma and substance use problems (Leon & Shdaimah, 2019). They may or may not respond to program participants from a trauma-informed perspective as described above.

The intersection of trauma and substance use problems and that intersection's complex relationship with street-based sex work is central to understanding the lives of women who come before the court with prostitution charges. Their experiences have implications for their service needs and for contextualizing the court-based diversion programs that are designed to assist them. As we have described above, prostitution-focused problem-solving courts typically incorporate processes designed to address trauma and substance use problems in their procedures and court orders. The nature of the criminal legal system and the tertiary expertise of professionals present challenges in addressing the complexity of trauma and intersecting substance use disorders—and may in fact exacerbate them.

5

"I've [Got] Hooker Court Every Month"

Shame and Shaming in Prostitution
Diversion Programs

Many people have written about shame and stigma in the context of criminalized behaviors, particularly anything that involves sex, including sex trade activities. In the criminal legal system, stigma is negotiated between the expectations of different PDP professionals and the expectations of people trading sex, who often need to make their actions intelligible to PDPs in order to secure the status of victim. The arena of intelligibility describes the conceptual space in which criminal justice professionals "identify which women are legitimate victims by making sense of their actions, affect, and experiences within bounded societal, political, and legal norms about gendered behavior, sexuality, and crime" (Corrigan & Shdaimah, 2016, p. 447). These can include expressions or evidence of trauma, contrition, and supplication that fit criminal justice professionals' understanding of what these should look like in public and private settings. The criminal legal system tends to take for granted that everyone views sex work as inherently stigmatizing and shameful. Few system professionals question the underlying assumptions that sex work, both as a construct and as an activity, is so deeply and unavoidably exploitative that it must be a choice of last resort.

Most women in our study do NOT in fact regard trading sex as the worst choice, instead finding it to be less shameful than other activities that colleagues or peers (often male peers) choose. Our respondents share a contested construction of what is shameful and why. PDPs often contribute to harmful narratives of shame rather than creating expanded choices to meet women's needs and obligations to self and others with dignity. Both PDP participants and PDP team members talked of struggles around feelings of worth and shame, linking these to the stigma of trading sex. Participants discuss how these struggles are reinforced or changed in the participants' interactions with criminal justice professionals and with each other, and how the struggles impact the participants' success or failure in the program. PDP team members (and often participants) reflect broader social views concerning women arrested for street-based sex work, views that do not recognize the women's agency as rational and moral actors (Shdaimah & Leon, 2015). These views limit women's opportunities and make the women prime targets for rescue and rehabilitation.

We describe and discuss our participants' experience of stigma and, relatedly, shame, and the impact of the two. We critically reflect on how stigma is both mitigated and reinforced by the programs that we study, often simultaneously. The PDPs' attempts to end engagement in prostitution often involve efforts to shame women into changing their behavior. These attempts stigmatize a choice and may cause further distress and suffering, perhaps unwittingly using harmful practices that further marginalize program participants socially, increase participants' psychological pain, and undermine their self-worth. Court and PDP staff generally intend to incorporate coercion and exhortation into treatment—and PDP participants often experience it—as expressions of concern and love. However, professionals whose interactions convey disdain shame PDP participants, a phenomenon that is also noted in the literature on regimes in which sex work is legalized (Armstrong, 2019; Blakey & Gunn, 2018; Samuel Centre for Social Connectedness, 2018). We explore PDP participants' own experiences of shame, and how these are viewed and replicated—even as they are contested—within PDPs.

Shame and Stigma

Shame is an emotionally painful experience in which one feels that the inner self is suddenly exposed or scrutinized. Lewis (1971) notes that a person experiencing shame feels helpless and small, as though they could sink through the floor, or die from shame. Shame can be healthy or it can be problematic. Healthy shame contributes to positive social functioning in that it helps people to be aware of themselves and their behaviors and to adjust in accordance with social limits. Parents use shame to correct behavior in their children and to facilitate the development of a conscience. The connective bridge in a healthy relationship between parent and child allows the shame to be a transitory experience. Healthy shame may also be triggered when a person experiences indignities from others; such shame results in appropriate boundary-setting and self-care. When an individual experiences frequent, long-lasting, and intense shaming, they may develop problematic shame, in which shame becomes internalized and the individual operates from a frame of shame (Kaufman, 1996). The individual has a sense of inner wounding and feels damaged or flawed and may also feel vulnerable, alone, isolated, and disconnected. Individuals attempt to defend themselves from psychologically painful shame using withdrawal, attacks on themselves or others (psychologically or verbally), and avoidance strategies (Nathanson, 1992). Such defenses can manifest in depression, interpersonal problems, and substance use problems. Internalized shame is common among those who have experienced childhood abuse, ongoing violence, or identity-based oppression.

Stigma is disapproving judgment toward individuals or groups based on physical characteristics, behaviors, or identity. Stigma, often understood as being labeled deviant, is created through interaction with other individuals and institutions, such as the criminal legal system (Goffman, 1963). A significant body of scholarship in sociology and criminology focuses on categories of behavior that are understood by the dominant groups to be so deviant that the behavior taints a person's identity, and the research describes how people manage, counter, or resist the resulting stigma (LeBel, 2012; Lemert, 1951; Sykes & Matza, 1957). It is well documented that the stigma associated with being labeled an "offender" has tangible impacts, as in the creation of significant obstacles to employment, housing, and government benefits and support programs (Pager, 2003; LeBel, 2012). This labeling leads to disconnection and isolation for the stigmatized person (Kilmer, 2016; Shdaimah & Leon, 2016), puts a significant strain on social support networks (Denney et al., 2014), and may spill over onto their families (Goffman, 1963; Leon & Kilmer, 2022). Stigmatization may even increase the likelihood that the person will engage in criminal behavior in the future (Lemert, 1951).

At the structural level, stigma concentrates disadvantage (Link et al., 2004). Attempts to manage stigma, whether through social withdrawal (Farkas & Miller, 2007), rationalization techniques (Rapp, 2012), or internalization, can negatively impact self-identity and mental health. In our previous work, we showed how women involved in street-based sex work manage stigma by providing each other with mutual assistance to meet their basic needs and as part of their ethical norms, in contrast to predominant characterizations of sex workers as morally deficient (see also Karandikar et al., 2022a). Relationships with other women involved in street-based sex work are a source of concrete support and encouragement, while simultaneously producing a counternarrative that challenges the women's stigmatized identities (Shdaimah & Leon, 2016). PDPs and the professionals who work in them impact program participants' ability to manage and cope with sex work stigma, including through their uses of shaming practices and the narratives that they offer respondents in coerced treatment, mandatory public and private meetings, and informal interactions.

Ronald Weitzer (2018) describes the existing literature on sex work stigma as being focused on how individuals manage and cope with stigma—and, to a lesser extent, resist it. However, there is little consideration of how stigma can be reduced or eliminated at the societal level. PDPs show the same short-comings; while they may help individual program participants manage stigma, they often do so in a manner that reinforces sex work stigma by coaxing individual change and a rejection of stigmatized identity as a remedy. Even practices that are intended to reduce individual shame are largely intended to sever program participants from their actions and their former selves, in-cluding networks of material and social support (Shdaimah, 2015). These sev-ering tactics reinforce a focus on engagement in the sex trade as a result of drug addiction and victimization *instead of* (rather than *also*) as an expres-sion of agency. Ava's experience illustrates the operation of shame and stig-ma in PDPs.

Ava, Project Dawn Court Participant

Ava, in her early 40s when we first spoke with her, is a White woman from what she described as "an affluent [suburban] community," with a degree in the helping professions and with long-term struggles with addiction, chron-ic illness, and an eating disorder. At the time of the first interview, she had been involved in the Project Dawn Court for almost five months and was proud of her hard-won sobriety. She recalls becoming addicted to drugs when she was 17, and explains that becoming involved in sex work at 25 was something she did

> strictly to support my heroin and crack habit, which I started doing in the mid-90s. . . . It's not something I would ever do clean and sober, if I wasn't . . . [trails off] I've only done it because I was desperate to get money for drugs. It's not even a thought; it was just something I did to survive. . . . It's not the way I was raised, it's not in my value system to do that. I want a life; I wanna be able to sit in my own skin and feel okay about myself . . . the abnormal became normal for me. Having an addicted personality and I guess doing prostitution, it was easiest for me. I wasn't somebody who could steal or whatever, so, yeah, 'cause my self-esteem's low.

Ava makes it clear that she does not feel good about her engagement in pros-titution, saying that she is looking forward to being able to "sit in [her] own skin" without shame. However, like other respondents we have written about elsewhere (Shdaimah & Leon, 2016), she manages some of the feelings around her engagement with prostitution by comparing the sex trade to other things that she is proud she does not do, such as stealing from her family or home invasion. Ava adamantly asserts, across several interviews, that she strongly disagrees with social constructions of prostitution as being among the most immoral behaviors. She, and others, described choosing sex work precisely because she sees it as relatively less harmful to other people and society, even though it may have been harmful to her. Therapy has called upon her to reckon with the harms to herself and her family.

Ava had a record of drug- and prostitution-related charges and mentions several experiences with incarceration and parole. With new charges hanging over her head and awareness of the stakes, Ava felt intense pressure to meet the requirements of Dawn Court, including paying off substantial fees, while also avoiding trading sex: "They say I owe this astronomical amount of money to the courts so I can't get cash assistance right now and I can't work 'cause I have to do all this therapy for Project Dawn to keep my medical assistance." In the midst of these obligations, Ava wanted to have the satisfaction and independence of her own earnings: "I do live with my family; they support me. I do get food stamps, but I'd like to be able to buy my own deodorant and stuff." Ava is clear that she chose to be sober before involvement in Project Dawn, which she pursued in order to address sexually related harms in her past that she describes as connected to her sex work involvement:

> AVA: I've never addressed any of this, like the sexual component to my history and just my upbringing. There was some inappropriateness and I've always had some issues. So maybe that's why prostitution was probably easier for me to fall into to support my habit. I don't know, but . . . And there was a few rapes and traumatic experiences that happened to me.
> COREY: While you were engaged in prostitution?
> AVA: Um hum; yeah. I never addressed them. So I'm trying to cover all the bases and stay sober like for the rest of my life and be employed and be functional, have a family. So I'm just giving this the best that I can.

Ava also mentions sexual violence she experienced related to prostitution, and therefore explicitly values the trauma-related treatment that PDC mandates for all participants. While not all PDC participants welcome trauma treatment, Ava and some other participants view access to the sexual violence–related trauma treatment as a benefit of the program, "the trauma therapy, I've *never* done that before. So I like the therapy aspect of it."

Despite engaging in PDC with openness to trauma-related therapy, Ava found that some of the court professionals' use of what she calls "aggression" undermined the efficacy of treatment by replicating dynamics that she had experienced from difficult customers while selling sex (see the discussion in Chapter 4 of probation officer John as the "bad cop" from Ava and John's perspectives). Luckily, Ava's rapport with other members of the PDC team and her self-advocacy, combined with some family support and her own clear vision of her future, prevented the experience of "being abused all over again" from derailing her. This exemplifies the risks of embedding trauma treatment within a coercive environment that can, retraumatize people, and trigger counterproductive shame.

Ava describes her experience in PDC as a "fearful process" because of such hostile interactions. The additional surveillance and expectations are weighted with severe consequences, whether it is having to stop medication that is working for her because it is not recognized by her probation officer,[1] or the fear of program failure. She seems remarkably resilient in her ability to weather these stressors that are built into the PDC itself, what she calls "going through the hoops," which compound the stress of trying to remain sober and successful.

Ava reveals system savvy and what we have described as "selective manipulation" (Shdaimah & Leon, 2015), the ability to determine how to get along and to avoid "making waves." She explains, "I act real friendly like I do, cause I've learned how to put a mask on since I was very young. But I don't trust any of 'em." These strategies may also be part of Ava's efforts to counter shame. Such realism may be unavoidable, given PDP participants' histories of negative experiences with the criminal legal system and other authorities, but Ava's story also shows that the most overtly coercive aspects could be handled differently.

Ava also appreciates the peer support created by Project Dawn Court:

> I think it's good that the women are there to observe everybody else's process. I think that's very helpful. It's encouraging. . . . It's definitely a learning experience, seeing "Well, that could be me." But I feel for a lot of the women; and I have compassion and empathy 'cause I've been in their shoes. 'Cause I've been homeless and out there. And all of us have come from the same place, regardless of where we were and where we're at now.

Like many women in our study, Ava found value in the communal aspects of Project Dawn Court, and she repeatedly recommended improving the program by formalizing mechanisms for connection and mutual support with others who have gone through similar experiences, outside the shadow of the court.

Nonetheless, Ava's appreciation of the group aspect of Project Dawn, which made her feel understood and connected, was tempered—and sometimes outweighed—by the way the frequent public court sessions kept her shame at the forefront:

> But I'm very ashamed of what I did out there. And I had to constantly medicate more and more and more to do that, to continue to do that. And I have issues with that now, like it really makes me feel like a piece of shit. I felt so degraded out there, and people would drive by and look at me, throw stuff at me. Like it's upsetting because it's really humiliating. [starts crying] And it's hard for me to come every month because I have to face this. And I'm just reminded of how much I ruined my life. And this whole prostitution thing *every month* I gotta . . . [trails off].

Ava's experiences raise the question of how to assess whether the public collective processes like the court meetings (and for some, group therapy) were on balance beneficial, either in general or at different points in participants' trajectories, especially if these are mandated activities.

Compounding her frustration at being dependent on family and unable to get a job due to PDC obligations, Ava complained that Project Dawn Court held her back by constantly evoking shame and humiliation:

> I wanna move on with my life. So I feel that's not a good part for me; at least for me it isn't, 'cause I try and live in the moment and not stay stuck in the past, to stay sober [crying throughout]. It's, maybe it's a healthy reminder of what I could go back to, but it's also just very humiliating just to be sitting in that courtroom [crying]. It's embarrassing. Maybe other people don't feel that way, but I do. You know, just what my charges are and just . . . It's humiliating. For me, it's not working for me. It's like having an opposite effect. Instead of being a deterrent, it's just bringing back all of the pain over and over again. I just wanna move on, you know. So that's the hardest thing for me. Like I dread the court days, cause it's like right in my face all over again [crying throughout].

While individual interactions may be destigmatizing, especially as participants and PDC professionals care for and support her, even for someone as self-possessed as Ava "it's bringing back all of the pain over and over again." Similarly, the court celebrations of success that are intended to motivate and honor the hard work of participants (and, through association, of court professionals), reinscribed Ava's shame: "I think it's healthy for some of the other women to receive their certificates and stuff, although for me, it's shameful. It just reminds me I've [got] Hooker Court every month." When pressed to articulate suggestions for what would make the PDC better, Ava blamed herself for feeling so much shame:

> Maybe I just have to get better with it and forgive myself, move on emotionally, and just come and deal with it. I don't know. I don't know if the other women feel like I do or I don't know if it bothers them.

Despite Ava's insights, she viewed her discomfort with the court and the public ceremonies as an individual failure. Rather than criticizing the court for shaming and stigmatizing, she frames her experience using the widespread narratives of pathology. PDP participants rely on responsibilization, which is the idea that individuals are primarily responsible for their circumstances and is a feature of neoliberal penality (Leon & Shdaimah, 2021). She seems to view even the problematic aspects of Dawn Court as bitter but useful medicine: "I know it's good for me." In subsequent interviews, Ava continued to experience court as shaming, but shared that the repeated exposure became easier for her to handle. She also appreciated the regular sessions because she looked forward to seeing a person with whom she shared "a bond" each month.

Ava distinguishes between what outsiders might see as two coercive aspects of PDC (see discussion in Chapter 3): her probation officer's hostile insistence that she disclose sexual harm, and the fact that sexual trauma therapy is mandated. For Ava, the hostility from a court professional was retraumatizing, while having to participate in sexual trauma therapy was ultimately helpful:

> The therapists there are very—they don't push, they're very, they let you kind of, basically, I don't know, for me, I told her I wanted to be pushed, just because of [my professional] knowledge and stuff. And I need to be pushed 'cause I'll avoid, I'll procrastinate, I won't bring stuff up, so I kind of need that; that's what works for me. But I just think that they're, even though it is mandatory and mandated, they are sensitive.

Ava notes that the sensitivity demonstrated by the trained treatment practitioner ("she has a Ph.D. and she knows what she's doing") made the lack of choice endurable. This sensitivity was lacking in her experiences with the aggressive probation officer, even if the professionals have good intentions. Ava's experiences suggest that diversion courts should reconsider how trauma awareness is infused into PDP teams, and in fact may need to set boundaries about which professionals utilize the trauma toolkit to enforce compliance (Franke & Shdaimah, 2022; Leon & Shdaimah, 2019). As Ava explains, the risks are high: "If you're pushing people to a point where it's too much, they're gonna self-medicate"; aspects of the diversion program may push participants back into misusing substances in order to quiet the shame or traumatization caused by the program.

Throughout her interviews, Ava repeatedly emphasized the importance of PDC and how she hopes it will continue. Even in her last interview, however, it is apparent that the PDP did not free her from the shame and stigma she felt upon entering. Concretely, her charges had not yet been expunged (making her ineligible for positions that required a clean record), her ongoing and stress-inducing struggles to obtain medical coverage continued, and she had unresolved and burdensome court fines and fees. She expresses a mix of optimism and realism: "I'm still alive, I'm here waiting for my expungement. Things are good, I'm not on the street, you know, not locked up or anything. So I'm not using. But that's about it." Some short-term and other promising employment leads were on the horizon. Ava was working at a grocery store as a stopgap while she went through numerous interviews, only to feel in the end that she had lost out because of her past: "And it's still so embarrassing like when I have to bring up my record. People just like zero in on that in interviews." Yet, at the same time, Ava shares in her final advice to future participants, "When you expose secrets and shame and all that, it has less power on you. So talking about it and trying to help somebody, by sharing your own experience." Ava's advice is consistent with the professional literature: When people have the control to share their experiences at a time and place of their choosing, it can help dissipate the shame (Brown, 2007).

Assumptions about Street-Based Sex Work

Although academics and advocates may debate whether sex work should be decriminalized, legalized, or regulated like other forms of labor, most professionals who choose to work within PDPs viewed the sale of sex as "abhorrent" behavior. Nearly all of them viewed prostitution as a survival strategy that they assumed no one with other options would choose: "I don't think anybody wakes up one morning and says, 'I wanna be a prostitute!' or as a child that's not what you dream of being," says Margo, a Baltimore prosecutor. Their personal beliefs about sex work and sex workers were largely reinforced by their work in these programs. Derek, a community advocate in a prior study, whom we cite in other work, explained that prostitution stigma has a special stickiness: "Uh . . . with *prostitution* [whispered] . . . if you were here before, it's gonna show up when you come back again . . . then of course they got it on record, then ok, we know this is what you do" (Leon & Shdaimah, 2021). Derek can't even *say* the word *prostitution* without whispering.

Dawn Court prosecutor Erin sees all forms of sex work as exploitation. Speaking in 2021, she explained that working with Project Dawn Court was a natural fit for her, given her experience working with victims of sexual assault. In retrospect, Erin has the understanding to better articulate her reason for refusing to prosecute prostitution cases, which was her conviction that punishing people for behaviors that they did not choose was illogical and unfair.

> I would look at these prostitution cases on my list and be like, "This is ridiculous." Like, in my head, I was always thinking, like, "Why? Why are we . . .?" They're not gonna come to court, they're gonna plead guilty, there's nothing punitive the criminal justice system can do that's worse—or to get them out of, like what's happening to them out on the street is just horrible. You could tell by their physical appearance that this was not a lucrative opportunity for employment, but I didn't have the language [although] I did have that background coming to be a DA from working in rape crisis centers as a lawyer.

In contrast, court coordinator Lily echoed views similar to Ava's in noting that individuals can choose to engage in sex work, and that it can be viewed as moral and rational. Lily also questions the premise of treating sex work differently than other types of labor:

> I feel very strongly about a woman's legal right to do whatever she wants with her own body. . . . Well, why shouldn't a woman be allowed to sell herself if she wants; why shouldn't that be her economic decision? And why are we making that illegal when we don't make manual labor illegal?

PDP professionals, given their beliefs that it is inherently exploitative or, less commonly, that it is a matter of personal choice, struggle with the contradictions in criminalization as the primary policy response for people involved in street-based sex work.

The primary lens through which PDPs view prostitution is as the product of childhood trauma and dysfunction. Like Ava, who praises the therapeutic dividend that she received after being coerced into treatment, many respondents revealed some of their shameful feelings for the first time in the Project Dawn Court and Specialized Prostitution Diversion programs. In PDPs, they were met with staff who did not view them *only* as the sum total of problematic childhood and poor adult choices but as people whose choices and judgment were compromised by things that other people (and sometimes systems) had done *to* them. PDP professionals repeatedly told them that they were worthy of love and that the things they did were not necessarily who they were.

"There's Got to Be a Way to Reach Down There and Let Them Know 'This Was Not Your Fault'"

"You Can Be a Better Person" (George): *Rehabilitation and Rescue*

When they hear tragic accounts of abuse and the failure of existing systems, professionals in PDPs respond with the belief that they can do something to help. They mobilize their newfound sympathy to address a subgroup of defendants whose needs fall within an acceptable range (Leon & Shdaimah, 2019; Shdaimah & Leon, 2015). PDP professionals, acting within their roles, convey to program participants that their engagement in sex work is primarily a result of past traumas and maladaptive behaviors, coercing them into programs to address these. Baltimore assessment professional George explains his philosophy: "There's got to be a way to reach down there and let them know, 'This was not your fault. You can be a better person. You can put this behind you.'" PDP professionals also engage in public exhortations designed to convince program participants that they are not alone, that they can be good people, and that they should no longer bury, medicate, or repress their experiences—that otherwise they will continue to engage in illegal behaviors caused by their traumatic pasts. PDPs work to accomplish George's vision in several ways: (1) coerced therapy, which we described in detail in Chapter 3; (2) empathetic reinforcement of program participants' humanity (stigma management); and (3) specifically in Project Dawn Court, reducing isolation through communal encounters.

Almost all of our participants had very bad experiences as children and as adults that either they did not reveal or were not believed, resulting in pervasive problematic shame. Through involvement in the PDP, participants often reinterpreted their actions through a lens of empathy for themselves, shifting some of the attribution for their engagement in stigmatized sex work and problematic substance use from poor individual choices to an understandable response to internalized shame and isolation. Nicole explains that in mandated therapy at Project Dawn she shared experiences of childhood abuse that she had long kept secret, initially for the sake of her family and, later, out of habit and shame:

> My bad choices led from things happening in my youth that I never told anyone about or got help for. It led to drug use and then that led to prostitution. I guess you just gotta take a chance and tell somebody. Like I have my one best friend that I didn't tell her 'til we were way older that I was even molested. I never told anybody. And that was the initial [reason] why I started using. And then as I got older,

when using got real bad, couldn't work, and then that part had to come in. And it didn't have to. None of that ever had to take place. And I guess even as a child I knew it. I knew it was right to talk to someone, but you have all that embarrassment and stuff and I just wasn't going to. Let alone then my mom would know; my mom would be devastated. It was a friend of the family. It would've killed her. So you don't always have to take the weight on.

Nicole believes that therapy helped to relieve her of shame. Encounters with her probation officer Ronny were pivotal. Nicole described Ronny as someone who genuinely cared about her, in contrast to prior encounters with criminal legal system personnel:

[Ronny] would look at you, and that made me really uncomfortable. But that's when I knew, "Alright, I gotta do work for this one." And because she took that time to look at me, I don't wanna say I wanted to make her proud of me, but I wanted her to feel like her job was worth it too. You know what I mean? . . . I passed two of my POs in the street the other day; they didn't even recognize me. C'mon, how many people [do] you know with [an obviously distinguishing feature]? Walked right by me like they didn't even know me. And really it was because they just were oblivious. [Ronny], I saw her at [a mall] a couple years ago. She came running right up to me and my boyfriend.

Since Nicole saw that arrest and "being put in the system was inevitable," she believed it was incumbent on "the system" to provide "more POs like [Ronny], for real."

Part of Ronny's approach is to induce Project Dawn participants to reveal their histories of abuse and trauma, which she views as root causes for engaging in sex work:

Most of them are holding onto a myriad of secrets . . . and it's an onion secret, so it's layer after layer after layer. They're holding onto their own secrets, they're holding on to someone else's secrets, they're holding on to the drug dealer's secrets, they're holding on to the mother who didn't love 'em secrets. I mean they just have so many secrets. And because of the activity that they're doing, that's a secret. So no one knows what they're really doing until you sit down and are able to actually begin speaking with them. . . . I start every interview off by telling the women that . . . there's nothing that I haven't heard before, and I want you to know that I've heard it all. There's just nothing that's really a secret. And you need to tell someone. And then I also tell them that the secrets are gonna cause you to go out and use and be rearrested; and in this environment, you cannot be rearrested. . . . Just start telling me your history.

In addition to the encounters that mitigate program participants' burdens of shame, PDP professionals provide explicit messages of genuine care, often countering participants' prior experiences with criminal legal system actors, social service providers, and broader society.

Hearing each other's stories makes people feel less isolated and alone, as Ava indicated in her appreciation for observing other people's processes during PDC sessions. As Toodles vividly recounts, the sense of shared experience and solidarity is healing and motivational:

Because when one of us go to jail, it's like we all go . . . 'cause we all feel that, we all feel that. To see somebody come through them doors, because we all walked through that back door [from lockup], you understand, to come to court. To be able to come through the front door, and then see one of us come through that back door, it kind of crushes us all. . . . So I think I've grown a lot from this experience. It's made me step back and take a look at myself.

PDP participants often appreciated finally sharing and being validated.

Many PDP professionals saw their work with women engaged in prostitution as a matter of life and death. In the context of prevalent violence, addiction, and overdose that led to a number of deaths of program participants and others across our studies—including at least two respondents and people we knew from court observations—these concerns were neither hyperbolic nor remote. Stories of abuse, violence, and deaths haunted workgroup members and motivated their involvement. John, a probation supervisor, exhorted his supervisees to work hard:

I always tell the officers, "If you don't get burned, then you're not doing your job." So we have tire tracks up and down our backs; but we have to extend ourselves . . . that's part of the job; girls are gonna run on you. But if a couple can stay, you do see results. And that's what I think, especially [Ronny], she works her ass off. If she didn't see results—but she sees it. And that's really big.

John urged persistence—even though he and his officers are often disappointed—because those efforts sometimes make a difference.

"I Take Good Care of My Kids"
(Brown Sugar): Rejecting Shame

Brown Sugar's experiences provide an important counterexample to the experiences of many others who we profile in this book. Although such counterexamples are outliers in many ways, they may be more prevalent among street-based sex workers, especially those who have not been arrested as frequently or who are unwilling to enter PDPs. Examples like Brown Sugar challenge the totalizing narratives that we so often see in the media, and that are replicated and reinforced through criminal and rescue targeting of those engaged in some of the most public, least remunerated, and marginalized forms of street-level sex work. The range of choices that Brown Sugar and other Baltimore Specialized Prostitution Diversion Program participants have, and the far lower program burdens, concessions, and penal risks that they are asked to take in comparison to their Philadelphia Dawn Court participants (see Table 2.1), are also illustrative.

Brown Sugar is a high school graduate who lives in Baltimore and is the mother of an infant, a toddler, and an elementary schooler. Now in her mid-30s, she shared the belief stemming from her late teens that people she had sex with should be generous:

> You sleep with somebody, and you gotta keep asking for something? If he cares about you, he's gonna do what he needs to do. . . . I meet with guys, go out, and I just be like "You gotta have some money." I ain't messing with nobody broke, and I run like that. I never had a boyfriend or whatever. . . . You have to have money to deal with me.

Brown Sugar's perspective reflects a nonsentimental way of denoting the continuum from illegal sex work to more traditional relationships or exchanges. Brown Sugar's characterization is important, particularly in light of her overall attitude that sex is like any other form of economic capital and is her best financial option. As we have noted elsewhere, for Brown Sugar, sex work was a rational choice:

> I take good care of my kids. So, I don't have a drug problem. I just love the money. That's the whole big thing. I just love the money. You know, you can be with somebody for an hour and make two or three hundred dollars—why not?

While many of our respondents were clear that sex work was the best way, as CeeJay explained, to get "quick fast money," Brown Sugar seemed to be among the least troubled by stigma or shame. This may be because, as someone who had a high school degree and did not use drugs or have physical or mental health problems, she likely had more choices for employment and for assistance. She may also have been better able to deflect some of the many shaming practices that the courts and service providers so often engage in and that are well documented in the literature even where sex work is legal (Armstrong, 2019; Weitzer, 2018).

When asked to reflect on how the SPD might help her, Brown Sugar shared that she had been rethinking sex work. "The whole game has really changed," making it less lucrative and more dangerous than it had been earlier in her 12-year career:

> People don't have the ability to pay like they used to. When you're used to getting like $1500 a day . . . What *happened*? Somebody comes up to you now and [says] "Oh, I got $20." The crackheads are down the street . . .[and that] changed the whole game. Now [customers] go chase behind crackheads now for $20 dates. So when you do go out there, they expect you to be on the same page.

She also considered her age and her maternal role:

> The game ain't promised forever, you know. You gotta have some kind of stability when you get older. You don't get no benefits with this. You don't get no insurance. [chuckling] You don't get the [work-based retirement plan]. . . . I don't want to be 60 years old, still on the streets working and . . . After a while, it takes a toll on your body. If you don't take care of yourself while you in the streets—if you don't take care of yourself, you're done. 'Cause you got nothing else.

When originally offered the option to enter the SPD, Brown Sugar reacted to the public defender with derision: "I was like, I'm not no crackhead. What you mean I got to go to a *program*?" However, she said that he explained, "That don't mean you're an addict. One person come[s] here for drugs or whatever, and one for something else, and one for something else. That's because the things y'all got in common is y'all prostituting." The deciding factor for Brown Sugar, unsurprisingly, was that the SPD was an alternative to incarceration.

> He said, "It beats sitting in jail—[the program is] 90 days. All you gotta do is show your face and participate. That's all you have to do." I said, "I can do that." Okay. I can do that. And, I'm gonna do it.

Like Ava, Brown Sugar opted for a program over incarceration.

However, Brown Sugar's assessment of the SPD, a pre-plea program that required only one weekly phone call with her pretrial agent and a weekly meeting with the SPD social worker to which she could bring her children, led to an obvious decision. This is in stark contrast to some of the many requirements that Ava had to subject herself to under the PDC: a *nolo* plea in which she gave up her right to contest charges, weekly probation appointments, monthly Project Dawn Court hearings, and many hours of intrusive treatment and surveillance.

Like Ava, Brown Sugar had a desire not to expose herself publicly as a woman who had engaged in sex work:

> People look at us like—when they look at you they know they're dealing with a prostitute. They look at us like, "Oh my God, she gonna try to get at my husband." I don't do those things, you know. A person would never know what I do. I don't dress like that. I keep it clean and simple. If I see somebody that I've dated, and they are with their wives, I keep moving. I don't need to try to speak to nobody. Don't nobody really know.

As we saw above, the shame of public exposure was one of Ava's most salient negative and demoralizing program experiences. Similarly, Brown Sugar was more receptive to the SPD precisely because it would help her avoid exposure. Also like Ava, Brown Sugar rejected the hypocrisy of outsider judgment that rated sex work as uniquely immoral, or as the worst kind of criminal charge that one can receive:

> "Oh, how you can do that [sex work]?" "Well, how you gonna let your children be hungry and you running around and wanta smoke coke all day?" And you talkin' about you don't prostitute, or you just selling drugs. I'd rather catch a *prostitution charge* than a drug charge. 'Cause now you're facing 10 or 15 years . . . [and] you got a felony on your case; you can't get housing. You can't get no public assistance. You got a felony, you're not gonna get nothing. You [have] to sign your kids over to somebody else so they can *get public assistance*.

The SPD was also less stigmatizing because it did not make as many assumptions about participants' needs and it allowed Brown Sugar to engage with services that she saw as relevant or that arose from her assessment. As she shared with us during a conversation punctuated by baby sounds, Brown Sugar used her 90 days in the program primarily to learn how to better "manage my money" and to talk with the social workers about her "daily life":

I thought at first it's going to be a loooong [drawn out] road to go. But it was so easy because you just follow directions and get to where you need to be. To really learn to be responsible and once you learn to be responsible . . . it's so easy. It's very easy. This whole thing, this is a good program. . . . It's better than being locked away. You just check in, talking about how you feeling, what's going on in your daily life.

Brown Sugar was not required to perform victimization, trauma, and contrition in particular ways or to divulge her deepest secrets (Corrigan & Shdaimah, 2016). Instead, Brown Sugar used the program to make changes that she was already considering, given her age and role as a parent of older children and changes to the sex work economy in Baltimore. She explained several times that what she liked most about her social worker is that Brigit treated her as a human being, and respected that Brown Sugar was honest with her.

It is hard to see how an experience with the much longer and more interventionist Project Dawn Court could have helped someone like Brown Sugar more than her SPD experience did, and there are many ways that we can imagine it might have harmed her. For example, Lily's reinterpretation of Christina's relationship with an older man as prostitution deprived Christina of both shelter and comfort and was likely experienced as shaming (see Chapter 6). Asking Brown Sugar to reimagine all of her relationships that involved any exchange of sex for affection, housing, or gifts as prostitution seems like it would have been equally devoid of benefit and potentially harmful.

Explaining why she did not plan to go to the SPD's graduation, Brown Sugar made it clear that she planned to continue to stay under the radar:

I just have, uh, not stage fright, but I hate to be in the room full of people. I mean I got myself into this, but I have no choice but to stand up there because if I didn't, I'd have a warrant. But now I don't want to be interfaced with that.

Conclusion

How might Brown Sugar's experience have been different if she were arrested for prostitution not in Baltimore but in Philadelphia—where for a third prostitution charge, she would be facing fines of up to $10,000 and incarceration of up to five years? Offered the Project Dawn Court, Brown Sugar likely would have opted in to avoid these harsh punishments. Yet she would have faced increased risks, including these:

- Child welfare entanglement due to heightened surveillance and reduced resources to care for her children, including lack of programming where she would be able to bring them with her or find an appropriate caregiver;

· Inability to work or engage in day-to-day activities of living due to the myriad requirements of individual and group therapy (whether she thought she needed it or not), probation, and other obligations; and

· Collateral consequences due to the tendering of a *nolo contendere* plea and the lower likelihood of graduating and having her charges expunged (or for it to take much longer, thus prolonging her difficulties in securing legal employment and housing).

In addition to these very practical fears, Brown Sugar likely would have been subject to repeated attempts—in public and in private—not only to shame her for selling sex but also to reinterpret all points on the continuum of exchanging sex for material and nonmaterial assets as a form of stigmatized conduct. This was the case with Nicole. When asked what she gained from Project Dawn, which she remembered fondly, Nicole said this:

> And even though I was terminated, a lot of what I learned stuck with me. I mean I still sell [sex] 'cause it's hard to get a job out here sometimes, and you just kind of revert back to what you know. But it's never the same after that. It's not. Um hmm. Don't do it. It's easy to do because . . . it's like a football player and football: You know how to play football. But it's not easy in the sense, you've done all that work [in trauma therapy]. And it's like once I started doing that work, doing the trauma therapy and all that, it changed it. It might be easy because it's like, yeah, you know how to play football, you know how to play. But to actually, like, go out in the field and play, it's not easy. And that's basically how I'm kind of thinking, you know. It wasn't easy to [sell sex] again [when] I've had to.

Nicole's relationship to sex work is changed because of the stigma she learned to associate with it, but she is nostalgic for Project Dawn Court and recalls her overall experience there as one of love and care. She is sad that she missed graduation, even as she feels somewhat sheepish for wanting to celebrate something that feels "ridiculous":

> When I was in it, I felt real goofy, "Oh Dawn's Court," goofy graduation and this little paper, um, the little . . . framed [certificate] like "Hey, Yay, you didn't prostitute!" [laughs], so silly. But when it was done it was like, I'm out of that. . . . They're doing something. . . . [PDC

is] like the pilot you know. It's new . . . these women, we're starting something here.

Nicole's participation in Project Dawn provided her with many things: therapy, a renewed connection to her peers from the street, and a network of professionals she can trust, including her therapist and probation officer. But the price is high: Nicole now feels bad when she trades sex out of financial necessity, which also signals that she was not able to find stable, sustaining means to support herself, even though she has family help. It is hard to reconcile the shame that Nicole continues to feel and that is amplified by her program experience with her positive assessment of Project Dawn Court, especially given how harmful internalized shame can be.

Toni provided a similar assessment that Project Dawn created harm by requiring program participants to be vulnerable without assuring their continued well-being:

You're letting them go after a year and fend for yourself. Well, that's not right. . . . What are you really doing to support them? Because it takes more than a year to get them on their feet. A year is not enough time to get somebody who's been trapped up in the system for 20, 30 years on your feet. A year's not enough. It's not. It's going to get them out of the wheel, but it's not going to sustain them for a lifetime. It's not going to sustain them for a lifetime of education, job placement, any of that. Yeah, they need to stay in [treatment] but where's the rest of the part? Where's the rest of the pie? Where's the rest of the pie? That's just a small slice. . . . [PDC] didn't really think about . . . how bad [people are] gonna feel about themselves when they fall and relapse. Because the ones that are gonna get hurt are the girls that fall on their face . . . and OD themselves when they fall and they fail.

PDP participants' continued precarity demonstrates that these short-term interventions do not address the "slow violence" that criminalized sex workers and survivors of human trafficking experience through "tracking into low wage labour" and "legal tenuousness" (Schwarz, 2022, p. 11).

Comparative anthropologists Brewis and Wutich (2019) provide a framework for thinking about whether shame and stigmatization should be used in the pursuit of public health goals, however lofty and beneficial. As with the court professionals in our study, many public health interventions calculate how to use what some might argue is "just enough shame": "Discussions of the ethics of using stigma as a health promotion tool argue for a 'sweet spot' that maximises the wanted behaviour change while minimising negative effects" (Brewis & Wutich, 2019, p. 2). Brewis and Wutich draw on their cross-cultural research to show the concentrated disadvantage that shame creates across various practices for those who are most vulnerable when they are the targets of ostensibly useful shaming. Through evidence from multiple studies, they demonstrate that the harms of shaming can reach deep into a person's being and are often counterproductive to public health goals, for example, by driving behaviors underground or by creating iatrogenic effects. They conclude that "Until there is compelling empirical counter-evidence of primum non nocere [first do no harm], shame-based stigma strategies—even if they ostensibly work to nudge much-needed healthier behaviours—should never be deployed as part of the global health toolkit" (Brewis & Wutich, 2019, pp. 2–3). As we have explored in this chapter through Ava's story, which documents ongoing long-term shame detailed throughout two years of interviews, harm is in fact being done through the PDP's use of shaming.

Our data are full of examples of ostensibly or partially helpful practices and interventions that might be delivered differently if Brewis and Wutich's dictum is the guiding principle. For example, what if people were offered mental health services and peer support groups outside of the court processes? Even if, as some of our respondents argue, the heavy hand of the coercive criminal legal system is necessary to force people into services that they do not want, might these be provided in locations and ways that minimize shaming? For example, for people experiencing mental illness, Parkinson and Whiter (2016) call for the delivery of art therapy in low-stigma settings, such as museums, an option that is in stark contrast to the experience of PDC participants who attend sexual trauma therapy and wait to give urine samples sitting next to people who have been convicted of sexual violence. Taking into account that the behaviors for which they are shamed have a long history of surveillance and regulation, it is hard to deny that PDPs are part of a long series of gendered norm enforcement at least as much as they are about "help" (Cohen, 2017; Global Health Justice Partnership, 2018; Lilley et al., 2020; Singh, 2018).

6

"To Be Normal": Building, Rebuilding, and Surveilling Relationships

Social Connection in the Shadow of the Courts

ike other PDP participants who are engaged in street-level prostitution, Project Dawn participant Amy is interested in what she refers to as a "normal" life (Shdaimah & Wiechelt, 2017). This includes being able to meet basic physical needs like shelter, food, and health, but also (re)building social relationships with family and significant others. Similarly, court personnel seek to (re)make program participants to create and maintain what professional team members consider appropriate relationships. Relationships among program staff and between program staff and court participants are sites where criminal legal personnel model their versions of mainstream normalcy—often in explicit and self-conscious ways. Normalcy for the court includes not only legal employment, stable housing, and desistance from illegal or problematic drug use and prostitution but also less tangible factors such as proper attire (i.e., clothing that is not considered suggestive) and proper demeanor (paying attention or not using cell phones during court) (Corrigan & Shdaimah, 2016). These manifestations of normalcy may be contested in public (i.e., in court hearings) and in private (i.e., "in booth" with probation officers or at team meetings).

We begin this chapter with an extended vignette that describes how Amy, a White woman in her late 20s, negotiates her different relationships and her vision of an ideal life against the backdrop of a reality that is constrained both by difficult personal circumstances and by the PDC stakeholders from whom she requires approval and support. We follow with critical reflection about how relationships are built, rebuilt, and surveilled as part of the PDP's ongoing project of support, rescue, and control.

"I Just Wanna Be Normal" (*Amy*)

Amy is a participant in Project Dawn Court. Our first interview with her took place in October 2011 when she was nearly finished with the fourth phase of the program and was scheduled to graduate in just a few months. Our final interview with her took place nearly two years later in August 2013, eight months after her December 2012 graduation. In this extended description, we draw primarily on the seven interviews conducted with Amy during this nearly two-year period. We also draw on data from PDC court observations, where, in addition to the interchange between PDC participants and staff, there are public and whispered expressions of judgment and support by participants and staff in response to Amy's and others' successes and relapses. Together these create a normative environment in which Amy and all other program participants are schooled as to which behaviors and relationships are acceptable.

At our first interview, Amy was already a veteran PDC participant. Her extended tenure was a result of program breaches and drug relapses that resulted in phase restarts, in addition to other sanctions, including incarceration.

Amy began using drugs at age 16. When she was 19, to pay for drugs, she began selling sex on the streets in the neighboring state where she lived, relying on guidance and advice from other street-based sex workers about how to sell sex safely. Amy's PDC obligations included trauma counseling, intensive outpatient treatment, and weekly meetings with her probation officer, all of which required her continued presence in Philadelphia. Her insurance provider and medical care for HIV/AIDS and hepatitis C as well as other health problems were located in Philadelphia. Amy talked about her family often and their importance to her. However, the sheer volume of program demands on her time combined with geographic distance made it hard to maintain regular visits. She and her family members were also constrained by financial hardship that made transportation unaffordable.

Throughout the interviews, Amy alludes to her parents' troubled relationship. She explained that they stayed together in order to raise Amy's daughter as well as two of her nieces, all of whom were in their custody. When Amy described her parents and sisters, she often lamented their worries about her. She described her mother as "frantic" with fear at times, to the point where her mother called the PDC probation officer and "got me locked up twice, my mom did." Amy's PDC probation officer, Ronny Landis, has been an ongoing link between Amy and her family:

My mom would call her when she hasn't heard from me for days. She would call her to see if she'd seen me or if I had gotten locked up; she'd call Ms. Landis to find out if I was in jail. She would call Ms. Martin to find out if my body had come up in the morgue and I just didn't have ID on me or they didn't know how to get in touch with my mom. She would call Ms. Landis when I fucked up, when I came to her house and I was fucked up and I left, and she'd call Ms. Landis and say, "Look, she has a warrant and you need to get her off the street 'cause she's gonna kill herself." My mom would do that.

While at the time Amy was "pissed" at her mother for having her arrested "to be spiteful," in hindsight, "Now I see that she did it so she could get a night's rest and so that I would get better, and I would have a chance to detox; 'cause I would detox every time I went to jail."

Amy describes her relationship with her father as frozen in teenage dynamics. While in the PDC, program staff helped them renegotiate their relationship:

It went really well because me and my father never had that close [adult] relationship, because of the fact that I started using drugs at 16, mentally my mind stopped. So all these years getting high, I had the mentality of a 16-year-old and he treated me like one. He talked to me like one. I didn't respect myself and they didn't respect me either.

Before Amy and her father reconciled, she had not seen him in two years. The last time they met, Amy had been gaunt from drug use and ill health:

That was a reunion that I had been nervous about. I didn't know how it was gonna turn out. But when he saw me, he started crying. Last time he saw me I was [extremely underweight]. He started crying when he saw me and my mom wouldn't let go of my hand.

Amy often talked about the importance of rebuilding her family relationships. She worked hard to regain family members' trust, but years of worry about her health, safety, and disappearances made this a rocky process. Amy understood their concerns and recognized the need to prove herself "through actions." Discussing her two drug relapses during the course of our interviews and the impact these had on her family, her tone was somber. Amy pointed out that unlike in prior relapses, she had not returned to prostitution and had not "picked up" heroin, which had been her "drug of choice," but instead took Xanax, stolen from her grandmother's friend and her sister and later purchased on the streets. She also pointed out that in her relapses she had

not run away but had attended her probation appointments, despite the knowledge that the positive urinalysis (evidence of her program breach) would likely land her in jail, as one of them did. Remaining engaged in the face of court
sanctions allowed her to maintain her family ties, as well as to stay in the
program. The court, even as it meted out the required phase restarts and punishments to Amy, praised her for maintaining her relationships with program staff and for her relative progress. Amy, in turn, viewed her ability to
remain in the program, despite rule breaches and what she saw as the non-
judgmental application of standard punishments, as proof of a caring relationship in which both sides continue to be there for each other over the long
term. This was parallel to the way she navigated her relationships with family members while she was in the program. From the quotes above, it is also
clear that Amy's family and PDC staff worked together to reinforce a network
of support and accountability that Amy (generally) saw as difficult but necessary for her own survival.

Amy frequently talked about her gratitude for assistance from program
staff, who kept close tabs on her different relationships. PDC staff, particularly her probation officer Ronny Landis, were key in helping her rebuild her
relationships with her daughter, her parents, and her grandparents. However,
program staff also supervise and control women's relationships. In monthly public court discussion, the PDC team debated the extent and nature of
Amy's involvement with her boyfriend Carlos and her involvement with her
family's health care needs. Probation and court decisions limited her contact
through disapproval of visits out of state due to a declared concern for her
potential relapse while away from her recovery network and supervision.
They also worried that she would take on too many family obligations and
prioritize those over her own recovery and PDC obligations. Using an explanation that is echoed by many of the program staff, Judge Kahan warned
Amy that she could not "make up" for all of the losses she incurred during
her addiction and her separation from family. She exhorted Amy that successful recovery is dependent on Amy focusing first and foremost on herself.
At times, Amy views court oversight and public discussion of her life and
relationship choices as a welcome expression of caring and support:

> AMY: The first day that I had [Judge Wallingford], she was very sweet.
> She asked me "How did I lose all of my teeth?" Right in front of
> the whole court. And it didn't embarrass me, it just showed—gave
> me a chance to show her—"I need your help. I need help."
> COREY: So that was ok that she asked that question? You didn't feel—?
> AMY: No, I didn't feel embarrassed. Because my teeth were knocked
> out by men. Dates who had turned violent. And drugs, rotting my

teeth out. And she wanted to know. She needed background history. And that was one thing that she got a chance to see—that gave her an opportunity to see what kind of life I had led, that my life was hard.

When we asked whether they ask questions like that in "regular court," Amy responded:

No they don't ask questions like that. Because they don't care. They don't pry because it doesn't matter [banging lightly for emphasis]. "It doesn't matter how you lost your teeth to me because I'm giving you this punishment." It didn't matter. It doesn't matter. Judge Richards took the time to care and Judge Hartwell pried because she needed to learn background history.

Amy's characterization of the court's questioning as an expression of caring was echoed by other respondents, who viewed PDC and SPD program staff as wanting to know in order to help. As Amy's quote suggests, many also felt that program staff would come to see them as whole people, rather than cases to be processed, as they got to know them better (Leon & Shdaimah, 2012). The public nature of court hearings also means that all other program participants are present for these exchanges, providing opportunities for support and approbation, as well as advice. Amy is keenly aware of other PDC participants' trajectories, is eager to be a model to others, and at various times explored pursuing peer counseling certification.

Conversely, there were times when Amy viewed questioning and oversight as an unwarranted intrusion. This was most often the case in regard to her romantic relationship with Carlos, whom she met in a recovery program. Amy chafed at the PDC team's concern, which countered her own assessment of the value of this relationship. Program staff urged her to keep her distance from Carlos, whom they viewed as a threat to her sobriety and program engagement. Not only was Carlos her romantic partner, but he assisted her ailing grandmother and was close to her daughter. When they were eventually permitted to live together, he also paid the rent.

Amy's disagreement with PDC stakeholders' vision of her relationship with Carlos is at odds with her ideal future, which is anchored in family life (see also Shdaimah & Wiechelt, 2017). She wants to be a good partner, daughter, sister, and granddaughter. In one interview, as an illustration of their connection and her daughter's longing, Amy described how her then-preteen daughter would snuggle close so that she could deeply inhale Amy's smell to remember it before they parted. Amy wants to help with her family's medical and caregiving needs, which variously included her elderly grandmother's ill health and her sister's brain tumor. Perhaps most central to this vision is living with her daughter and Carlos:

> My ideal life is getting a house that my daughter wants to live in and not having to worry about money on a daily basis. And some people may think, "That's it? That's all you wanna do? You don't wanna have a yacht? You don't wanna travel to Vail? You don't wanna do this [or] that?" "No. I don't need any of that stuff." I don't need to do any of that stuff. I just want a life comfortably with my daughter and my husband and stay clean and go to work every day like a normal person does. I just wanna be normal. I'm 31; I'm 9 years away from being 40. This is crazy, you know? I wanna put my life on the right track before it's too late, before I'm too old to do anything about it.

In interviews with Amy six and eight months (respectively) after she finished the program, many of these dreams were no longer possible. Her grandmother died, taking away not only an important relationship but also her housing. Her father was in treatment for cancer. She did not have the financial means to live near her family. Carlos left her, moving in with a former girlfriend in another state. Although he paid two months' rent to help her "get on her feet," time was running out. She lost her local fast-food job due to absences for health problems (a job that was insufficient to pay her rent and sustain her in any case) and she was desperately searching for other work. Amy said she was lonely, missing Carlos and her family. She was also unable to talk to her family about Carlos. Her mother stopped all conversation on the matter by cursing him out, and her daughter was too young and too sad about his leaving to be a confidante.

Relationships as a Rich and Complicated Web

Amy's story over a two-year period exemplifies how the PDC views, shapes, and regulates relationships as well as how the participants' relationships interact with their involvement in the SPD and the PDC. These include relationships with family members, intimate partners, other street-based sex workers, and criminal legal system personnel. Amy's trajectory illustrates the range and complexity of relationships: She has worried parents whose own relationship is characterized by discord, a sister struggling with addiction and ill health, a grandmother whom Amy lives with and cares for when sober, and a daughter who is being raised by Amy's parents together with her sister's children. Amy and PDC program staff often discuss her family relationships as a motivation for her continued success in the program and as an impediment to sobriety and desistance from prostitution when Amy is feeling overwhelmed or judged or is away from treatment due to family obligations.

Amy's description of her relationships with men illuminates the role of partners, some of whom influenced her initial and continued engagement in prostitution, and the court's dim view of nearly all of participants' relationships with men, regardless of the role that the men often play in providing necessary emotional or financial support. Also present, although less prominent in Amy's narrative, is the importance of relationships among women engaged in prostitution, who provide work advice and support, as well as their attempts to reduce their involvement with prostitution and drugs. Like many of the women in the PDC, Amy has interacted with other program participants in other venues. They have met in jail, in rehabilitation programs, and on the street. Interactions are characterized by mutual assistance, explicit and modeled encouragement and support, and critique of self and others (Shdaimah & Leon, 2016). Relationships with other program participants can also be perceived as a source of risk. Amy's interviews shed light on the way that relationships with program staff are also a source of both support and frustration.

Amy's experiences in each of these domains are corroborated by the experiences of other study participants. Who women turn to and provide support for, and why, are key factors that shape whether they succeed according to their own and others' criteria for success. Their decisions around such support are also shaped by systemic and societal hurdles. Although the court-affiliated programs assist individuals with their behavior, rarely can they provide the resources, such as housing and employment, necessary for long-term survival. PDPs police relationships in ways that indicate that they are not fully attuned to how reciprocity and trade-offs operate within a context of needs, constraints, and opportunities.

Relationships within the Context of Diversion

Relationships are seen by program participants and professional staff as a hindrance to program goals or a facilitator of those goals. What often seems clear and obvious to PDP staff is actually more complicated when better understood within the context of program participants' opportunities and constraints, and these understandings are often contested sites within the compassionate court. We divide these relationships by type: Relationships with Family; Relationships with Children; Relationships with Intimate Partners; and Relationships with Program Staff.

Relationships with Family

As it did with Amy, family often plays an important role in diversion program participants' decision-making. Family obligations and relationships are what led some participants to sex work in the first place and may also make it a continued best option. This may be particularly true of participants who have criminal records, especially for the stigmatized offense of prostitution, which makes it harder to secure legal employment. One study in Poland (Ślezak, 2015) found that in families where sex workers had lower status, earning money was a way to gain love and status within the family structure. Approximately one-third of female sex workers in a study conducted in Taiwan were motivated by family obligation (McCaghy & Hou, 1994). Similarly, our own research indicates that women will engage in prostitution to support themselves and their families when they perceive it to be the most feasible and moral option available (Shdaimah & Leon, 2015). Ava saw prostitution as her best option to support her addiction without harming her family:

> It's such a stigma, prostitution; you know "she did *that*?" But to *me*, stealing from my 75-year-old mother who's on Social Security is *worse* than that. [crying] . . . I would rather harm myself than somebody that I loved and cared about. Or even a stranger. Knocking somebody over the head and stealing their wallet. People do that without [pause] batting an eye. I've seen it. . . . My sister showed me an article too, in [*Town*] *Times* . . . on heroin and addiction and the [journalist] said, "One night I remember *crawling* in my parent's bedroom, crawling across at night while they were sleeping, crawling across their bedroom floor just to get at their wallets." And then a comment that got sent said, "And some will go further, even to the lengths of prostitution!" . . . A lot of women I've spoken with out there . . . told me the same thing. "I'd rather hurt myself. I'm not stealing, taking my baby's diaper money. I'm not selling my food stamps that my kids need." So I guess it was an ethical thing for me. And I didn't want to involve my family and the people that love me in my addiction.

In addition to prostitution as a moral option in light of her family relationships, Ava also traveled to the city to sell sex so as to avoid having her suburban family members find out and be ashamed. This choice, made to protect her family, further isolated her from support. During one difficult episode, it took many hours for her son and her sister to come into the city and find her, a delay that resulted in a disfiguring disability in her arm where she had fallen asleep, alone, on an inserted needle.

Family may be a source of assistance. Often this assistance was symbolic. Ariella's decision to enter the PDC and comply with obligations was made with "motivation from outside, like grandmom, my aunt, my sisters, my kids. I was tired of disappointing them, tired of disappointing myself." Echoed by those respondents with supportive families, Ariella's family members were a steady source of support. Ariella had a relative who was a corrections officer in the women's prison and served as a connection to family while she was incarcerated. She lived with her mother in a well-kept home in what has been called a solid Philadelphia "middle neighborhood" (Philadelphia Reinvestment Fund, 2017). Ariella's sister, whom she described as "my biggest fan," came to court with her. Ariella described her sister, who would "have 3 years clean in July," as "my inspiration."

Assistance may also include, as it did for Amy and many other program participants, caring for children on a permanent or temporary basis (Sloss et al., 2004). Family members provide housing (Kurtz et al., 2005), a common need among study respondents who completed inpatient drug rehabilitation programs and were on long waitlists[1] for public housing with no source of income. However, for Amy and many other program participants (Shdaimah & Bailey-Kloch, 2014), family is not only a source of support but also a source of risk. Family is often seen both by program staff and by participants as a source of emotional pain and "triggers," which can precipitate program breach in the form of addiction relapse. In some instances, this is because interactions may give rise to feelings of guilt or shame (Chapter 5). Judge Kahan's exhortation of Amy not to overwhelm herself trying to make up for lost time or assuage her guilt through helping family to the detriment of her own needs was an oft-repeated refrain. These tensions and the ensuing frustration are illustrated in the following exchange in open court between Gina and Judge Kahan. Gina had appeared before the judge in various cases and their shared history extended to well before the PDC:

JUDGE KAHAN: In all honesty my concern—we've known each other for a long time and you have been working so hard—we were trying here to see if there's some way to keep the [treatment] bed that you have while you could spend more time with your mom. It's not exactly what you're asking for and in your mind it might not at all be what you're asking for, but we want to avoid putting you in a position where it makes it harder. Spending more time with mom—she's a real positive influence and she's a reality check but making this change is going to be really hard this month. This is going to be a difficult month for you and you're not putting additional pressures. Because I know you and your first focus is on your mother and that's a terrific daughter and you're going to show your mother all the progress you've made, but . . . [Judge Kahan

continues to explain why leaving residential treatment is a bad
idea and suggests talking to court coordinator Maya.]
[Catherine gives Gina her Phase 2 certificate.]
GINA: Thank you.
JUDGE KAHAN [to Gina]: Thank you.
[Gina runs out of the courtroom holding her certificate. The bar sep-
arating court personnel and people whose cases are currently being discussed from those who are observing and waiting swings
back and forth after Gina flies through it on her way out of the
room. She breaks into sobs as she runs out. Sara and later Christina follow her out.]

This extended vignette provides a sense of the good intentions and tensions
on all sides. Judge Kahan is proud of Gina's progress and recognizes how ten-
uous her recovery is. She respects and understands Gina's connections to her
mother but rejects Gina's request to return to her mother's home just as she
is set to begin sexual trauma treatment, which is considered by court staff
to be a risk for relapse and renewed engagement in prostitution. Gina is aware
of the need to keep it together in court but can barely contain herself as she
flees the courtroom. Sara and Christina's peer support is a common occur-
rence, born of personal knowledge and solidarity (see Shdaimah & Leon, 2016;
see also Bowen, 2015).

Some family relationships are inherently problematic. For example, a
number of respondents described abuse or exploitation by family members
that would be considered trafficking under current legal definitions.

PDC participant Keisha drew meaningful social support from her family, even though their smoking and drinking would have raised red flags for
PDC staff:

> [T]hrough my whole process my family has been supportive. I have
> some that still smoke weed and they drink beer, but they respect my
> recovery; they all for me. My family's seen me out there for so long,
> this is the day they finally get to see that I did it. And my mom and
> my dad, everybody like, "We so proud of you. Keep it up."

However, Keisha also found family relationships difficult. She helped care
for her mother who suffered from COPD that required ongoing medical interventions and refused to stop smoking despite Keisha's pleas. While she
kept in touch with her adult children, "the only time they call me is to see if
I got any money." Keisha attributed a drug relapse and loss of housing to a
break-up with her previously supportive boyfriend over night-shift employment. Upset at losing her housing along with the relationship—Keisha said

"I'm not gonna be living with my mom for the rest of my life; no." The totality of frustrations led Keisha to conclude "I'm pushing everybody to the side. I'm sorry, mother, kids, everybody. Because I got to; that's the only way I'm [going to] keep going, and be able to get exactly where I wanna be later on in life."

Program staff view recovery from addiction and building a new life as precarious endeavors, and they wish to help program participants navigate a complicated balance of connection and necessary self-protection. PDC participant Vitality/Tranquility described her "kinda/sorta" helpful social network, explaining: "sometimes they can be supportive, sometimes they may not be. They may not be there at all." Working with her JJPI therapist "in trauma therapy I've learned what good boundaries are [and] I've gotten better coping skills." Describing herself as "a work in progress," Keisha negotiates her own kinda/sorta helpful social networks using "boundaries that I put in place for myself and not allowing myself to put expectations on other people neither." The court, with input from PDP public defenders, prosecutors, therapists, coordinators, and probation officers, has ultimate say over where (and with whom) participants live and how they spend their time. However, staff decisions are also intended to provide the involved participants with a model of how to figure out a proper balance and set boundaries.

Relationships with Children

Like relationships with family members, pregnancy and children can provide an impetus to leave or stay out of prostitution or may precipitate involvement (Månsson & Hedin, 1999; Karandikar et al., 2022b). Few studies have explored the complexity of motherhood and prostitution, but existing research shows that children and women's roles as mothers can be a source of pain and pride and a means of demonstrating care that is shaped by the stigma and criminalization of prostitution (Reno et al., 2020; Toquinto, 2017). In the case of Baltimore and Philadelphia PDP participants, the experiences of pregnancy and motherhood was also shaped by long-term drug addiction, perhaps even more than prostitution (Shdaimah & Bailey-Kloch, 2014; Gesser & Shdaimah, 2021; see also Bailey-Kloch, 2017).

A number of Baltimore and Philadelphia program participants were pregnant or gave birth while in the program. Among those who were parents, the majority had children who were being raised by family members through informal arrangements or who had been removed from their care by the state. Although we did not explicitly ask for information about children or parenting, 14 of our 18 PDC participants, unprompted, initiated discussions or mentioned their children, as did 4 of the 11 SPD participants. Brown Sugar provided one of the most explicit articulations of how her decisions about prostitution related to her parenting. Her children were both the reason why she engaged in prostitution, despite her assessment of its risks, and the reason why she was pleased to be in a diversion program. Brown Sugar's decision-making changes as her circumstances and her children's developmental stages evolve, but it is consistently rooted in the moral and practical imperative of parenting. Brown Sugar actively rejected stigmatized conceptions of prostitution as inherently wrong:

> My kids is what I'd die for. . . . I tell anybody, "I'd go to jail for my kids." I'm not going to let my kids be hungry, be homeless, none of that. I'm not doing it. Being walking around with signs in the street, with my kids, as cold as it is, no I'm not doing that. If that's wrong, well then it is what it is. The government's only going to give so much money, so you've got to do the next best thing. What they give you; it's not enough to pay your gas and electric. You need a phone. Your kids can't be in the house without no phone. The gas price is still going up, so what are you going to do now? . . . So everything I did, I worked for it, it was for this house. It is what it is. And I accept the fact of what I've done. And I'm pleased with my actions. I [am] pleased I completed it. I'm pleased that this program gave me another chance to be with my kids and not behind no bars.

Similar to consideration of other family relationships, prostitution may be perceived as the only—or the best—means to make sufficient income to support one's children, particularly for single mothers or low-income families (Zeglin, 2014; Rosen & Venkatesh, 2008; Shdaimah & Leon, 2015).

Brown Sugar's praise of the program as an opportunity to avoid jail time reveals the double-edged sword of engaging in illegal behavior to support one's family. Throughout her interview she noted the stigmatized nature of prostitution and her desire for her children to lead a better life as reasons that she was now looking to cease working and sought "stableness" since acquiring a house. Fear of arrest and violence was also part of her calculus.

> But now I'm just like "we can struggle together." My kids are the most precious things and you don't want to miss nothing and that's what I look at now. I don't want to miss nothing. I don't want to miss her making a frown. When she gets her first boyfriend, what to tell her. I want to be around to see that. And sometimes the streets can cut your life kind of short.

Brown Sugar also worried about the messages that her daughters were taking in as they got older:

I have two girls; I don't want them to live my kind of life. That's why I try in every way I can to hide it from them, shield them from it. My daughter knows something about me. She knows something, but she don't know, really exactly. All she knows is that mommy likes to wear boots, knee boots, so now when she sees me getting ready to get dressed, she says, "Oh Mommy, put your knee boots on." And what she sees is sneakers. I try to keep sneakers on my feet at all time. I don't want her to get no ideas.

The stigma of sex work can lead people to hide their involvement in sex work from family, friends, and home communities, which may create additional barriers to seeking and engaging services that may help people who would prefer to leave the sex industry (Lazarus et al., 2012). Stigma may also lead to secrecy and stress that strain family relationships, even in countries where sex work is not criminalized (Sanders, 2005).

Similar to Brown Sugar's calculus, Hankel et al. (2016, p. 414) observed that "motherhood, as well as separation from their children, caused women to make complex decisions about how and where they engaged in sex trading activities." In their study of 126 women in a midwestern U.S. city, they found that mothering responsibilities can interfere with women's ability to comply with requirements of many drug or prostitution rehabilitation programs. PDC program staff sometimes disagreed with participants and with each other regarding what they considered to be legitimate maternal obligations. For example, PDC participant Elena was the subject of debate during a court hearing that she attended with her infant. Elena's probation officer Catherine argued against the recommendation of Maya, the court coordinator, who wanted Judge Kahan to impose the usual phase restart sanctions for Elena's having missed required therapy appointments:

> Catherine was upset that Elena's graduation date will be delayed because she missed mandatory appointments at the end of her pregnancy and for childbirth, noting that she has been coming to therapy with Diane with her baby. Catherine says that Maya wants her to restart her phase, but Catherine objects to women being penalized for maternity leave. (PDC field notes, August 2013)

Catherine and other program staff wanted to support program participants' parenting and felt empathy for defendants' children. Many also saw motherhood as a positive identity that would inspire defendants to leave prostitution. CeeJay, who was pregnant, had lost custody of her other children but was motivated by the expectation of being able to parent. She opted into Baltimore's SPD because "I had me another chance to be a mom, to stay straight, stay focused in order to raise him." CeeJay extended her SPD participation beyond the required 90 days, one of many precautions she took to prevent drug relapse, which she believed could be easily activated at any time:

> Yeah, like right now being on this corner [where the courthouse is located] is a huge trigger. It is. So when I'm almost finished with Brigit, I'm going to call my sister back so that way she will be out front or coming around the corner when I get out there because I know everybody on this corner. And drugs and money don't have no person or place. They will ask you and give you regardless of person or place. And unh-unh, I can't afford it. I'm not chancing it. I'm already at a stage whereas though when I have my baby, I can keep my baby. I'm actually at that stage, so no. I can't do it. . . . I'll be a mom of a newborn! Oh my god! [sigh] This will be the first baby after eight years that I will be taking care of. That's a huge gap. [And] I'm petrified.

Many program staff also viewed mothering responsibilities as a source of concern. Similar to the way Judge Kahan cautioned Amy not to overextend herself with her family of origin, program staff exhorted participants to avoid taking on responsibilities that could interfere with program obligations or recovery. The empathy they expressed for participants' perceived desire to "make up for lost years" was tempered by the concern that trying to do so could jeopardize their recovery. They encouraged program participants to explore their experiences and feelings around motherhood in therapeutic settings, and they often helped participants locate or reconnect with their children or children's guardians. In some cases, program staff helped participants negotiate new relationships with their children in much the same way that Amy's probation officer liaised with her father in this chapter's opening vignette. PDC participant Lorraine, whose children were raised by her mother, explained that it has taken her a long time to reconcile with having lost her status as a mother:

> It took me 30 years, not being the mother 30 years. Like Mother's Day, my roommate's son called, and I looked at her and I said, "Happy Mother's Day." I'm not expecting any phone calls today, because it is what it is. My mother will be getting those calls. And I'm alright with that because I did this. And they've had to build [their lives], cope. Now all of a sudden I want a Mother's Day card, a call? C'mon. I'm realistic in my expectations. . . . I don't expect to be the mom; I'm more like the distant aunt. . . . They don't even know me; I don't know them. That's how distant I've been. And it's an acceptance piece.

Lorraine's quote reveals a mixture of pain and acceptance. Preceding this quote, she explains that while she did not want her mother to raise her children, she also did not want to take responsibility for them herself. In addition to Lorraine managing her own expectations, her now-adult children have learned to manage their expectations of her. They are happy she is in the program but they take a wait-and-see attitude. "I know they're happy to see that I'm getting help.... 'Mom's trying it again. Let's see how long it goes.' ... They're cautious. And I respect that."

Relationships with Intimate Partners

Relationships with intimate partners are often characterized in the literature as a hurdle to exiting prostitution. Under the models that inform much of the desistance research, romantic relationships can hinder the process of identity transformation that involves developing a conception of self beyond prostitution (Ślezak, 2015). This may be because women engage in prostitution to support themselves and their intimate partners or as a result of coercion (Decker et al., 2013). Sometimes this occurs within the context of a violent relationship, which literature indicates may be more prevalent among street-based sex workers than among the general population (Hankel et al., 2016; Muldoon et al., 2015). Prostitution can also be a means to exercise limited agency or power within a violent or abusive relationship (Decker et al., 2013). This was the case for Elana, a participant in another study of Baltimore street-based sex workers (Shdaimah & Wiechelt, 2012b) who began engaging in prostitution when she charged her husband for sex in order to have a sense of control after his repeated sexual violence.

However, our interviews with PDC and SPD respondents often revealed more complex relationships than are reflected in the literature or in the responses of program personnel. CeeJay answered our question about what led her to begin engaging in prostitution with "an addiction problem . . . and a man problem." When asked what she meant by "a man problem," she explained:

I was with a man, an older man [pause] that had a drug habit. I never had a drug habit. So when I got with him and I started falling in love with him, being around him too much, I fell into the drug habit. He introduced me to the drugs. And after that he fell ill. I don't like seeing him like that. So I turned a couple dates, and it just went on from there.

Many of the program personnel, as well as many advocates and researchers, might frame CeeJay's story as one of exploitation. The age difference combined with the use of her earnings from the sale of sex to support his drug habit would lead many to classify this as a form of trafficking or pimping. Criminal justice personnel sometimes referred to people with whom PDP participants had social relationships and who also benefited from their sale of sex as "sneaker pimps," a term that recognizes these multifaceted relationships. This could include family members, or friends, but most often it was with intimate partners. Whatever discomfort an outsider has with CeeJay's classification, her description was similar to those of many respondents who viewed these relationships as characterized by love and mutual support. Although program personnel often dismissed such interpretations as the result of dysfunctional family patterns and self-delusion, to see them only in that light ignores respondents' relational opportunities and constraints as well as their sense of loyalty and service to others. A number of respondents told us that they often refrained from talking about such past and current relationships due to a fear of being judged and having existing relationships brought under scrutiny.

Such fear was indeed warranted, as we can see in the extended narrative below from Lily, talking about her experience as a PDC coordinator in a follow-up interview about eight years after she had left the PDC. In a 2021 interview, Lily shared her current understanding of demands that she made of Christina to leave a "man who she lived with part time." Lily forced Christina to leave because she was convinced that "these men are the problem"—so convinced that she said, "Well, Christina, you can't be in this program if you have that boyfriend or that guy." Lily juxtaposed the ambiguity of the situation, which was not illegal and therefore was subject to discretion of the PDP, with her own certitude at the time.

When Lily took Christina to retrieve her belongings, the man and his interaction with Christina did not match the image of the problematic relationship that Lily had envisioned, which was that "either he was a john or a pimp and there was nothing in between."

> This guy was like 76 years old, like clearly existing on Social Security. . . . There was no money, right? It was very obvious. And he looked happy to see her and then really sad when she said she was leaving and gave her a kiss. And just said, you know, "Be good, Christina, I'll miss you." And she was crying in the car and I remember—it makes me really sad. I was so wrong. [tearing up] Right? And I remember thinking about how I was, sort of dragging her away from like the only safe place she had. I didn't think that then. Then I was like, "You need to toughen up, this guy sucks." But looking back on it, you know, like, "Oh God, what was I doing?" I was so wrong. This was like her safe haven. It was clean. It was where she could shower. She could keep

her clothes there. This guy wasn't gonna beat her up or charge her or steal from her, you know? He just liked the companionship and because I didn't see things as gray, so early on I really think I hurt [pause]—I hope sometimes that she went back there.

Lily summarized: "The grays get lost in . . . the criminal justice system. The whole point of a problem-solving court is . . . allowing a judge to have the opportunity to explore those grays."

As we have reported (Gesser & Shdaimah, 2021), ambiguity and "grays" are reflected throughout PDP participant relationships and such ambiguity is inconsistently recognized by professional PDP stakeholders. The very same relationships may evolve over time, or can be simultaneously helpful *and* detrimental to women's self-chosen goals. Toodles's relationship is a good example. In her first interview, she said that she left prostitution because "I was cheating myself out of having a good relationship with somebody that wants to be with me." The importance of their relationship overrode her desire to spend money on drugs:

One day I was surprised that my account said $75. So the disease of addiction said, "Well, you can take $20 and go buy some crack." But I went downtown and got my boyfriend, I had it all planned out, I went and bought my boyfriend some underwear for Valentine's Day. . . . I have one boyfriend, one partner; I haven't tricked [in months].

In a later interview Toodles described a boyfriend who had become violent, and she said that she was selling sex in order to buy drugs for both of them. While it was not clear whether this is the same boyfriend, it does show how love and loyalty can be both helpful and harmful to women's attempts to comply with court requirements and, to some extent, reinforces the compassionate court's wariness of romantic relationships.

In addition to concrete and immediate decisions like the ones Toodles made based on her relationships, relationships were part of a larger picture of home life. Relationships with intimate partners were important for a variety of reasons. Respondents explicitly shared their desire to be good wives or partners, a vision that was part of the ideal lives that they were working toward. Similar to the description Amy gave when she was asked why she was motivated to stop using drugs and selling sex, Jerri explained that she "had a boyfriend and we were gonna try to get a life" (see also Shdaimah & Wiechelt, 2017). Jerri's goals were overarching and long-term. Romantic or sexual partners also served short-term goals or addressed immediate emergencies, as when Ava was eager to escape her family of origin:

I was still living with my mother, my son was young, my mother was very critical and harsh and nothing I did was right. I wanted to get out of there so bad. . . . This guy who was quad[riplegic] was renting out his basement in exchange for taking care of him. There was a place I could bring my son and just get away from my mother.

Ava, who like Amy described an emotionally difficult and possibly abusive home life, is very clear that she perceived sexual involvement with the man who provided her and her son with a place to live as the best choice. While the courts or outsiders may disagree, respondents often found the sale or exchange of sex to be their most practical and ethical option. Referred to as "bounded agency," the idea of exercising some control within highly constrained situations is well documented among women who engage in prostitution (Baylson, 2017; Shdaimah & Wiechelt, 2012b).

The value of romantic relationships was often a point of contention between criminal justice personnel and program participants. For example, during one hearing the prosecutor Erin said to a program participant, "The men you choose to hang out with will be your undoing, and hopefully JJPI will help you think about what you can change going forward. We all know that everyone agrees. Is that what you want?" In this case Erin is expressing true concern based on the stories that she has heard from program participants. Similar to what we have seen with other relationships, this is due to their fear that women will be triggered or enticed into drug use or prostitution, or abused and exploited.

While these concerns are indeed justified in light of the data in this study and others, criminal legal system personnel do not consider participants' intimate relationships within a larger constellation of participants' lives but through the narrower lens of program imperatives. They therefore failed to see the value of these relationships as important, if imperfect, resources for women. Program staff openly express their reliance on stereotypes, which influenced their judgment and had the effect of "othering" both the program participants and the men with whom they were involved. The gap between their judgment and their understanding had a very concrete impact on some program participants; for example, PDC program participants were required to vet their living arrangements with the probation officer and the court. During one court observation, Judge Kahan warned the court to stay away from what she referred to as "creepy men." As a counterexample, she singled out prosecutor Jack Arnall, the only male among the PDC team, indicating that program participants should be looking for partners like him. While it was not entirely clear what type of man she intended Mr. Arnall to represent, he was an employed White lawyer who came to work in a suit and tie; did not outwardly manifest addiction; and presumably, since he was employed at the State's Attorney's Office, did not have a criminal record. It was not clear how this exhortation was received by program participants. However, as we observed the exchange in open court, it invoked for us what we heard from some program participants and probation officers: City workers dressed just like Mr. Arnall purchased sex on their way to or from work.

The irony of this statement was twofold. On the one hand, it reveals a naivete regarding what we know about people who may appear to be upstanding models of behavior but who in fact may engage in activities that are deemed criminal or deviant. What separates "them" from the women in prostitution and their clients and partners are rather the outward appearances often drawn from cultural scripts that are a product of race and class privilege that allow them to "pass" as models of virtue. In fact, these individuals might be more blameworthy (in the framing of a system that criminalizes sex work), since they are exploiting others who, due to poverty and limited options, have no choice but to engage in sex work. Judge Hartwell shared a more empathetic version of this dim view of program participants' significant relationships as part of a dysfunctional environment:

> They're decent women; they have just had bad circumstances, but they're nice as they can be . . . but they are just messed up. They get in their first apartment and it's a big deal for them. I don't know about you, I don't know what your background is, but I was raised in a two-parent household; both parents [are] college-educated. So I know what matching sheets and towels look like. But I can't imagine getting it for the first time at 30 years old. So it's a big deal, something to celebrate. They've never seen that before. They didn't have houses, they have bed bugs, they live with these "reject" men, they got kids by these nuts, their kids have problems, and they should. I mean you can't live with that crap and be normal. Ain't none of us normal. When you put that weight on it you just, you know. . . . But you can't give up.

Judge Hartwell is empathetic and blames a lack of role models and a poor environment that includes "reject men" and the children that women have "by these nuts." Her characterization is less othering, as it invokes the idea that anyone could find themselves in the predicament of program participants given such adverse environmental conditions (see also Leon & Shdaimah, 2019).

These explanations do not explain why the fullest weight of punishment, surveillance, control, and judgment remains squarely on those selling sex. The added irony of both Judge Kahan's and Judge Hartwell's characterization of the men in program participants' lives is the flip judgment of the "reject men" who do not look like Mr. Arnall. With all the concern for exploitation and violence expressed by the courts, women in the PDC had relationships with their peers: people they met in shared spaces of recovery and low-income neighborhoods where they lived and worked. Their stories of limited opportunities and struggles similarly reflect the well-documented experiences of racial and class-based marginalization that are too often missing from dominant narratives of sex work, trafficking, and prostitution (Majic, 2015). The men with whom PDC participants were involved (with or without permission of the courts) arguably had more in common with the program participants and were the best material and emotional partners available to them.

Conclusion

Perhaps the most blatant, overarching disconnect—which is an ongoing source of tension in court-affiliated programs—surrounds the focus on the individual as the site of intervention. Criminal justice personnel and the related programs construct participants primarily as lone actors making personal decisions. They are often viewed as having been selfish people who abandoned traditional family structures and responsibilities to pursue drugs and deviant lifestyles. Accusing them of abdicating their roles as dutiful daughter, monogamous wife, or maternal nurturer, program staff largely understand participants' relationship motivations in one of two lights: (1) as trying to make up for lost time and obligations that cannot, in fact, be recaptured or (2) as "falling back" into what are seen as bad habits and problematic relationships, often with deviant others with whom PDP personnel believe they should cut ties. These understandings reveal a focus on the program participant as an individual, disconnected, and calculated actor.

Such individualistic and calculated approaches to relationships run counter to how PDP participants see themselves: as people embedded in intersecting and complex networks. Unlike program personnel, participants perceive these networks as neither wholly "good" or "bad," nor do they feel practically or ethically able to make black-and-white decisions about whom to cut off and why. Social service providers should consider shifting their programmatic focus to include women as mothers and significant others, irrespective of their custodial relationship to their children or their residence status with a significant other. As demonstrated in the experiences of PDP participants, women are clearly impacted by these important roles, making it less effective for programs to focus on women's rehabilitation and health from a purely individualistic perspective. In other words, since many women see themselves as defined by their relationships to others, it is vital that social service and treatment programs include an emphasis on family and community. Failing to include these foci may decrease the effectiveness of programs serving women who are engaging in sex work (Muldoon et al., 2015).

Beyond concerns regarding efficacy as it may be variously defined, ignoring the context of relationships provides an incomplete and less accurate conceptualization of why women make the choices that they do. Ecological or person-in-environment frameworks that are implicated in social work, social psychology, and symbolic interactionism also reveal the larger structural considerations that influence women's relationships. Ironically, an oft-recited aphorism in many recovery programs—and echoed in Project Dawn Court and the Specialized Prostitution Diversion program—is "people, places, things."[2] Although this seems to acknowledge the embedded nature of PDP participant experiences, it is all too often focused on the individual choices, *as if* PDP defendants have limitless options and capabilities to choose the context in which they live and work, and their social environments and influences emanate only outward from these choices. By design, PDPs that are firmly entrenched in the criminal legal system further circumscribe women's choices, often without regard for the potential impact that such requirements and prohibitions have on PDP participants' lived experiences. A relational, dynamic, and intersectional lens reveals the complex interplay between individual and systemic factors as they relate to women's relationships under the authority and surveillance of the PDP.

7

"Figuring Out What Should Happen"

Transformative or Conforming Practice?

Looking back on her involvement with Project Dawn Court, court coordinator Lily shared conflicted feelings about her role as a founding member, noting that "my feelings have evolved."

> I still have a hard time figuring out what should happen or what should have happened because I know that everyone who was involved in creating the Project Dawn Court really had the same goals in mind, which was to try and help women who didn't want to be involved in prostitution figure out a different path.

Lily worried that she had facilitated harm, in that her work shored up the criminal legal system as a site of control. The minimal help she secured for participants came to them with the risk of incarceration and other symbiotic harms, especially as it involved heightened and prolonged surveillance: "I came to the conclusion that, in fact, the court was ending up hurting women more than helping them [and that] the criminal justice system, in my opinion, is inherently a broken machine."

Lily also worried about the harm she may have caused to individuals—for example, when she forced Christina to end her relationship with the man who provided her with housing and seemed to genuinely care about her well-being (discussed in Chapter 6). Lily regretted her zealous intervention, designed to teach Christina to reframe her relationship with this older man as an exchange akin to prostitution. With an additional decade of personal and professional experiences, Lily now views the PDC's good intentions as mistaken:

> What we are all trying to do is be paternalistic and coercive to these women in the hopes that we could get them to change their lives, something they wanted to do, but we weren't going at it with the right tools. And I don't personally think that . . . anything of a coercive nature is gonna help someone change their lives in the way that you need them to, to actually really change. . . . So looking back, I don't think I would have been involved in the same way and I don't think I would have structured it in the same way.

Alongside her rethinking of Project Dawn Court and her own involvement, Lily believed that there should be more focus on providing for all of people's needs:

> And—but that doesn't mean that this isn't a population that needs a specific type of help or needs certain tools. I just think that our concept of what holistic means has changed. Mine has. And it's kind of a question mark, whether or not there can be anything holistic about the criminal justice system. . . . I don't know how to reconcile all that.

Lily was not the only program professional whose views had changed:

> I still do a lot of work with Erin when she needs an attorney to take a case. . . . I just recently represented a juvenile who was being used as bait in a Backpage case, and they wanted to charge her as an accessory to robbery. And Erin who's come, I think, very full circle in terms of how she views these women—you know, Erin was a district attorney—starting as "this is a criminal" and now sees them entirely as victims. But [Erin] still feels like "no one should be allowed to do this," you know, still feels like this should be, I don't wanna say criminalized but not decriminalized. Well, decriminalized but not legalized. And that's different from where I am but it's also very different from where someone like Judge Kahan is, or Judge Hartwell or Judge Richards, or whoever started this program. . . . Erin and I agree a lot that there are all these people talking about "how these trafficked women are victims and all this stuff and they shouldn't be arrested and we should be arresting more johns." And if you feel that way, then get rid of prostitution as a crime. I think that's a no-brainer.

Although Lily, Erin, and the three former Project Dawn Court judges may differ on the legal status of sex work, all see it as exploitation. Similarly, Lily indicates that all of their views had shifted through their work with Project Dawn, which reinforced their collective discomfort with punishment as a focus of intervention.

Perhaps Lily's most radical shift is acknowledgment of her own positionality, which brings a growing discomfort about deciding for others and "what is right" more generally:

> The district attorney up in Boston said recently that there's almost nothing worse than a PD, a White, liberal PD. And I think a lot about whether or not my role in and of itself, even now as a criminal defense attorney doing this for indigent people, is not systemically problematic. I might think that I'm doing a really good job for someone and clearly, I'm trained and I have the pedigree and I—all this stuff, I'm "qualified" [using air quotes], whatever that means. But is my engagement . . . just as problematic as everything else in the criminal justice system? So, I put that as a question mark too, and I don't know the answer to these things, but I do think about that.

The complexity of what is right, as Lily considered her own positionality, becomes more tangled by Lily's growing array of identities, which now includes parent and homeowner. While she has gained empathy for many viewpoints through her work, reconciling these creates an added burden:

> I don't know how I['d] feel about this whole situation if there were women prostituting on my corner. And I would highly doubt that I would feel so "evolved" [using air quotes] about everything and feel like "decriminalize and all this stuff" if it was impacting my day-to-day life. . . . There are neighbors who feel literally preyed upon because this is happening in front of them. And I don't know that I necessarily think that that's unfair . . . or wrong. And if my daughter was seeing that every day as we went to school, I might be like, "You need to come and arrest these women to get them out of here" . . . that wars in my heart with other parts.

Lily's ambivalence is heightened when she thinks about relationships she developed with PDC participants. These relationships are characterized by nagging worries about people she came to care about—even as these relationships are tainted, in hindsight, by what she now sees as a flawed narrative of rescue and the harmful consequences it engenders.

On the other hand, I also think a lot about [exhales], like I also think a lot about how there were women in that program who I know I made their day better, I know their month better. Like, I know I took them out to eat and we had fun. Toodles is someone who, until two years ago, I was in contact with, and took her out every year for her birthday.

An openness to other women's experiences, and learning about and trying to address "root causes" through onerous and incomplete interventions are at the center of problem-solving justice. But it is precisely this openness that makes Lily's work in the criminal legal system ultimately untenable:

I left being a PD basically because I wasn't doing a good job anymore. I was working so much and I was so involved in all the injustice and the unfairness and I felt like it was so unfair how people who had private attorneys were treated differently . . . and I was gonna work so hard for all my clients, and honestly it just kind of broke me down. . . . I would cry with clients when I was seeing them in jail because of how unfair things were, but that's not what they need from a lawyer. That's not what they need from someone who's going to be advocating for them.

This chapter focuses on the motivations, vision, and goals of PDP staff ("program professionals"). As Lily's narrative shows, these are structured, constrained, and informed by larger normative understandings of individual agency, sex work, and the role of the criminal legal system as they interact with the program participants' on-the-ground realities. Program professionals discussed a variety of motivations that range from practical reasons to ethical concerns regarding punishing people whom they perceived as victimized. PDPs provide a means to resolve such concerns and provide assistance within the purview of their professional roles and agencies. Program professionals draw on related discourses of trauma and trafficking. These discourses are largely consonant with what the program professionals have observed in their work with street-based sex workers who are arrested for prostitution in Baltimore and Philadelphia, itself an artifact of policing practices that target outdoor sex work in particular neighborhoods.

PDP professionals respond to the dissonances between their criminal justice roles and their personal and professional ethics, and like other street-level bureaucrats (Anasti, 2020; Lipsky, 1971) they use moral entrepreneurship within their circumscribed decision-making authority (Hasenfeld, 2000). Drawing on their expertise, they allocate limited resources to a subset of potential beneficiaries in line with their determinations of deservingness (Corrigan & Shdaimah, 2016; Rowen, 2020; Schwarz, 2022). While some defendants therefore benefit from sympathy, problem-solving justice also constructs ideal subjects, a feature of neoliberal governance that absolves the state of responsibility for individual and social welfare while creating a more compliant citizenry (Dewey & St. Germain, 2016; Fording et al., 2011; Leon & Shdaimah, 2012). Program participants are instructed on how to dress, how to act, where to live and with whom, often without a longer-term plan (e.g., Chapter 6). Toni, a PDC graduate, said this:

> They want to fucking get you sober, and they run you through a program and they really have no safety net beyond that. They give you no way to really sustain you. They give you no educational tools, they give you no way to ground you in ways to give you employment. Most people who are out there that are working the street came from nothing. No way to get employment. . . . What the fuck are you gonna do with that? Live in a fucking room? And that's what you're supposed to do for the rest of your life? . . . there's some of us like me that want more out of life. You know how many times when I was at [trauma therapy] they wanted to stuff me on [an] SSI check? And give me medication and just think that I was gonna settle for that for life? That ain't me. . . . And people come . . . into the jail and say, "I got this great program for you." And they sell it to you and then when the year's up, they forget that you existed. And then you're left out there to your own devices, and what do you do? You go back to what the fuck you know. And where is Dawn Court then? In the jail, suckering somebody else into the program, forgetting all about the person that they suckered into it last year.

While only a handful of professional stakeholders would likely state these concerns as baldly as Toni does, most are aware of the inadequacies of PDP interventions but view them as incrementally better, as we discuss below.

"They're Decent Women; They Have Just Had Bad Circumstances" (*Judge Hartwell*)

Regardless of whether they believe that sex work should be criminalized, most program professionals presumed that people arrested for street-based sex work engaged in the work as a matter of choice. Influenced by their tertiary trauma knowledge and the public discourse that so often conflates sex work and trafficking, most were empathetic to diversion program participants and were frustrated by the limited tools of prosecution and incarceration provided by the criminal legal system. Treatment courts allowed Judge Hartwell to act on intuition and on recommendations from probation officers in appropriate cases.

> A lot of the women were on my probation; some for years. Some I had to send to jail for short periods of time and then we put them back on probation. Some recidivised[1] then would get probation; some would recidivise and I'd give them incarceration. So it just depends. And it depended on what the probation officer said, what the women said. If the women were narcotic addicts, I always try to get people treatment; 'cause I believe in treatment as opposed to incarceration for things that you can get treatment for . . . you just have to get a further, a deeper understanding of what makes people tick. And talking to 'em helps you understand who they are. They have stuff going on just like you and I do.

Judge Hartwell believes that given the right therapeutic tools and guidance from caring court professionals, "something is going to turn around." This is based upon her understanding that women who are engaged in criminalized sex work are basically good people who have not been given a chance to develop and grow: "They're decent women; they have just had bad circumstances. . . . They are as nice as they can be, but they are just messed up."

The street-level bureaucracy literature emphasizes how individuals manage dissonance between their personal and professional values and workplace constraints. The desire for specialized programming comes from their inability to adequately handle challenging cases with existing legal tools. As Simon, a Baltimore public defender, notes:

> They're more difficult problems, more deeply ingrained problems, and it's nice to see a program that's gonna say, "Alright, we'll take the tough ones and we'll try to work with it." So there's a lot of good that has come from that.

PDPs are adaptations created by program professionals like Judge Hartwell and Simon to resolve dissonance. In previous chapters we have explored PDPs' contradictory logics, specifically how professionals rely on coercion, surveillance, and responsibilization while they also recognize structural inequities and demonstrate care for their clients. Judge Hartwell's sentiments to this effect were echoed by all program professionals and often were features of the SPD and PDC that program participants praised the most.

In contrast with professionals outside of PDP workgroups, who would be unlikely to take Toodles out to celebrate her birthday as Lily shares above,

PDP professionals respond to interactions with program participants by mobilizing sympathetic understanding. Sympathetic understanding and caring concern help justify carceral protection, which is the largely unreflective use of punishment for purposes of rescue (Musto, 2016). Public defenders and therapists, who we might expect to be more suspicious of criminal legal system solutions to addiction, trauma, and mental illness, also often valued PDP within the current landscapes. Philadelphia court coordinator Maya makes this observation:

> All I can do is process what I'm in touch with. So, within the criminal justice system, I really think that the Project Dawn Court had the best intentions, and I think that it's moving in the right direction of how we should be handling this. The criminal justice system as a whole I think does not.

As we consider the ways that PDP professionals made sense of their work through what we have called *targeted sympathy* (Leon & Shdaimah, 2021), it is important to recognize that those stakeholders we interviewed chose to work in PDPs as an aspect of their regular duties, often volunteering to staff specialized programs or caseloads. Some were key members of teams that created these programs. They chose this work because of a special interest in people in prostitution. Our findings revealed a set of preconditions, derived from stakeholders' professional experiences and personal beliefs, that led them to sympathize with (certain) women engaged in prostitution. Targeted sympathy is a rationale or post hoc rationalization rather than a deliberate strategy or intentional approach selected to address resource scarcity. As Figure 7.1 illustrates, program participants who fit PDP professionals' assumptions "enjoy" the benefits of targeted sympathy channeled into particular responses within a system that remains largely unchanged.

Program professionals' involvement in diversion programs allows them to operationalize their understandings and reinforces underlying assumptions about prostitution defendants and what they need. Targeted sympathy enhances the ability of these professionals to use their discretion to help, but they use their discretion to elevate a narrow set of acceptable problems and interventions. This perpetuates certain assumptions and creates other problems.

Program professionals encounter dissonance between their personal or professional moralities or sensibilities and their prescribed roles (Whittle, 2017). PDPs allow criminal justice stakeholders an opportunity to respond within their existing professional roles to what they see as unjust or ineffective practices in systems that they generally see themselves as unable to change. Multiagency team members' belief that they can help people who they believe

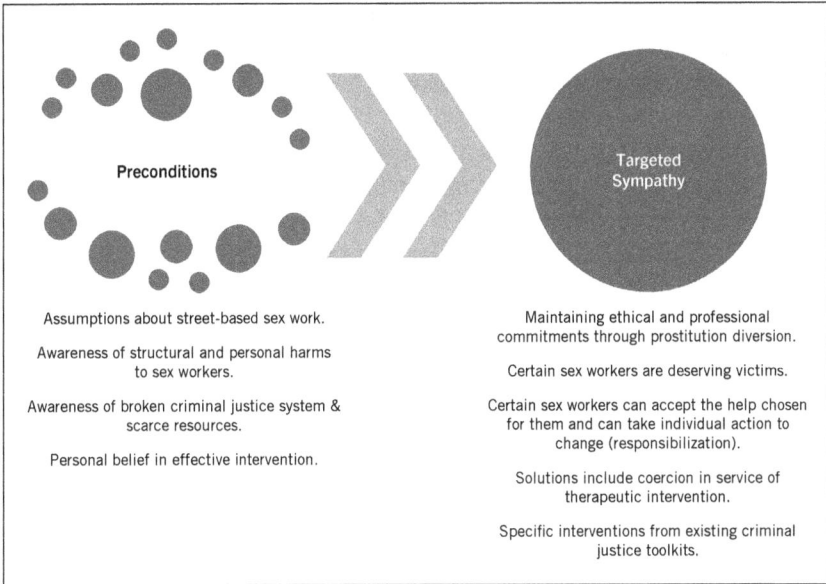

Preconditions

Assumptions about street-based sex work.

Awareness of structural and personal harms to sex workers.

Awareness of broken criminal justice system & scarce resources.

Personal belief in effective intervention.

Targeted Sympathy

Maintaining ethical and professional commitments through prostitution diversion.

Certain sex workers are deserving victims.

Certain sex workers can accept the help chosen for them and can take individual action to change (responsibilization).

Solutions include coercion in service of therapeutic intervention.

Specific interventions from existing criminal justice toolkits.

Figure 7.1 Targeted Sympathy

are just like them, but who have not been given the chance to reach their potential, opens them up to the possibility that traditional criminal justice practices are unfair or unjust. The more holistic view made possible by PDPs may facilitate their recognition of program participants as situated within larger structures of disadvantage. Criminal justice–involved individuals come to be seen just like other people who can successfully be improved through the use of empathy, treatment, and the guidance of criminal justice stakeholders and their community-based allies.

Limits of Empathy

Program professionals were divided on how critically they viewed their respective diversion programs. Some of them, like Judge Kahan, saw it as unequivocally beneficial. Her comment:

> There is no downside. I mean that's really, if you start from the standpoint that there is no downside and there is no harm in trying, then you'll see the benefits relatively quickly if you have the proper people in the program and the proper people working the program. And that there's a clear benefit in terms of the cost of incarceration. There is a clear benefit in terms of stopping the cycle of recidivism and unbelievable personal benefit and satisfaction in seeing the change in the

people who come in drug addicted, hanging on street corners, with attitudes, you know that can fill this room on a good day, to recognizing that there is a different way.

In contrast to the "attitudes" often seen in her courtroom, Judge Kahan finds it gratifying to work with the "proper people" who are ready to benefit from the PDP. However, it is not always clear who the "proper people" are. An added benefit for Judge Kahan, who is also an administrator, is the cost savings, which may help PDP professionals maintain support for the program. Indeed, the state of Illinois, for example, required each jurisdiction to submit treatment court reports that included "Aggregate Criminal Activity of Successful Program Graduates, first year post," and "Reduction in cost/jail utilization" (Mark Kammerer, personal communication, 2012).

Just like Judge Kahan believes that certain defendants are suited for the opportunities of diversion programs, program professionals and participants alike remarked on the suitability of PDP professionals. PDP professionals appreciate opportunities to collaborate across roles beyond what happens in typical courtroom workgroups. However, they face challenges in striking a balance between a nuanced professional stance and the teamwork called for by problem-solving justice. Grace, a public defender, said this:

> I was super excited when they asked me to do Project Dawn . . . [because] I do very much believe in the work that's done. It's just to me, personally, it's a challenge between my defender attorney side and my humanitarian side and wanting to provide those resources and the help and . . . everything that the court provides. But as a defense attorney, you kind of have to also understand, you know, it's not up to me to take care of anyone. It's up to me to make sure they are properly represented in the courtroom. . . . It's definitely a challenge, but at the end of the day, I am the defense attorney and I have to be wearing that hat, and that's really the bottom line. There's really no . . . [shrugs] [The reason] I do what I do is because I want to help people . . . and [I have a] desire to give them whatever it is that's missing. . . . But at the same time, you know, that's not my job. There's other people in the program whose job that is.

As Grace explains, her professional obligation as a defense attorney places limits on her work with clients. Project Dawn provides her with resources, including the opportunity for collaborations that provide more resources and support that are unavailable to clients who are not in the PDC. Although she sometimes must forgo collaboration due to her obligation to represent her client's wishes even when she may in fact *agree* with other PDC professionals, in most cases good working relationships and the shared goal of helping PDC defendants provide her with enough opportunity to find "what is missing."

Adam, an outreach worker with the Philadelphia District Attorney's Office, underscored the importance of having criminal legal system stakeholders with knowledge of local conditions and empathy involved in addressing prostitution. He thought that Judge Kahan was the best choice to head it:

[Judge Kahan] had a background in mental health court as well, so she—of the possible options for judges, she was the most acclimated to what the current conditions [are] in terms of the toxicity of the local drug supply, the severity of people with a substance use disorder and the frequency of co-occurring mental health issues that were compounded with that. She had more of a nuanced understanding of how that impacted people's lives, more so than the average judge that could have been pulled for that, you know? Because of that, she was not quick to levy bench warrants on people who didn't show up for court. She would push back sometimes on the desire for more harsh sanctions. She had a level of understanding that was connected with that.

When we talked with PDP professionals about what makes program professionals suitable for diversion program work, they largely described their perceived ability to reconcile tensions around how to manage people arrested for sex work. Most of these tensions derived from differences of opinion regarding how to balance victimization and agency and, relatedly, between rehabilitation and punishment. Workgroup members who coalesced on a vision that saw these ideas as compatible, either from the outset or in dialogue with other workgroup partners, were generally viewed as well suited for PDPs. When asked about the team-based aspects of the SPD, social worker coordinators Brigit and Gerrie gave this response:

BRIGIT: No, no, let's be clear. It was never a team.
GERRIE: Yeah, let's, yeah.
BRIGIT: "Who was on the project" is more accurate.

Brigit and Gerrie attribute lack of cohesion to an absence of clear leadership or clear orientation to help determine key aspects of program implementation, particularly in terms of eligibility criteria, treatment of defendants, and responses to program violation. Gerrie noted, "It was difficult with parole and probation. You know, the officers would want to violate people over things and we would be like, 'Wait a minute, let's hold the reins on that.'" Gerrie said that part of their role was to remind overzealous diversion program team members of the diversion program mission, like when a state's attorney "wanted them to say [that someone was] in violation and you were like 'No, no, it's not their fault!'" As was the case with court coordinator Maya in Project Dawn Court, social worker coordinators Brigit and Gerrie were the keystone professional stakeholders in the SPD. Like Maya, they were the only program professionals who were hired on dedicated funding streams when the diversion program was created. This reinforced their sense that it was their role to provide the guiding vision.

Brigit and Gerrie cultivated program professionals whom they viewed as allies. Brigit described Miss Anita, a seasoned pretrial agent with many years of experience working in traditional criminal legal system roles, as a key partner who became a primary contact for some program participants even though her official role was more limited:

> Miss Anita literally stopped in her tracks and listened. I mean, I can see it. I can feel it. And she said, "What?" And she listened. . . . I think that she, underneath, was really a social worker, but nobody ever told her. She just, she went along being the monitor, you know, the regimented person. And her humanity, if you will, came out when we kind of said to her, "They like you if you would just listen to them." . . . And she did. And she really, really, really became very invested in the project and in the women. [Miss Anita] and I, I would say we were a team.

Similarly to Gerrie and Brigit, who spoke of needing "to shape and mold and gently guide" the other stakeholders, John Keats, speaking of Project Dawn Court, underscored the need to shore up rehabilitative perspectives in the face of a tendency toward punishment:

> After [the first PDC public defender] Jan left, the people who took over the project from the Defender's Office, they were very aligned with the DA's perspective, so I felt like there was not any countertension there, which could have been legally healthy for the participants.

Conflicts among professionals also included the marginalization of, and sometimes outright aggression toward, program professionals who were considered overly rehabilitation-oriented, and such conflicts ultimately resulted in their removal or resignation (Franke & Shdaimah, 2022). Jack described his understanding about why he was brought in to replace Emily as the Project Dawn prosecutor:

Talking to people in the program, I think they were concerned that Emily was just too emotionally involved in the situation, where, you know, she was getting just too invested personally in the cases and having trouble balancing when to be a prosecutor and when not to be a prosecutor. Because it gets tough because you're the one who's in there saying, "Judge, send this woman away to jail for five years or two years, or for one year," or wherever it might be. And that's a really tough burden, especially when you start, knowing the woman, the women.

Jack came to worry that he himself had become "overly involved." He recalled, "People went to the hospital, I would call them. People had, like, you know, kids graduating in high school or something, and I'd bring a present." Jack viewed this as good and bad both for him as a prosecutor and for PDC participants: "It was good, because I really understood what issues were going on their lives, but it was bad because you get too close." For example, Jack explained that his knowledge could push him toward punishment. In the case of a PDC participant who was HIV positive, "I know she was sleeping with them and I know she wasn't wearing protection or anything like that. And, man, I hammered her every chance I got." Jack's use of what would otherwise have been personal information to respond punitively to a participant practicing unsafe sex results from the blurring of adversarial roles. It also reveals variation in appreciating what it means to send someone to prison: while it weighed heavily on Emily, Jack framed incarceration as having "a little bit" of a problematic impact. But Jack is also reflective: "I think I'm almost glad that I left the program when I did because I feel like I was too close and I was losing some of that edge," likening himself to other professionals who "might have been just too involved in these people's lives where you kinda lose that outsider perspective and forget the hat that you wear and the role that you play." Jack indicates that fidelity to professional roles should restrain the amount of interpersonal knowledge and involvement that professionals utilize even in problem-solving programs, but he is not clear about exactly what this balance looks like.

When asked whether the blurring of role alignments was not in fact one of the goals of team-oriented diversion programs, Jack responded,

You're exactly right. I think that's part of the goal. But I think the other thing is that typically these programs are done in six months to eighteen months. Two years was a long time for a program. And, like I said, there was women in Dawn Court for three, four, or five years. Yeah, that was a problem. You know, people were torn, because you're like, "At some point, you gotta let this woman go, right?" At the same time, you're like, "If I don't, if I lose my grip on her, she's dead.

She's done. She's not gonna last on her own." So, I think people were afraid to, you know, let them go.

Jack cautiously suggested that not only public defenders but also other program professionals, including Judge Kahan, were overly involved in participants' lives. He attributed their loss of fidelity to a general "change of mentality of the system to not send women involved in sex crimes to prison or jail . . . that began to weigh on [Judge Kahan]." Jack's frustration was exacerbated by a string of public defenders who often stuck to their traditional roles rather than cooperate with the Project Dawn team. He observed:

Jan Netter would literally walk into a courtroom and if I wanted to sanction a woman to 48 hours in custody, [for] kind of like a little refresher course, you would think I was sending her away to five years in state prison in Erie, Pennsylvania. Like everything was the most traumatic thing you've ever seen. And, I mean, the show after show was just [pause] it was exhausting. Quite frankly, it was just utterly . . . exhausting. Like, they had to stand on the soapbox every single time and cry [throws hands up], "Ohh, we're sending everybody to state prison! We're sending everybody to state prison!" And I'm like, "We're not. We're asking for 12 hours of community service. What are we talking about here?" Everything was a political statement. I was like, "Jan, your problem's with Harrisburg. Don't yell at me. I'm just following the law."

Sociolegal scholars and pop culture alike have long recognized the role of showmanship in court proceedings. Problem-solving courts build the performances of oversight, caring, responsibility, and contrition into their proceedings. Jack signals here his frustration with colleagues he seemed to find overly performative, on their "soapbox." In contrast, Alice was so fed up with individual actors' inability to see the criminal legal system as an inappropriate response that she ceased recommending PDP to nearly all defendants and eventually left. She was baffled that even though other professionals emphasized the centrality of victimization, this did not disrupt the individualized damage-centered ethos of diversion programs (Shdaimah & Leon, 2018).

The whole way that people would think about these women and what they deserve and how bad they are . . . invades people's unconscious interpretation of their actions. Like, "You're willing to risk this [punishment] and you're a seriously bad actor here because look at what we're saving you from by letting you in here. And you should be grateful."

Alice protests the cruelty of combining the philosophy of rescue, which de-
nies the participant's agency, with the philosophy of individual responsibility, which relies on it. Similarly, former trauma treatment therapist Ace referenced Project Dawn Court's inherent contradictions:

> It never made sense. I was like "You're telling me simultaneously that
> these people are victims and they had no choice and also saying, not
> only are you arresting them and punishing them, you are also threat-
> ening them?"

Alice and Ace make explicit the combination of responsibilizing and interventionist logics that defines diversion programs.

As we explored in Chapter 3, ungrateful program participants or those
who defy program strictures may not continue to enjoy the material, emotional, and legal benefits of PDPs—what Ace referred to in the same interview, with heavy irony, as the "opportunities." Like Maria, who was shuttled
from Project Dawn into mental health court, participants recognize the burden of support at the price of unremitting surveillance. Even as Ace prob-
lematizes this notion of opportunity, Ace recognizes PDC as a "weapon of
the weak" (Scott, 1985), meaning it is an important tool for those with no
other recourse:

> People [in Dawn Court] got opportunities, "opportunities" [making
> air quotes], and it is, it is, it depends on who you ask, but access to
> some kind of treatment, access to some kind of housing, no matter
> how bad the place is, and also keep in mind that a lot of these wom-
> en found motivation in wanting to get their kids back. So no matter
> how punitive, this was one way that there was gonna be someone may-
> be out there who could potentially write a letter maybe advocating
> for them to get their kids back. It wasn't always a thing, but often.

One way to understand Ace's difficulty deciding whether opportunity is a
reality or a euphemism is to pay closer attention to the difference between
individual choice and the constraints within which such choices are made
(Baylson, 2017). Project Dawn and the Specialized Prostitution Diversion
program may in fact represent important opportunities for individuals with
limited choices. Ace's discomfort and that of others stems from their frustration that these diversion programs—alternatives to incarceration—are
the best choice. Such choices are structured by systemic factors and bureaucratic imperatives, including the continued criminalization of sex work and
underfunded and incentivized mental treatment that is treated as a private
good.

Uptake of reform can be influenced by its compatibility with the interests of powerful stakeholders. McCoy (2003) describes how after the mandatory sentencing that was a hallmark of the war on drugs had curtailed judges' discretion, drug courts were seen as a tool to reassert judicial authority. Similarly, the policy backdrop informs PDPs. Availability of money and training may drive a response to prostitution that is shaped by trafficking discourse and that refers to existing or well-funded services designed for victims of trafficking (Boonyapisomparn, 2017). Bureaucratic imperatives and resource scarcity also explained which people are targeted through eligibility criteria and program offerings in the SPD and PDC. Jan, a Philadelphia Public Defender, said this:

> If you target that type of low-level offender, someone's going to come around and cut your budget like nobody's business and say "What are you, nuts?! Give these people probation for like a tenth of what you're spending." . . . To prevent that from happening, we targeted those who cost the system a lot of money 'cause they're in jail. But even then, we've had a hard time because Philadelphia's so budget-strapped that we get [responses like] "Oh yeah, she's approved for inpatient 28 days." 28 days!?—[to treat] a lifetime of abuse. Decades of addiction. "But you can straighten it all out in 28 days, can't you, sweetheart?"

Not only do defendants "cost" the state significantly more when they're incarcerated than while they're in a community-based program like Project Dawn, which functioned as an alternative to incarceration but with the threat of a return to prison as a prime motivator. Also, their participation in treatment programs provides a stable source of funding to those providers precisely because their therapeutic engagement is coerced.

The call and response of grant provision and fund-seeking reinforces, and is reinforced by, discursive constructions of sex work and exploitation. Philadelphia's Project Dawn Court and Baltimore's SPD coincided with the need for treatment programs to ensure viability in a fee-for-service environment by guaranteeing a steady stream of mandated "clients." John Keats, who held an administrative oversight role with the main trauma treatment provider, explained that the steady supply of clients who are mandated to show up for treatment made a partnership with Project Dawn appealing to his employer:

> I think that working in the criminal justice context has obvious benefits to clinics because they get steady referrals where the court can heavy-handedly say, "If you don't go to this clinic, we will hold you in contempt. And you might be sanctioned. You wanna go 30 days

up on State Road? Watch, I will do it." And they will come. "You don't take this lie detector polygraph? I will send you up to State Road. You better go to the clinic and do it." And clinics say, like, "Well, we get the clients to come in. They don't no-show. Everyone, it's a win-win, right?" It really threatens integrity.

John and Ace both noted the pressures created by fee-for-service models. As Ace explained,

> We were all being encouraged to double-book people so that if one doesn't show up at least our chances of seeing someone in the hour we had was higher, but when we asked the question of "But what if both show up?" the answer was "Well, you know, they wait and eventually someone won't show up and you can see them." Like that level of absurdity, "Yeah, don't worry about these people's lives or time or whatever, they can wait a few hours and see you when it's the open slot."

Sofia recalled case review meetings in which "billable units" received more focus than the clients: "They were talking about [billable] units more than, like, the intention of the actual service that was being provided to support folks navigating addiction issues and remaining unincarcerated." The realities of the financial benefits for clinics that work with a coerced population are in stark contrast to the individualized treatment ideal that motivates professionals in problem-solving justice, and also contrasts with the genesis of the assessment unit within which Sofia worked, which grew from a federal intervention aimed at lowering Philadelphia's incarcerated population. Bureaucratic imperatives also ran counter to professional ethics, especially when agencies relied on court referrals as a source of income. John Keats described how therapists under his supervision asked whether they should participate in the level of information-sharing demanded by the court. They asked him,

> "Hey, we got this call, asking for all these files to the Court. Can we release that? It's kind of weird." So we started noticing it more and more. And yes, some therapists were not as concerned, some were very concerned, but as the program grew, we had so many therapists involved in it. . . . I would say that the majority of them at some point would express confusion or concerns or not really knowing how to navigate the politics and working with the courts. And, in all honesty, I think, you know, from where I am now looking at MSW [master of social work] curriculum, I mean there are few programs to prepare clinicians to do forensic work. I mean there's few MSW programs where people learn about what's a subpoena, what's the difference

between probation and parole, how do you navigate confidentiality when you're working with someone who's coerced into treatment, who is there per a court order? What are your expectations and duties and roles? So I felt that lots of the people we brought on board to do this work were not prepared to do it either.

As was discussed in Chapters 3 and 4, this reality presents challenges to professionals who come to this work without preparation for the "neoliberal delivery of care model" that Sofia, an assessor with an unrelated bachelor's degree, described as a "trial by fire." The political and financial benefits to be gained by clinics that work with court-mandated clients like those from Project Dawn Court require professionals to have a clear grasp of the ethical boundaries and to have enough experience or other sense of empowerment to be able to work within these pressures. For some, this becomes untenable.

Conclusion

The way PDP professionals make sense of their work demonstrates what we identify as targeted sympathy. Like street-level bureaucrats in myriad organizations, PDP professionals must allocate scarce resources and resolve ethical conflicts about their roles and their usage of discretion. While they would say they are sympathetic to everyone, our analysis identifies the ways in which these PDP professionals in fact target their sympathy guided by their assumptions about appropriate behavior and appropriate victimhood. Targeted sympathy is mutually reinforcing and bidirectional: As governmentality scholars note, how a problem is constructed shapes the resources or solutions that will be mobilized (Valverde & Mopas, 2004). Targeted sympathy as an overarching approach implicates specific strategies to determine who is deserving and what they get, as well as which aspects of their needs and hopes are addressed. In this manner, the targeting is normative and paternalistic.

Supposedly innovative programs in institutional settings replicate rather than disrupt the norms of women as victims. As sociolegal scholars of sex work have argued elsewhere (Dewey & St. Germain, 2016; Leon & Shdaimah, 2019; Majic, 2015), such interventions are securely anchored within criminal justice and adjacent therapeutic programming and thus they reinforce norms about sex workers as victims even as they may subtly shift those norms. Carceral protection (see Musto, 2016) in the form of ongoing and heightened surveillance is justified by the underlying assumptions regarding victimized women who sell sex—assumptions that leave systemic forces unexamined. Mirchandani (2005) also contends that problem-solving courts can make some progressive reform—just as the bureaucrats in the domestic violence court that she studied taint the feminists in the collaboration, so too do the feminists taint the bureaucrats. Our findings show that targeted sympathy has a tangible impact both on the professionals and on the people in the program, creating incremental change without broad impact.

As other scholars have found, PDPs are predicated on understanding sex workers as victims and assuming that they engage in undesirable work for survival. Simultaneously, prostitution diversion programs rely on responsibilization, expecting sex workers to bootstrap themselves over systemic hurdles despite having virtually no resources. Targeted sympathy focuses our attention on the situation-specific interventions that workgroup members make and that they consider to be within the bounds of their roles.

Professional PDP stakeholders see coercion as a primary contributor to ineffective desistance policies that mitigate punitive responses by introducing rehabilitative components. However, our critical analysis reveals the limitations of ostensibly empathetic understandings of victimization and exploitation. PDPs rely on a framework of rescue that limits agency and valorizes courts and PDPs as saviors to legitimize their use of coercion, as is widely reported in trafficking interventions. They also rely on neoliberal frameworks that situate the locus of responsibility for change with the individual program participants, who are asked to learn to heal and move on from individual forms of victimization and trauma such as dysfunctional families and previously untreated mental health concerns. Such assumptions are also reinforced by bureaucratic imperatives and agency structures that reap financial and reputational benefits from coerced services within existing programs, logics, and pathways.

Even when some PDP professionals recognize economic and structural oppression, such oppression is largely a taken-for-granted backdrop with which program participants *and* PDPs must cope or work around.

8

"Better Than Nothing"?

Our study of court-affiliated prostitution diversion programs is book-ended by the optimistic beginnings of Philadelphia's PDC and Baltimore's SPD and the criticism that emerged a decade later. Our first wave of data collection, from 2011 to 2014, took place in the very early days of both programs. PDPs were part of a proliferation of problem-solving justice models, which were touted as rehabilitative criminal justice programming that saw coercion as an opportunity to help. These efforts were supported by a broader narrative of sexual trafficking that has fostered sympathy and a desire to rescue people who get arrested for sex work. Indeed, sex work and trafficking are often conflated under a definition that views all forms of sexual labor as "icky" and exploitative (Blakey & Gunn, 2018; Parmanand, 2022). It is evidenced in other U.S. jurisdictions by the naming of diversion programs that are aimed at those arrested for sex work as "human trafficking courts," ignoring the contradiction that anyone who meets a definition of *trafficking* due to age or coercion should not be arrested for a crime (New York State Unified Court System, Office for Justice Initiatives, n.d.; Musto, 2016).

During our data collection in 2021, a very different picture emerged. Our interviews showed much more contention and ambiguity among stakeholder groups, which were deeply divided on the balance of harm and help both for individual participants and at the broader program or policy level. These interviews indicated stakeholders' concerns about oppressive systems that shore up racialized, gendered, and classist hierarchies under the cover of an ostensibly neutral system of crime control. In this final chapter, our "vignette" is a composite of our own reflections that reveals our evolution through the register of our distinctive voices. In writing this book, we brought different and some overlapping perspectives, partly due to varied training and research emphases. Corey is a legal and social work scholar who uses a phenomenological lens to understand how frontline workers and targets of social policy make meaning and change in a bleak policy landscape. Santhi is a qualitative researcher and sociolegal scholar in dialogue with critical and feminist criminologies on stigmatization and symbolic effects of law. Shelly is a social work scholar with extensive practice experience who uses both qualitative and quantitative methods in her research on the intersections of trauma and substance use in diverse groups. We converge on a similar pragmatic hopelessness. This reflects our shared journey to understand a compromised effort within a deeply problematic social, political, and economic reality. Despite meaningful successes, PDPs have failed many individuals and do not challenge harmful norms that discipline women.

Shelly

I came to the work on this project via a connection Corey and I made at a meeting of the Problem-Solving Court Steering Committee in Baltimore City that came together to address citizens' concerns about prostitution in their neighborhoods and legal and judicial concerns about the revolving door between the streets and jail for the women. I was a field liaison between one of our social work students and YANA Place, a social service program serving women engaged in street prostitution in Baltimore City, and its Executive Director asked me to attend the meeting to be an ally with her to advocate for the women. Upon arrival, Corey and I connected to see how we could collaborate to bring the women's voices to the discussion. I was also invited to join the steering committee.

Corey and I developed a study to learn about the experiences of women engaged in prostitution in Baltimore City and hear their views on whether a court-based program would be helpful and what components would actually be helpful to them. Corey and I spent nearly a year in the YANA Place drop-in center, where we conducted focus groups and individual interviews. Many of the women shared stories with us about their experiences of childhood abuse, intimate partner violence, and violence in the streets. Most also either were working on their significant addiction issues in a nearby treatment program or were actively using alcohol or other drugs in a harmful manner. Most supported a court-based program that would help them rather than putting them in jail. They wanted the judges and other court personnel to understand why they engaged in prostitution and what challenges they faced in their lives. They wanted assistance with their health and social needs. Above all, they wanted to be treated like people who had worth.

The Baltimore Specialized Diversion program came into being with some of what the women said they wanted incorporated into the design. The women worked with a social worker to help them identify their needs and link them to services that could help them address those needs. When I met with this social worker, I was struck by her deep caring for the women and by her efforts to empower them in their choices for supportive services. I accompanied Corey on a court observation one day and saw a very stern and jaded prosecutor who made statements to the judge about the women's compliance or lack thereof. I saw the judge require a woman to enter a guilty plea in order to participate in the diversion program. This was a clear violation of the processes set out in the design of the program; the women were supposed to be able to enter the program without increased judicial risk. The judge and the prosecutor had a great deal of unchecked power; that is, no one could challenge them on their lack of adherence to the spirit and specified processes of the program. It was unsettling to see that the careful effort to include the women's voices and needs in the program design could so easily be undone by capricious court officials.

I also had the opportunity to observe the Project Dawn Court. I had a lot of conflicting feelings that day as well. On the one hand, the women's successes were highlighted and celebrated and I could see their pride and joy in their accomplishments. Most of the women seemed to appreciate the connection and support they had with one another. On the other hand, I observed police officers in the hallway giving the women judgmental glances with audible disparaging remarks about the women and the program. I saw a prosecutor use an authoritarian and tough-talk approach with one of the women. The woman said that she knew he was using "tough love" and that that would make her more likely to change than softer approaches would. The judge seemed caring and supportive with most of the women, but used the large heavy door on the side of the courtroom that led to the holding cell area as a warning of what would happen if you did not comply. And in fact, the judge did have a woman who was out of compliance taken through that door by an officer. There were moments during this visit to the court when I felt happy and excited for the women in their own celebrations of their success, and moments when I felt disgusted (such as when I saw the police officers' negative glances toward the women) and dismayed to see the potentially harmful use of "tough love" and the threats of incarceration used by the prosecutor and the judge.

As I read the narratives of the women who participated in the SPD and PDC, I was reminded of the stories I heard back at YANA Place. The women shared their experiences of horrendous trauma in their childhoods and in the streets, as well as the pain of their addictions. The difference is that they actually got to use a court-based program. It was heartening to read that some felt support and caring and saw opportunities to improve their lives. That was, after all, our intent from way back when we brought the voices of the women to the steering committee discussions. But the narratives also show that some of the women felt shamed, some felt they did not have much choice, some feared being taken through that door. Despite their best efforts in the programs, many of the women struggled to get to the place where they wanted to be in their lives. They needed more support and opportunities for things like housing and vocational training. I am left thinking that while prostitution problem-solving courts are probably better than nothing, much more trauma-sensitive practices need to be incorporated in the court operations and a wider array of social service and health programs made available to participants. Ultimately, policy changes that would decriminalize prostitution, empower women, and provide services outside of the court would create the choice, power, dignity, and opportunities that the women deserve and need.

Santhi

This work grew out of my role in 2010 as the academic researcher on a state mental health and criminal justice task force. Through the task force, I conducted biweekly participant observation in the Peterson County mental health court and visited all the mental health units in each prison across the state. Through those connections, I was asked to join a nascent effort to collect data about potential needs and supports for people involved in street-based sex work. Specifically, when a judge I deeply admired asked me to assist, I was happy to be part of something new that would "do something" for the people I had been talking with and that addressed some of the factors that made them marginalized and vulnerable.

Most formatively, one of the first tasks of this needs assessment was to create and conduct a brief survey of incarcerated women, asking about their involvement in sex work and the kinds of programming they would like to see. When I walked the units, going door to door within the prison to ask women to share their experiences and information, I tried to balance the invasiveness of asking about trading sex for basic needs, access to health care, housing, and employment by offering something back, so in my introductory spiel I highlighted the chance to try to shape future programs and policies. At the time, I felt that I was "giving voice" to people who were deeply stigmatized; now I recognize the White savior impulses and other problematic aspects of forefronting my own agency over theirs that were wrapped up in that conception. That day, and throughout later data collection in interviews and focus groups, I was also struck by the willingness to contribute that was evidenced by some of the women I spoke to that day. A woman emerged from her small cell in isolation to talk with me about her sexual assault by an officer and her efforts to hold him accountable, against all odds. Other women—some lounging in the more-open (and crowded) shared units; some standing in the middle of the recreation area in their towels, waiting to check out a razor—pointed out their pregnant cellmates and talked about how little was available to support them, foreshadowing the poignant and terrible work by Signe Toquinto (2017), featured in the volume Corey and I would later edit with Katie Hail-Jares, on the experience of being "dead-already" as a pregnant person in street-based sex work. When I asked about programming, women called for assistance that would allow them to parent their children, specifically asking for free legal counsel and for livable wages and safe places to raise their families. Many women also offered to provide peer support to each other. They wanted a one-stop center that would be welcoming and inclusive rather than restricted to women who met a narrow set of conditions, and they hoped to contribute their own experience and expertise.

The role of mothering continued to resonate through my later involvement in this area. When I had the chance to use our book to teach the sociology of law in the same prison six years later, my incarcerated students (a group that happened to include the woman in isolation who had reported her rape by an officer), we had rich, painful, and pointed classroom discussions about how norms of sexuality and femininity shape who can access resources and who is accorded a place in policy-making. When I asked them what to say to a group of lifelong learners who'd asked me to deliver a guest lecture, they said, "Tell them we are mothers, we are students, we are workers, just like them."

Ultimately, these issues of validation and exclusion remain central to my concerns about problem-solving courts, and about prostitution diversion programs in particular. In Peterson County, the diversion court ultimately created after I presented my needs assessment ignored nearly all of the needs we documented and solutions we suggested, in favor of a court nested within the criminal legal system. I ended my involvement at that point, so I cannot say how that short-lived prostitution diversion program compared with Baltimore's SPD or Philadelphia's Project Dawn. But I can say that there are still very few beds in emergency housing for women in our state, let alone women with children. There are no legal aid resources available to help with child custody issues. No new avenues for employment or housing assistance have emerged. There is no welcoming and inclusive one-stop center. It is likely that some of the people involved in the Peterson County PDP used the attention and resources they received to find some measure of success, and probably avoided some time in detention. But for me, the fact that there have been no systemic shifts or improvements, combined with the risk that the PDP's incremental benefits for a small number of participants and professionals has undermined any will to make broader change, leaves me angry and pessimistic about the value of problem-solving justice.

Corey

In December 2021 I visited Project Dawn Court (PDC). It was the first time I had seen anyone in person since the start of the COVID pandemic. Fresh in my mind were the interviews I had been conducting with program participants and other stakeholders, many of whom were no longer engaged with Dawn Court, and who hold wildly divergent assessments of whether PDC is good or bad, and in what ways. I was struck by how good it felt for me to be in this space, and the warmth that is there. There was a genuine feeling of camaraderie among many of the women in the program and care emanating from the program staff. As someone who sat on the benches with program participants monthly for three years, and in subsequent visits, this was familiar, and I was eager (COVID-caution to the winds) to share hugs. There was also a sense of sadness and nostalgia that something is ending. This court meeting was also a farewell party for the retiring judge and a longtime therapist who is leaving for new career options. The program is small, with participants who have been in Project Dawn for years. The "spigot" has literally been turned off by self-proclaimed progressive district attorney Larry Krasner, who will not bring charges for prostitution against those who sell sex, and who is the target of dismay and anger. Although there may have been folks in the room who think this is good, none shared this publicly. Program graduates and participants and the professional stakeholders were vehemently opposed and broke into diatribes in conversation and in their prepared farewell messages in open court. Most saw this as abandonment: The concerns of women who need help will once again go unheeded. They viewed Larry Krasner and his progressive vision as part of a larger, ongoing "discourse of disposal" (Lowman, 2000).

This narrative of abandonment shows both how important PDPs are and how they are also doomed to failure. This group of program participants and most program stakeholders—nearly all women—have created a space where (some of them) find a semblance of common ground. Even those who most decried the program, and women who were removed from the program, made meaningful personal connections. They found mutual hope, concrete assistance, and in some cases friendship. But few of the women were left better off. There are still insufficient resources for assistance that would help people who would prefer not to sell sex on the streets of Philadelphia or Baltimore to leave this option behind. There are also insufficient resources to help most of those who have stopped selling sex, either by choice or by mandate, to thrive. I was upset with myself for being nostalgic, and upset by how easily I could be lulled by the familiarity, warmth, and kindness of individual women to blunt and suspend my own critical stance. What does this say about the mutual eagerness to make connections among people whom I imagine do not usually connect—across class, race, and stigma? Is that the real purpose of this court? To make everyone here feel just a little bit better about an overall lack of empathy and isolation? And where is the line between a prurient curiosity and a desire for connection, especially in this space where sex and suffering are the main topics of conversation? What are the systems that place these women, myself included, into this space of longing and desire? How are visions of mothering and other forms of women's work implicated in this peculiar blend of maternalistic rescue that focuses on nurturing while tasked with a mission of preparation for the world? This role largely involves making sure that those in our charge are ready—ostensibly for their own safety but also for the "good" of a larger society—to conform to normative conceptions of how, where, and with whom women can present and use their bodies and their sexuality. Is one of the reasons that we cannot imagine large-scale change somehow built on this fear of abandoning and being abandoned?

As a benefit of our unusually long research engagement with the program, we can provide updates on the people who are featured in the preceding chapter vignettes. Maria, who we focus on to illustrate the many facets of coercion that operate on and around program participants, was transferred from Project Dawn Court to Mental Health Court. Fearful of new people, she was relieved to retain the same probation officer and public defender and she was hopeful that family members could facilitate her relationship with her children. Maria sought a balance between structure, freedom, and support that was elusive within her current tangle of treatment and criminal legal system requirements.

At the end of our interviews, Ava was living with her sister and seeking employment. Her son lived with her mother in a nearby suburb. Ava still struggled with shame for being in Project Dawn, pride in her ability to retain important family relationships, and a mix of trepidation and determination in the face of past and future adversity. Mental and physical health problems left her vulnerable, and she was isolated as a result of pre-emptively cutting herself off from her peers. Nicole, who remained positive about Project Dawn Court despite having been terminated from the program and stayed in touch with several PDC participants who were longtime friends, died from a drug overdose in 2017 in her mid-40s.

In the last interview with Amy, she was on the verge of losing her housing. She may have still been selling sex and using drugs, both of which put her at risk of arrest and jeopardized the likelihood that she could have her charges expunged. She also had a history of chronic health problems. Amy became an advocate and was loved and lauded by her family for sharing her story with others and working to repair her relationships. She died in her mid-30s.

In 2014, a few years after she graduated from PDC, Toodles was sent to state prison for "using a knife" on a front-desk worker at a shelter. Toodles sometimes called PDC coordinator Lily, who sent her cards periodically and put money on her prison tab, but Toodles had been out of touch since about 2017. Toodles's experience was characterized by ups and downs in her circumstances and her feelings about her future; these were mirrored by recurring cycles of relapse and recovery, punctuated with arrest and incarceration. Toodles reached out to reconnect with Lily just as we completed this book. The following I-poem was crafted from her participation in a focus group that took place after Toodles had graduated. She explains that she views PDC and its various stakeholders as a touchstone:

Toodles

> I was doing really really well, maintaining my sobriety, hanging in there
>   with my recovery house, which I still love today even though I'm
>   not there
> I'm still hanging in there
> I do remember each and every one of y'all from being incarcerated
> I love y'all and that's the reason why I keep coming
> I'm starting off as a newcomer again in the program of Narcotics Anon-
>   ymous and just getting myself back together because
> I did relapse in January
> I call myself missing it
> I congratulate myself because even though when I finished probation
> I didn't use
> I mean
> Still, I bounced back
> I'm not gonna stay stuck in my process of relapsing
> I'm saying
> I would like to say my job
> I felt that it was unfair, but I did it to myself because I didn't come in
>   for 2 days
> I thought because it was occupational/vocational rehabilitation that
>   they will stand behind you
> I got my last check from my job

I was surprised that my account said $75
I went downtown and got my boyfriend
I had it all planned out
I went and bought my boyfriend some underwear for Valentine's Day
     because my last check I smoked the whole thing up and my welfare
     check
I came home broke. He said, 'Lay you ass down,' which I did, and 'take
     a shower and get in the bed'
I've been in the bed ever since
I know
I need to get plugged back into outpatient.
I don't wanna go back the way they want me to go back.
     I'm not doing IOP* all over again
I'm just not gonna do it because
I do have the tools
I just need to get
yesterday as I bought his underwear, I contemplated going down where
     I used to get high at
I had a phone call
I went to work yesterday.
I am a floater until they hire me permanently, but that's better than
     nothing
     *Intensive outpatient therapy
     Crafted by Maggie Buckridge

Catherine Heathcliff reflected on the decline of PDC due to COVID-19 and de facto decriminalization. She worried about women who were on her caseload especially given the rise of opioid deaths, and her inability to "put a stop to this."

CATHERINE: . . . and let somebody sit [in jail] for two weeks and think about if they want to get sober and stuff like that. And it's just not happening and it's just a revolving door, it seems to be more now. You know, we had about 8, 9 girls die since you left . . .

COREY: were those people who were in the program or these are people who are sort of past the program you know either graduated or—?

CATHERINE: Both. So you know, we had one girl who was released early actually by accident from custody and probation normally when a person is released by accident from custody, I mean you have to go back and do your sentence. And that didn't happen and she overdosed and died. She got out, went and used, and then died.

And I'm not blaming people. I'm just saying there is something to saving somebody's life when you put a stop to . . .

After Lily left her role as PDC coordinator, she worked as a public defender representing people arrested for prostitution, among others, and then in private legal practice. She remained in touch with a number of PDC participants, including Christina and Toodles, for years after she left PDC and continued to provide pro bono legal services for women in sex work. Erin, no longer a prosecutor, forged a path for herself as a public advocate on behalf of women who she described as victims of commercial sexual exploitation. She also remained in touch with some PDC participants, including Sara. Although they were ostensibly on different sides of the criminal legal system, Erin and Lily sometimes collaborate. Both are also convinced that the harm that they have seen done to women who sell sex is the product of a patriarchal society that continues to disadvantage women individually and structurally, a society where women must continue to fight in gendered spaces on the streets and in the larger political arena. Alongside their respective advocacy efforts, both are also involved in legal education.

In addition to the above reflections and updates, this concluding chapter offers the opportunity to underscore some of our key insights. The following sections provide brief summaries of what we hope readers will take away from this study.

Professional Stakeholders' Investment and Limitations

Program participants and professionals were profoundly moved by personal connections, but also by a mutual personal admiration. Emily appreciated program participants' "resilience, strength, courage, tenacity [pause], bravery, vulnerability, humility. I could really go on and on" and was one of many respondents who likened staff and participant connections to friendship and family. This may have gotten in the way of a larger systems critique but was nevertheless a key feature of PDP professionals' and participants' experiences. Professional stakeholders were provided an opportunity to better align their values (about feminism, their beliefs on the nature of sex work, etc.) with their work and role imperatives. Emily viewed Project Dawn Court—at least in the idea—as a career highlight:

It was a really unique environment, it was a very special space, that I was honored to be a part of, and I told the ladies many, many times, "Listen, girls, I'm learning much more from you than you're ever going to learn from me, you have helped me more than I'm ever going to help you."

Most program participants similarly respected and were fond of professional stakeholders. Even when sanctions were levied, most saw program staff as carrying out their roles, often remarking that they did so without the demeaning treatment that program participants so often received (Leon & Shdaimah, 2012). Vitality/Tranquility saw PDC, with all its limitations, as an opportunity to "allow help to help me wherever the help comes from, however it is."

Personal Investment Is Nice but Not Enough: Continued Economic Precarity

The sense of being loved and respected often did little, however, to alleviate economic precarity. Toodles's situation highlights this conundrum. After we had finished our interviews, we were periodically in touch. In one of these exchanges, Toodles shared that despite working multiple jobs, she did not make enough money to meet her needs. On one trip into the city on the train, Corey brought her a bag that included tampons, produce, and goods that she would not need to store or heat up due to her precarious housing situation. Lily had paid Toodles's rent on at least one occasion. While Toodles was resourceful in calling on support, no one should have to rely on the care and concern, albeit genuine, of professional strangers to meet their basic needs. Even more upsetting is that at the time Toodles was working at least two jobs: She shuttled through the Amtrak station to clean the toilets for one and worked at a fast-food stand for the other; Toodles seemed literally trapped in an endless hamster wheel of the Amtrak station, never earning enough so that she can rest or leave.

Our study adds support to the call from scholars and advocates worldwide to demand much more if we truly want to solve the problems created by our social and political structures. As critical antitrafficking scholar Corinne Schwarz (2022, p. 12) writes, "The slow violence that the state perpetuates through its unfettered commitments to global capitalism, environmental extraction and precarity-inducing social stigmas is the power dynamic that must be dismantled to solve the problem of trafficking."

Uncertain Equals Unsafe: Knowing the "Dos, Don'ts, Wills, Won'ts" (*Maria*)

Uncertainty violates the sense of safety and security that people should have in the world. The women involved in PDPs seemingly leave the uncertain world of street-based sex work and drug use and engage in the structured "safe" world of the court. Yet, in some ways the street feels more certain because the players and the game are known. Once the women enter the court-based program, they must contend with the uncertainty of financial precariousness described above, which leads to the unsettling fear of not being able to meet their own basic survival needs.

On top of material uncertainty, PDP participants grapple with the uncertainty engendered by the capricious authority of the court; at each court appearance, one could just as easily be punished as cheered. The judge and other court personnel wield a great deal of power over the program participants and are people who, prior to court involvement, are completely unknown to them. The women are compelled to tell their story over and over again to people they do not know who could take away their freedom in an instant. Over time, the women may become used to certain court personnel and feel more secure in this disempowered situation because they "know" them and their expectations; then, when court or program staff change jobs, the table shifts. Maria did not like the judge over her case to change, explaining, "I try to keep the same people that I know in my circle because I'm already used to them. I know what's gonna happen, what ain't gonna happen." Maria's comments capture the danger that participants perceive as they face a system and individuals who have tremendous power over their safety and security, which are two necessary conditions for growth and change. Individuals who feel uncertain about their safety become guarded and afraid. Neither of these states is conducive to growth and healing. In effect, the uncertainty of the court recapitulates trauma.

Heightened Vulnerabilities with Limited Protective Mechanisms

As well-meaning and helpful as the PDPs can be, they do not erase many prior vulnerabilities and in fact they create new ones. In a focus group with eight SPD participants, respondents were animated about how unhelpful the *nolle pros* status is when they seek employment, chiming in to amplify each other's observations. They are waiting for expungement that may provide them with more opportunities, even as their prior strategies for making ends meet through sex work were foreclosed.

> RESPONDENT: The [*nolle pros*] you can expunge all you want, it ain't going nowhere. For real. I got the paperwork, and I've been going back and forth to court and everything. That's the only thing that

really disappointed me about the program. You know, if you get a *nolle pros* . . .

RESPONDENT: It's still going to be there.

RESPONDENT: You pay the $35; it's still there. And mine's been there for two years and I've been trying to get my stuff off my record and it's just not happening. It's not happening.

RESPONDENT: What?!

RESPONDENT: Some people don't know what *nolle pros* means so if you go to an employer

RESPONDENT: It's like we're charged with something.

RESPONDENT: They'll see *nolle pros* on your record and I'm trying to explain, "You know I wasn't never . . . "

RESPONDENT: They think you got a charge or something.

RESPONDENT: And it still looks bad.

This focus group exchange suggests potential net widening, especially for programs like PDC (although not SPD), which require that participants give up legal rights and therefore may present a fundamental affront to participants' dignity, even when they know that such legal rights are at best elusive (Baylson, 2017; Wahab & Panichelli, 2013).

Perhaps more concerning is the stripping away of protective strategies that have been adopted by women who are deeply marginalized and attempt to make the best use of limited resources and difficult circumstances. While such strategies are important for survival on the streets, a major focus of the courts is to change behaviors and attitudes as part of the effort to create actors who can act appropriately in socially sanctioned environments. However, many of the women do not have the resources that would enable them to fully participate in such environments, and they are actually made more vulnerable in some ways after these well-intentioned, individualized efforts that take place in a social vacuum. In Chapter 5, we discussed Nicole's new sense of shame after trauma treatment about exchanging sex for money when she needs it; we are troubled by our knowledge of Nicole's death due to overdose. The removal of protective adaptations in the face of continued vulnerabilities is also evident in a more mundane example: When Amy began working at a fast-food restaurant, she was paid by check. Without a bank account, Amy would have to go to a check-cashing establishment that would garner a high fee from her low wages. But when Amy opened a bank account to save these fees, the full check amount was confiscated by her bank: It turned out that years before, Amy had defaulted on a payment. For Amy, a cash exchange for far fewer hours of work would better help her pay rent and visit her family in another state.

The Rules Are the Rules

It is clear that community-based programs in Baltimore and Philadelphia are not designed to meet the existing needs of program participants. SPD and PDC were able to somewhat expand the pool of helpful resources and facilitate access to services, such as when Maya created trauma training opportunities for Philadelphia treatment programs (see also Cohen & Shdaimah, under review). However, many respondents' most basic needs remained unmet. Some, like SPD focus group participant Barbara, were desperately seeking assistance:

> I was an addict—and I know this sounds stupid, y'all . . . I wanted to get pregnant, I wanted to get pregnant because it seemed like when we were children, we got more options.

As Barbara explained later in the same conversation,

> My apartment building burned down July 5th. I did a lot of footwork on my own as to try to look for housing, try to get *this* thing, *this* voucher, this, and everybody turned me down because I was a single woman. . . . They offer housing, but you have to have a child.

Barbara became optimistic that her housing situation would resolve due to her own "footwork" and Brigit's assistance without her having to have a baby:

> I [had] said, "I'm going to have another baby because I'm going to juice[1] this city for everything I can get, [like] housing." And it just so happens, I caught the [prostitution] charge, and with Miss Brigit, I juiced it for everything I could. I got so much out of [the SPD]. I got my housing, I got my ID, I got my birth certificate, my social security. . . . I'm in computer class now . . . and, I still have Miss Sue's number because, I'll be like, "Well what do you think about this?"

In contrast, Brown Sugar reaped no benefits from the program, which was primarily geared toward helping people with addiction services and mental health services. Just as Barbara said that she was a lower priority as a nonparent, program rules made it hard for Brown Sugar to access needed housing (despite her status as a mother) without a specified disability or drug addiction:

> I didn't get anything out of this program. . . . I must have to be on drugs to get some assistance, because we [are all selling sex], but I need

assistance for my kids, that's why I was doing it. . . . Ms. Brigit, she had nothing to offer me. She was even telling me—our appointments were like 5 minutes because she was like, "I don't really know what to tell you."

While PDC and SPD respondents are required to be compliant and truthful, probation officer Catherine Heathcliff notes that "first and foremost they are survivors." When respondents are unable to meet their needs, they employ the limited strategies that are available, even if these created new problems or resulted in harm to themselves (for an extended vignette featuring Lorraine and two other participants about their coerced exiting, see Gesser & Shdaimah, 2021). When Lorraine was close to the end of her fourth Project Dawn phase, she described a 12-hour program breach that included use of cocaine. Invested in her own recovery, reconnecting with her children, and her success in Project Dawn, she immediately tried to access detoxification services: "I called [the court coordinator] and told her I was trying to get into detox . . . [but] I couldn't get in without [a doctor's] note. Plus, you had to have heroin in your system." When met with these bureaucratic hurdles, Lorraine purposely "went to [the Avenue] and got dirty. I [took] some heroin . . . in order to get in. There's no detox for cocaine . . . you have to be dirty for Benzos. Heroin. Something along them lines." The appalling lengths that participants had to go to in order to work around programmatic obstacles mirrors what their program professional counterparts also describe in terms of extreme efforts to blunt the impersonal and ill-fitting bureaucratic obstacles to meeting human need (Whittle, 2017).

The Dangers and Limitations of Compassion

Playwright Karen Hartman started her research for the play *Project Dawn* (Hartman, 2017) in the final year of our ethnographic work. Many PDC stakeholders brought family members to attend the world premiere in 2017 (People's Light, 2022), eager to have an opportunity to convey what PDC was like through this evocative medium. Two theatrical devices illustrate the tensions between empathy and otherness that characterized both PDC and SPD. The first is Hartman's casting of all actors in dual roles: Each played a program participant *and* a criminal legal system professional. To make these dual roles even more visible, actors sometimes transition between roles on stage. In a 2017 performance, for example, we see "senior therapist Ruth" turning a circle to don a veil, symbolizing her transition to Dawn Court participant Krystal. This casting and stage direction highlights the fluidity of the "this could have been me" ethos, which is one of the important components of empathy in PDPs that we have described (Leon & Shdaimah, 2021; Wiechelt & Shdaimah, 2011).

Despite—or maybe because of—the evocation of empathy through shared humanity, it is clear that some kind of distance or boundary must be maintained between a fluid "us" and "them." Hartman provides such a counterbalance through the character of the public defender Gwen, who (coincidentally?) is also the only program professional whose role as a mother is explicitly named. She is portrayed as a functional alcoholic and an absent mother, and we see a boundary blurring when her oldest daughter runs away. We later witness public defender Gwen and the prosecutor Kyla roaming the streets in search of Gwen's daughter. "Gwen almost trips on a figure hunched under a blanket" to discover that it is Bonnie, who is "nodding off." Gwen attacks a confused Bonnie, screaming and kicking, until Kyla forcibly restrains her. We see Gwen breaking under the weight of empathy, her own fear, conflation of Bonnie with her daughter, and her sense of helplessness in the face of larger forces. This cautionary tale shows the dangers of overempathizing, and the need to maintain a social distance. It also shows the high cost of caring and working in a Sisyphean system where the price for potential assistance and some form of friendship is the fear and horror that learning about and caring for another can engender.

Appendix A

Original Study Description

The first wave of data collection from 2011 to 2014 was in the very early days of both programs. In this section, we describe the original research study (the protocol approved by the University of Maryland's Institutional Review Board (UMB IRB), including interview guides, is available from the authors); see Appendix B for the follow-up study, Appendix C for an alphabetical listing and brief description of the program participants, and Appendix D for the same for the criminal legal system professionals.[1]

OVERVIEW

This study examined court-affiliated prostitution diversion programs (PDPs) that had been newly implemented in Baltimore, Maryland, and Philadelphia, Pennsylvania. Corey Shdaimah served as the primary investigator and conducted all of the PDC interviews, with research assistance from Deborah Svoboda who at the time served as a Ph.D. student research assistant and primarily conducted the SPD interviews. Shelly Wiechelt, who has expertise in addictive substance use and trauma research and treatment, aided in the research design. Corey, Chrysanthi (Santhi) Leon, and Shelly analyzed the data together, drawing upon conceptual frameworks elaborated in prior collaborative and individual work.

The study sought participant and stakeholder perspectives on what motivates them to participate in the program and how participants negotiate with court professionals to meet their needs. This research study was designed to contribute to the broader policy debate regarding the risks and benefits of alternative criminal justice models, including under what circumstances and with which populations they are most likely to be effective, beneficial, or harmful.

STUDY DESIGN AND PROGRAM COMPARISON

The study employed a primarily qualitative longitudinal design, using interviews and focus groups with a sample of Baltimore City's Specialized Prostitution Diversion program (SPD) and Philadelphia's Project Dawn Court (PDC) clients, that took place during and after their participation in the SPD or PDC, and with program staff and professional stakeholders, such as attorneys and probation officers.[2] We supplemented these with observations of courtroom processes and interactions with program staff. The study provides conceptual comparison of two programs: While the PDC shares some traits with the SPD (for comparison of program features, see Table 2.1 in the text), such as consequences of successful completion (*nolle prosequi* of cases, meaning that prosecutors declare that they are voluntarily ending a criminal case), the PDC provides a useful comparison as it differs from the SPD with regard to a number of program features that have been identified in the problem-solving court literature as salient, including length of program, level of judicial involvement, and the need to plead guilty in order to participate. These differences are important for this study as they may impact (1) client decision-making, (2) professional stakeholders' perceptions of clients, and (3) the negotiations between the two groups regarding program implementation and compliance. The study had several components:[3]

1. Qualitative Interviews with Program Participants

We interviewed SPD and PDC participants over a series of one to five interviews per person (depending on where they were in the program), during and after their participation in their respective program, to explore their perceptions of that program and their encounters with professional staff. The interviews took place in a private location either at the courthouse or of the respondent's choice (these included quiet coffee shops, private rooms provided by programs that participants were enrolled in, participant homes, and residential programs). Program staff referred most SPD respondents; Corey recruited most PDC respondents during court observations.

Potential program participant respondents were informed that participation was voluntary and would in no way affect receipt of services or program participation. Staff were instructed to share study information at the end of their meetings with potential respondents, in order to convey that participation (or nonparticipation) would not impact receipt of services. This was reiterated to all referred participants before and during the consent process.

In all cases, in order to avoid coercion, program staff were not informed of whether any particular individual participated in the study. We collected basic demographic data as part of the interview, which otherwise comprised open-ended questions. In order to assist with follow-up with the study participants, all study participants completed a locator form.[4]

It is important to note that the study underwent review by the Institutional Review Board for vulnerable populations. Program participants were included under the federal category of "prisoners" due to their criminal justice involvement (probation, incarceration, and court). The University of Maryland also considers individuals with posttraumatic stress disorder (PTSD) as a protected category, and so the study was reviewed under this category of vulnerability. As an additional precaution in this regard, Shelly Wiechelt, who has expertise in substance use and trauma research and treatment, aided in the creation of the research design.

Steps taken to minimize risks to respondents who may be suffering from PTSD included the following:

1. Short, standardized study instruments were used to assess trauma; these instruments are widely used to obtain research-relevant information while not eliciting any detailed or specific information about traumatic events, in order to reduce the likelihood of retraumatization (see list below). Corey and Shelly had used four of the five instruments successfully in prior research with a similar study sample.
2. Interviews and focus groups did not focus on past traumatic events but rather on participants' experiences in the SPD or the PDC.
3. All participants were in ongoing counseling as part of their program requirements and therefore were connected to supportive services that they could access if needed.
4. Corey and Deborah were prepared to immediately discontinue the interview and offer referrals for counseling if a participant became upset or distressed; they brought a sheet with referral numbers and instructions relevant to each site/state in the event of a disclosure of a participant's intent to harm herself or others (suicidality or homicidality).[5]

Protocols and processes for both waves of the study were evaluated by the UMB IRB, which included the steps taken to protect the respondents in the Baltimore and Philadelphia programs while still naming the programs in order to be useful for these stakeholders as they consider future programming. This is consistent with our prior published research.

We explored concerns around trauma, substance use, and stigma by administering five brief standardized questionnaires once during the second interview, for descriptive purposes:

- The Addiction Severity Index Lite version (McLellan et al., 1980).
- The PTSD Checklist—Civilian Version (PCL-C) (Weathers et al., 1993)
- The Stressful Life Experiences Screening Questionnaire (Stamm et al., 1996)
- The Trauma Symptom Checklist (Briere & Runtz, 1987)
- The Internalized Shame Scale (Cook, 1987)

Interviews lasted from 30 to 90 minutes, were audio-recorded, and were transcribed verbatim. We provided $20 per research activity to each program participant (e.g., interview or focus group but not observations). The amount was designed to provide some compensation for time and effort but not unduly influence participation.

2. Qualitative Interviews with Program Staff and Professional Stakeholders

We also interviewed professional SPD and PDC stakeholders, including program social workers, public defenders, prosecutors, probation officers, and judges. In both the SPD and the PDC, professional stakeholders from a number of different organizations were involved in the creation and implementation of the program for diverse motivations, and their beliefs about prostitution and about clients likely influenced the culture of the program and their interactions with clients and their responses to those clients.

In recruiting professional program staff, we emphasized that their decision to participate was voluntary and that we would not report to other staff members whether or not they participated. Where staff requested information or follow-up to confirm study participation with supervisors, we provided the requested information for them to share for approval. Recruitment at both sites was cleared through gatekeepers.

Interviews with these stakeholders explored their personal and professional beliefs, resources constraints, and the culture of constituent organizations. We asked about their involvement in the SPD or the PDC, respectively, their understanding of prostitution, and their views on program participants generally and in specific cases. Interviews lasted 45–90 minutes, were audio-recorded, and were transcribed verbatim. Professional stakeholders received no compensation for their participation.

Importantly, all interviews (participants and program professionals) were semistructured, meaning that we deviated from the questions to follow the lead of respondents. PDC interviews were much more free-ranging. While this may be related to their being conducted by Corey, who had more interview experience and felt more comfortable deviating from the questions, it largely derived from the longer-term and multifaceted relationships that formed due to the longer length of program participation in the PDC than in the SPD (minimum of 1 year and minimum of 90 days, respectively), as well as the shared interactions that took place during observations (see below).

3. Observations

Corey conducted observations at Philadelphia's Project Dawn Court and Corey and Deborah conducted observations at Baltimore City's Eastside District Court (Shelly and Santhi also observed PDPs related to their work). Both locations are where clients initially sign up for the program and have regular meetings with program staff. These observations provided a sense of how the SPD and PDC work and of program participants' experiences. More importantly, they allowed the study of formal and informal interactions between and among clients and program staff, which include negotiation around program implementation, individual treatment plans, and program infractions. No observations were conducted that heard privileged interactions between clients and their attorneys. Partway through the study, the protocol was amended to allow Corey to observe public defenders' interactions with prospective PDC participants at Philadelphia's Riverside Correctional Facility (three such observations were conducted). Corey also accompanied the second PDC probation officers on a "train-ride and walk along" observation to the primary site where PDC clients were arrested and, often, housed or attended required PDC activities. Another observation was conducted with a probation officer while she met with probationers "in booth."

Observation data provided an important source of rapport-building and shared knowledge at the PDC site, where mandatory monthly court meetings were held that Corey attended every month throughout the duration of the study for approximately 3–5 hours each time. Observations often led to questions during interviews and provided a means to gain insight into both the proceedings and the respondents' subjective experiences. The SPD had no such comparable venue where program participants and staff gathered, and so observations were made in general spaces where some participants might be present. For court observations, Corey chose to sit with program participants in the open court, although she was also invited to sit in the "jury box." This allowed for listening to and participating in informal conversation with program participants, and also to avoid the perception that the research was allied with the program staff or the program. Corey generally brought baked goods to all hearings to distribute to program staff and participants during breaks. Notes were recorded by hand or tablet when permitted by the bailiff.

4. Focus Groups

We conducted one focus group each with SPD and PDC program participants, some of whom had also participated in interviews. The collective group dynamic allowed for dialogue between group members, so that participants could share their views through dialogue with others (Kruger, 1994). Focus group participants were not informed regarding whether others participated in interviews. We asked participants to respect others' confidentiality and refrain from discussing anything that came up in the focus group upon leaving the group. We provided food and $20 per participant.

While we also intended to collect SPD entry and exit documentation from the court, these were not made available. We collected available, generic program materials, including forms that SPD participants were required to sign upon entry; we also collected the colloquy signed by PDC program participants, and other program materials such as program booklets from PDC graduation.

More information on the sample can be found in our other published work and in Appendixes C and D of this book, which include the interview dates. Interviews were held with 13 and 6 professional staff from the PDC and SPD, respectively. Of the PDC program participants, 18 were interviewed between one and seven times; of the SPD participants, 12 were interviewed between one and four times (one was deemed ineligible). One focus group each was held with PDC participants (N = 8) and SPD participants (N = 6). Demographic information, such as race/ethnicity and age, was included in the interviews.

CONFIDENTIALITY

For all components of the study:

1. Participants were asked to refrain from providing identifying information, and all references to participants used pseudonyms that they chose. In the few instances where respondents did not provide a pseudonym or provided a pseudonym that we were concerned would be deductively identifiable, Corey created pseudonyms.
2. We removed or altered any identifying information that was provided inadvertently, or when participants requested that we do so.
3. Participants were informed that we were required by law to report child abuse, adult abuse, or previous sexual abuse and therefore were specifically asked not to discuss these. Since answering whether a person has ever been abused would not elicit enough information to require a report according to the law in either state, we used standardized measures that asked this question without eliciting details.

DATA ANALYSIS AND STUDY RIGOR

We used a number of different methods to analyze the data for different purposes. In the earliest stages, we analyzed qualitative data to build and generate both descriptive analysis (Sandelowski, 2000) and theory (Charmaz, 2006), rather than starting out with a specific testable hypothesis (Padgett, 2017). In light of our limited knowledge of program participants' and professional stakeholders' experiences, this method was best suited to understand their perspectives on court-based interventions. This type of analysis can also point to further directions for research and is likely to flag connections and concerns that otherwise might not be readily apparent to policy-makers and researchers.

We also employed the constant comparative method of data analysis to allow us to revise the interview guides, when necessary, and for purposes of member checking with the same participants (possible due to the longitudinal nature of the study) and other study participants.

We used NVivo qualitative data software to assist in the analysis. Initial analysis was conducted with peer groups comprised of Corey, Shelly, and an MSW graduate research assistant. They performed independent coding initially and then created a combined coding scheme through dialogue, revision, and consensus from the independent initial analyses in order to enhance rigor of the analysis (Padgett, 2017).

Corey, Santhi, and Shelly conducted targeted secondary analysis and thematic analysis and used Saldana's (2009) qualitative longitudinal matrixes (with Nili Gesser) for different purposes, as described in relevant publications; Jonas Rosen contributed to analysis for Chapter 6. We use extensive quotes to provide readers with the participants' own language, and limited edits to those needed for clarity but not grammar, allowing respondents' own colloquialisms to come through and attempting to avoid linguistic imperialism (Phillipson, 1992).

In addition to member checking, peer debriefing, and prolonged engagement, we enhanced study rigor through triangulation of methods and sources.

Scores derived from the standardized measures were used not for clinical assessment purposes but instead to describe the participants' experiences of stressful life events, PTSD symptoms, trauma-related symptoms, substance use behaviors, and shame. We compared their scores conceptually rather than statistically, due to the small sample size, with scores of the general population or subgroups for which there is available data.

FOR FURTHER INFORMATION ON PROSTITUTION DIVERSION PROGRAMS AND THE STUDY SITES

- For an overview of key aspects of prostitution diversion programs, see Shdaimah, C. (2019). Prostitution diversion programs. In F. P. Bernat, K. Frailing, L. Gelsthorpe, S. Kethenani, & L. Pasko (Eds.), *The encyclopedia of women and crime* (Vols. 1–3). Wiley-Blackwell. https://onlinelibrary.wiley.com/doi/10.1002/97811 18929803.ewac0423
- For more details on the PDC and SPD, including a comparison chart of key features, see Leon, C., & Shdaimah, C. S. (2012). JUSTifying scrutiny: State power in prostitution diversion programs. *Journal of Poverty, 16*(3), 250–273.
- For information on the backdrop and origins of the PDC, see Shdaimah, C. S. (2010). Taking a stand in a not-so-perfect world: What's a critical supporter of problem-solving courts to do? *University of Maryland Law Journal of Race, Religion, Gender, and Class, 10*(1), 89–111.
- For information on the backdrop of prostitution processing in Philadelphia, see Baylson, M. (2017). Victim or criminal: Street-level prostitutes and the criminal justice system. In K. Hail-Jares, C. Shdaimah, & C. Leon (Eds.), *Challenging perspectives on street-based sex work* (pp. 156–161). Temple University Press.
- For information on the PDC, see the editorial remarks provided in Muraresku, L. (2017). "Just to be there": A probation officer's reflection on Project Dawn Court. In K. Hail-Jares, C. Shdaimah, & C. Leon (Eds.), *Challenging perspectives on street-based sex work* (pp. 41–50). Temple University Press.

Appendix B

"Looking Back, Looking Forward" Follow-Up Study

The follow-up study from 2020 to 2021 was designed to explore the perspectives of criminal legal system program participants six years after the original study ended, in a changed political and social environment, especially as these changed or evolved over time. This longitudinal qualitative study included a convenience sample of 21 professional stakeholders and 3 graduates from Project Dawn Court and 2 professional stakeholders from Baltimore's Specialized Prostitution Diversion program. In order to yield a relatively comprehensive variety of perspectives from different time periods, we identified participants from the initial study through publicly available information and snowball sampling to connect with any current or former program stakeholders and program graduates. We contacted respondents via email to determine if they were interested in the study and willing to participate in it, and in the case of snowball sampling, we followed up in the manner indicated by the potential respondent.

We conducted confidential virtual interviews using a semistructured interview guide, but we largely tailored the interviews to the individual respondents. Interviews lasted between 45 and 90 minutes and were recorded and transcribed verbatim. We requested permission to follow up with the research team for purposes of clarification or with follow-up questions, which we did as needed.

In order to protect confidentiality and maximize respondents' comfort level in sharing candidly, we referred to respondents by their chosen pseudonym; those who had participated in the prior study are referred to by their original pseudonyms. We also did not share with others who consented or declined to participate, even when potential respondents were referred through snowball sampling. We told respondents from the outset that they could review their transcript for confirmation or if they wished to amend or delete anything. Two respondents ultimately requested deletion of small portions of their transcript, and another respondent offered a correction. Participation in all cases was voluntary; we reminded respondents of this from the outset and explained that this also related to any question that they chose not to answer and that they could discontinue the interview at any time for any reason (or no reason). We also asked respondents to select a private and confidential location for the interview. Program participants received a $25 electronic gift certificate for a vendor of their choice as compensation for their time and effort; professional stakeholders received no compensation for participating.

Upon agreement to participate in the study, we shared a copy of a letter of explanation that contained all the elements of consent so that respondents could review it prior to the interview. Before the interview commenced, the interviewer asked the participant if they had any questions about the letter of explanation or the study and asked for verbal consent prior to beginning the interview.

The University of Maryland Baltimore County Institutional Review Board determined the study, HP-00091255, to be exempt under 45 CFR 46.101(b).

Appendix C

Project Dawn Court and Specialized Prostitution Diversion Participants

Participant	Interview Month/Year
Amy (PDC) was nearly 30 when we first interviewed her, and she lived in a neighboring state. She identified as White and had one teenage daughter. We provide an extended vignette with her in Chapter 6. She volunteered with local high school students to provide drug addiction prevention programming. We learned that Amy passed away in her mid-30s, a few years after graduating from PDC.	11/11 12/11 8/12 10/12 1/13 7/13 9/13
Angela (PDC) was interviewed only one time, as she was reincarcerated during a PDC hearing in the presence of one of her adult children, and we lost touch. She identified as White, and she was 53 during our interview.	3/12
Ariella (PDC), who identified as Black, was in her late 30s at our first interview. She lived with family. One of her relatives was a corrections officer at the prison where she had been incarcerated, who provided an ongoing family connection.	9/11 10/11 4/12 5/12
Ava (PDC) is a White woman who was in her early 40s at the time of the first interview. She has the highest level of education in our sample, pursuing graduate work in a helping profession. She also had one of the more financially stable support systems in our sample. We feature her experiences in the Chapter 4 extended vignette.	9/12 11/12 7/13 9/13 7/14
Brown Sugar (SPD) is a mother of three in her mid-30s who identifies as Cherokee, Puerto Rican, and Black. We quote her extensively in Chapter 5, and she is one of the only respondents who did not struggle with addiction or mental health concerns.	10/11 12/11 1/12

(continued)

Participant	Interview Month/Year
Casey (PDC) is one of a small number of veterans in PDC. She identifies as White and is married. She was frustrated at having to live apart from her husband while in addiction treatment.	1/13
Candy (SPD) is a White woman in her early 40s who married young and began selling sex in her early 30s, first as a stripper and then in a massage parlor, which she learned about from other workers who "opened a whole new world to me of sex for money" when she was "on crystal meth." She was in the SPD after being evicted and on the streets and was scared of being incarcerated.	12/11
CeeJay (SPD) is a Black woman in her 20s with multiple children. She was pregnant during her participation in the Baltimore diversion program and was hopeful that the program would enable her to avoid incarceration, love herself, and parent the child she was expecting after having others removed from her care. She was wary of other women she met on the streets.	9/11 11/11 12/11 1/12
Christina (PDC) is a White woman in her late 40s who has been trading sex for 30 years, and who entered the United States illegally. Helped by a lawyer who was connected to PDC, she is working with a lawyer, also connected to PDC, to obtain a special visa based on her entry into the United States as a trafficking victim; obtaining this visa would make her eligible for benefits. However, they have been stymied by a lack of records and detailed information about the long-ago circumstances.	10/11 8/12 8/12 9/12
Daisy (SPD) is a White and Indian woman in her early 30s. She sold sex to purchase drugs, which helped her "block stuff out." She was interested in the SPD to try to "get clean" because she didn't want to "end up dead like a lot of them or being an 80-year-old out there getting high." Program expectations seemed clear and she liked the social workers.	11/11 1/12
Gina (PDC) is a Black woman in her mid-40s. She was in school through the 8th grade and then completed her GED when she was forced to by a judge while incarcerated. She has been on Judge Kahan's docket before, and often shares notes that her mother has sent to the judge.	11/12 2/13 5/13
Jean (SPD) is a Black woman in her early 40s. The arrest that precipitated her entry into the SPD was for the only time that she sold sex, which was in order to get back home from the street where there is Baltimore prison.	12/11
Jenn (SPD) is a White woman in her late 30s. She was homeless during the first interview in November 2011, and hoped to be housed by Christmas. The SPD was looking into her Section 8 status. She was happy to be pregnant at our last interview and looking forward to moving into a home with her boyfriend of over 10 years, and being a good mother after having her first child removed from her care and struggling with fertility.	11/11 1/12 2/12 3/12

Participant	Interview Month/Year
Jerri (PDC) is in her early 30s and struggles to find appropriate housing for herself and her infant child. She is a White woman with no clear network of support. One of the PDC legal professionals shared with the team that she saw Jerri begging for change near the courthouse months after her PDC graduation.	10/11
Keisha (PDC) is an African American woman in her late 30s and is a mother. She helped care for her ailing mother and lived with family, who were demanding but also supportive. Keisha lived with her boyfriend while in PDC. When their relationship ended, she moved back in with family but was eager to live by herself. For a more detailed analysis of her experiences in Project Dawn Court, see Gesser & Shdaimah, 2021.	6/12 (Observation notes from prison) 12/12 4/13 9/13 10/13 7/14
Lex (PDC) is a White woman graduate from PDC and chose to work in and with the same criminal legal system and child welfare systems that she had previously had to engage with involuntarily. She opposes prosecutorial efforts to decriminalize prostitution. PDC staff is intensely proud of her, as she is of herself, and they have ongoing relationships. She was in the process of adopting a foster child when we spoke.	2/22
Lorraine (PDC) is a White woman in her mid-40s whose parents raised her two children in another state. She has a GED and is eager to find employment that gives her sufficient income to sustain her own housing. She views herself as a natural leader and has been offered roles in her recovery housing and workplace that validate her abilities and work ethic. For a more detailed analysis of her experiences in Project Dawn Court, see Gesser & Shdaimah, 2021.	5/12 10/12 3/13
Maria (PDC), profiled in Chapter 6, identifies as Hispanic. She is in her late 20s and wants to live with her three children and have more control over her life. She was transferred to mental health court as an alternative to being removed from PDC.	2/12 8/12 10/12 10/12
Myesha (SPD) is an African American woman in her mid-40s who has lived in Baltimore for about a decade. She was angry at being arrested for prostitution by an undercover police officer who picked her up in the car while it was raining. One of the best things about her experience in the SPD was when social workers Gerrie and Brigit arranged for her to spend Christmas with her family out of state. Although they wanted her to stay, she had to return to Baltimore in order to not be in violation of the SPD.	11/11 1/12 2/12
Nicole (PDC) was a White woman in her late 40s who had been removed from the PDC when she was determined to be incompliant with the program. Nevertheless she thought highly of the program, and remained close to several women who were in it and whom she knew from the streets. Nicole died of an overdose in 2017.	3/12 11/13

(*continued*)

Participant	Interview Month/Year
Pink (SPD) is a White woman in her early 50s who quit school three days into the 12th grade. She began selling sex in her early 40s to get money to buy drugs, initially taking money up front and running away. When she was last arrested, she had not sold sex in a while and only did so because she was approached by a police officer. She learned about the SPD from a friend who'd participated. Pink cited the notoriously poor Baltimore transportation—"having to come up here every Thursday on the god-darn bus"—as one of the most difficult aspects of the SPD.	10/11 11/11 1/12
Powder (SPD) is a woman in her mid-30s whom we did not ask to identify her race or ethnicity. She began sex work as a dancer and an escort when she was 17 where "you can make $800 a night. Nowhere else can you make that kind of money that quick. And you only work 4 to 6 hours." When she became involved in drugs "everything went downhill." She hopes to go back to college, and the SPD is helping her figure out how to repay the $2000 that she owes so that she can continue her education.	10/11
Sara (PDC) is a White woman in her mid-40s and has four children. She considered the death of her oldest son, and the support and structure that she received from PDC in response, as pivotal to her continued engagement and success. As a former victim of human trafficking, Sara has lobbied around issues of trafficking and works within the local recovery community. With the help of the PDC staff through a long and complicated process, she regained custody of her younger children and was in touch with her daughter, who gave birth to Sara's first grandchild.	10/11 12/11 3/12 4/12 4/13
Sharon (PDC), a woman who is African American, White, and Indian, and almost 40 at our first interview, came to a focus group and then joined the study shortly before graduating. She began selling sex in part due to the excitement, especially when she was able to take measures to ensure safety, but was now eager to return to her desk job. We share her nonjudgmental and carefully calculated support of other PDC members in Shdaimah & Leon, 2014.	3/12 4/12
Sheena (SPD) is an 18-year-old college freshman. She sold sex to take care of herself during a stint in foster care when her mother could not care for her. Her tenure in the SPD was extended after she missed appointments due to trouble sleeping and getting up in the morning. The SPD helped her work on getting her driver's license and navigate independent living through the foster care system. She was looking forward to having her *nolle pros* charges expunged.	1/12 2/12 4/12 5/12
Sheila (PDC) is an African American woman in her early 50s who has attended some nursing school. She is friendly with some of the other women who are close in age and have shared experience with time on the streets and in programs, and who provide mutual support when they can.	5/12 10/12 6/13 9/13 2/18

Participant	Interview Month/Year
Silver (PDC) is an African American woman who has been selling sex for about 15 years, primarily in order to obtain money to buy drugs. We only interviewed her once, due to concerns about her mental health and the location of the interview in her room in a locked, dark courtyard that made Corey feel unsafe.	10/12
Sky (SPD) is in her mid-30s. We did not ask about race or ethnicity. She was already in a drug program before starting the SPD, and was happy with that program and with the SPD primarily because it gave her "something to do with my time. Something to look forward to. Because now that I'm not getting high anymore, it's like I don't have no life, nothing to do. But I can come here and get up and have somewhere to go." Sky praised the SPD for helping her with whatever she needed. This included bus tokens.	1/12 3/12 4/12 5/12
Toni (PDC) is a White woman in her mid-40s who completed two years of college. She has five children, one of whom she had recently lived with at our last interview. While conducting observations, Corey accompanied her to Family Court at the PDC coordinator's request so that Toni would not have to wait alone during court proceedings for her son to be adopted by his foster family. At the time of our follow-up interview, she was living with her boyfriend and working.	2/13 6/13 2/21
Toodles (PDC) is an African American woman in her mid-40s who was attending community college at our first interview. Eager to learn, she also worried about having to pay off loans. Toodles struggled financially, working multiple jobs to meet basic needs, including housing. We expand on her story in Chapter 4.	9/11 11/11 12/11 10/12
Vitality/Tranquility (PDC) is an African American woman whose age we do not have recorded. While she liked many features of Project Dawn, it is not clear to her why anyone should have to be stigmatized or arrested to receive services.	12/21

Appendix D

Criminal Legal System Professionals

Pseudonym	Role	Date
Ace (PDC)	Trauma Treatment Therapist	6/21
Adam (PDC)	Outreach Worker	2/22
Alice (PDC)	Public Defender	12/12 11/20
Miss Anita Martin (SPD)	Pre-trial Officer	4/12
Belle (PDC)	Trauma Treatment Therapist	3/21
Brigit Larkin (SPD)	Social Worker	8/11 12/21
Caroline (PDC)	Women's Recovery House Administrator	5/21
Catherine Heathcliff (PDC)	Probation Officer	11/12 3/21
Daniel (PDC)	Trauma Treatment Administrator	3/21
Diane (PDC)	Trauma Treatment Therapist	12/12 1/21
Dolores (PDC)	Women's Recovery House Social Worker	5/21 6/21
Donna (PDC)	Women's Recovery House Social Worker	5/21
Emily (PDC)	Prosecutor	5/21
Erin Archer (PDC)	Prosecutor	4/12 9/20
George Jenson (SPD)	Paraprofessional Assessor	1/22

(*continued*)

(*continued*)

Pseudonym	Role	Date
Gerrie (SPD)	Social Worker	4/12 12/21
Grace (PDC)	Public Defender	10/20
Judge Hartwell (PDC)	Judge	4/14
Jack (PDC)	Prosecutor	2012 8/20
Jan Netter (PDC)	Public Defender	11/11 12/20
John (PDC)	Probation Supervisor	11/11 2/21
John Keats (PDC)	Trauma Treatment Administrator	4/21
Kacey (PDC)	Public Defender	12/20
Judge Kahan (PDC)	Judge	4/12
Lily (PDC)	Coordinator	9/11 9/20
Margo (SPD)	Prosecutor	9/11
Marta (PDC) (notes only)	Public Defender	5/21
Maura (PDC)	Public Defender	12/20 6/21
Maya Norris (PDC)	Court Coordinator	6/12
Judge Richards (PDC)	Judge	7/12
Ronny Landis (PDC)	Probation Officer	11/11
Simon (SPD)	Public Defender	9/11
Sofia (PDC)	Forensic Interview Recovery Administrator	8/21

Notes

INTRODUCTION

1. See Chapter 1 for a discussion of Maynard-Moody & Musheno's (2003) use of law abidance and moral abidance.

2. We visited this program, observed proceedings, and spoke with the presiding judge in 2010.

CHAPTER 2

1. Of a subset of 431 cases from January to August 2010, 221 (49 percent) were eligible for the SPD. Of those eligible, 93 (42 percent) accepted the offer and 14 (6 percent) rejected it; 58 (26 percent) were interested in the program but were turned away due to space limitations.

2. Of the SPD-eligible sample, 51, or 24 percent, did not appear in court. We were told by many of the criminal justice personnel as well as program participants that it is common for prostitution defendants to avoid court dates.

3. TurnAround, Inc., is a program that works "to combat domestic and sexual violence" (http://www.turnaroundinc.org/).

4. "Boyfriend, guy, a guy giving drugs"

5. Unless otherwise specified, information on the program in this chapter comes from program documentation on file with the authors, or from informal interviews with PDC program staff, in which the information was verified.

6. I-poems are a practice of feminist research intended to center participant voices (see Appendix A). Buckridge et al. (2022) innovated the use of focus groups rather than individual interviews as the basis for I-poems; Buckridge takes this one step further in crafting this "We-poem" from Shdaimah's focus group, pulling statements in which participants commented on shared experiences and affirmed each other. The We-poem pre-

serves the words of the participants in the chronological order in which they appeared, with very minimal edits for clarity and confidentiality.

7. Here we use the term *probation office*, as this is the stance of both of the probation officers who held this role as well as their supervisors.

CHAPTER 3

1. This is the term that our respondents use to describe the judge with whom a defendant's cases are concentrated, including new charges. Like Maria, all defendants require permission from their back judge in order to be released from their docket and put into the PDC.

2. *Blackouts* are periods during which participants cannot leave an intensive inpatient program or have contact with anyone outside of the program, including family members. Blackout periods were typical for PDC participants' entry into treatment programs or after relapse; they were also standard for many inpatient programs.

3. The *show cause* hearing was instigated by the prosecutor's petition to terminate Maria from PDC. As outlined in Chapter 2, entrance to PDC requires a *nolo contendere* plea, meaning that defendants do not contend the facts outlined in the charges, with sentencing held in abeyance while defendants are in PDC. Successful completers have charges dismissed without prejudice; unsuccessful defendants are sentenced.

CHAPTER 4

1. Pages 58–59 are adapted from Corrigan and Shdaimah (2016).

2. While *suffer* may sound journalistic or hyperbolic, we purposely use this language rather than a more neutral term like *experience* because it is grounded in the narratives from defendants and criminal legal system personnel, conjuring horror and empathy regarding the objectively difficult life circumstances that people describe.

3. The DSM is the primary source of psychological and psychiatric diagnoses used by clinicians in the United States. It is also widely used by medical institutions and personnel as well as insurance companies (including publicly funded insurance) to determine eligibility and financial coverage for care. The DSM is periodically reviewed and revised to incorporate new data and understandings of diagnoses, including different cultural notions of what constitutes pathology. Experts make diagnoses by assessing people according to the number and type of diagnostic criteria set out for any given diagnostic category.

4. Tertiary expertise is the widely available—often bastardized—knowledge that originated with primary experts but has since become part of the dominant culture, providing ways of thinking available to many (Swidler, 2013).

CHAPTER 5

1. Ava's prescription for Xanax was written with the scientific name, which her probation officer did not know, causing him to insist that she take a different prescription drug. Ava complied, but the alternative didn't have the same benefit for her as the Xanax had, and she persisted in advocating for herself, eventually receiving permission to resume the Xanax.

CHAPTER 6

1. Some of these waitlists have been closed for years (Philadelphia Housing Authority, 2020).
2. We are grateful to Nancy Franke for this keen observation.

CHAPTER 7

1. Judge Hartwell uses the word *recidivise* instead of *recidivate*; the latter is a colloquial term commonly used among frontline criminal justice professionals.

CHAPTER 8

1. By *juice*, Barbara means that she took full advantage.

APPENDIX A

1. All respondents were required to be over 18 (no minors) and proficient in English.
2. At the outset of each portion for which consent was required (all interviews; focus groups; prison observations), Corey or Deborah reviewed the potential risks and benefits of the study. Participants were informed that their participation was voluntary, and they may end it at any time and that SPD/PDC services were not contingent upon participation or nonparticipation.

The consent form was written at a seventh-grade reading level to make it comprehensible to a wide range of education levels and was reviewed aloud with participants, so that those who cannot read would not have to disclose this. The only portion of the consent form that was above a seventh-grade level was wording required by the UMB IRB.
3. Interview and focus group transcripts and audio files were stored on a password-protected computer. Locator forms and consent forms, which were the only documents with identifying information, were stored in a locked file cabinet. Locator forms were destroyed upon completion of all relevant participant interviews. All transferred files were sent using the University's secure transfer service (Accellion). Part of the data is available in the QDR database (Shdaimah, 2020b).
4. Participant locator forms were shredded upon completion of final interviews.
5. No interviews were discontinued due to participant distress, although we chose not to conduct a subsequent interview with a participant who had chosen an interview location that Corey realized, after the interview, made her feel unsafe.

References

American Psychiatric Association. (2013). *Diagnostic and statistical manual of mental disorders* (5th ed.).

American Psychiatric Association. (2022). *Diagnostic and statistical manual of mental disorders* (5th ed., text rev.).

Amnesty International. (2016, May 26). *Amnesty International policy on state obligations to respect, protect, and fulfil the human rights of sex workers.* https://www.amnesty.org/en/documents/pol30/4062/2016/en/

Anasti, T. (2018). Survivor or laborer: How human service managers perceive sex workers? *Affilia, 33*(4), 453–476.

Anasti, T. (2020). Street-level bureaucrats and ethical conflicts in service provision to sex workers. *Ethics and Social Welfare, 14*(1), 89–104.

Armstrong, L. (2019). Stigma, decriminalisation, and violence against street-based sex workers: Changing the narrative. *Sexualities, 22*(7–8), 1288–1308.

Bachman, R., Rodriguez, S., Kerrison, E. M., & Leon, C. (2019). The recursive relationship between substance abuse, prostitution, and incarceration: Voices from a long-term cohort of women. *Victims & Offenders, 14*(5), 587–605.

Bailey, K. M., & Stewart, S. H. (2014). Relations among trauma, PTSD, and substance misuse: The scope of the problem. In P. Ouimette & J. P. Read (Eds.), *Trauma and substance abuse: Causes consequences, and treatment of comorbid disorders* (2nd ed., pp. 11–34). American Psychological Association.

Bailey-Kloch, M. G. (2017). Poetry in street-level prostitution. In K. Hail-Jares, C. S. Shdaimah, & C.S. Leon (Eds.), *Challenging perspectives on street-based sex work* (pp. 136–152). Temple University Press.

Bailey-Kloch, M. G. (2019). Mothers engaging in street-level prostitution: Lived experience [Doctoral dissertation]. University of Maryland, Baltimore. https://archive.hshsl.umaryland.edu/handle/10713/11485

Bailey-Kloch, M. G., Shdaimah, C., & Osteen, P. (2015). Finding the right fit: Disparities between cisgender and transgender women arrested for prostitution in Baltimore. *Journal of Forensic Social Work*, 5(1–3): 82–97.

Barron, J. (2019, December 6). Climate of vulnerability: What a recent prostitution sting reveals about Commissioner Harrison, policing, and sex work in Baltimore. *Baltimore Beat*. http://baltimorebeat.com/2019/12/06/climate-of-vulnerability-what-a-recent-prostitution-sting-reveals-about-commissioner-harrison-policing-and-sex-work-in-baltimore/

Bateman, V. (2021). How decriminalisation reduces harm within and beyond sex work: Sex work abolitionism as the "Cult of Female Modesty" in feminist form. *Sexual Research and Social Policy*, 18, 819–836.

Baylson, M. (2017). Victim or criminal? Street-level prostitutes and the criminal justice system. In K. Hail-Jares, C. S. Shdaimah, & C. S. Leon (Eds.), *Challenging perspectives on street-based sex work* (pp. 136–152). Temple University Press.

Beaujolais, B., & Dillard, R. L., (2020). Court-affiliated diversion programs for prostitution-related crimes: A comprehensive review of program components and impact. *Violence and Victims*, 35(4), 562–588.

Begun, A. L., & Hammond, G. C. (2012). CATCH Court: A novel approach to "treatment as alternative to incarceration" for women engaged in prostitution and substance abuse. *Journal of Social Work Practice in the Addictions*, 12(3), 328–331.

Berg, H., Jones, A., Patella-Rey, P. J., & Schwarz, C. (2022). "Nothing about us without us": An interview on the sex worker syllabus. *Ethics and Social Welfare*, 16(2), 1–7.

Berman, G., & Feinblatt, J. (2005). *Good courts: The case for problem-solving justice*. The New Press.

Blakey, J. M., & Gunn, A. (2018). The "ickiness factor": Stigma as a barrier to exiting prostitution. *Journal of Offender Rehabilitation*, 57(8), 538–561. https://doi-org.proxy-hs.researchport.umd.edu/10.1080/10509674.2018.1549177

Blakey, J., Mueller, D. J., & Richie, M. (2017). Strengths and challenges of a prostitution court model. *Justice System Journal*, 38(4), 364–379.

Blunt, D., & Wolf, A. (2020). Erased: The impact of FOSTA-SESTA and the removal of Backpage on sex workers. *Anti-Trafficking Review*, 14, 117–121.

Boldt, R. C. (2010). The "tomahawk" and the "healing balm": Drug treatment courts in theory and practice. *University of Maryland Law Journal of Race, Religion, Gender and Class* 10(1), 45–71.

Boldt, R., & Singer, J. (2006). Juristocracy in the trenches: Problem-solving judges and therapeutic jurisprudence in drug treatment courts and unified family courts. *Maryland Law Review*, 65, 82–100.

Boonyapisomparn, N. (2017). "HIV is not a major concern": Trans identity, public-health funding, and sex work. In K. Hail-Jares, C. S. Shdaimah, & C. S. Leon (Eds.), *Challenging perspectives on street-based sex work* (pp. 101–13). Temple University Press.

Bowen, R. R. (2015). Squaring up: Experiences of transition from off-street sex work to square work and duality—concurrent involvement in both—in Vancouver, BC. *Canadian Review of Sociology*, 52(4), 429–449.

Bowen, R. (2021). *Work, money and duality: Trading sex as a side hustle*. Policy Press.

Brewis, A., & Wutich, A. (2019). Why we should never do it: Stigma as a behaviour change tool in global health. *BMJ Global Health*, 4(5), e001911.

Brewis, J., & Linstead, S. (2000). "The worst thing is the screwing" (1): Consumption and the management of identity in sex work. *Gender, Work & Organization*, 7(2), 84–97.

Briere, J. (n.d.). *Trauma Symptom Checklist 33 and 40.* http://s1097954.instanturl.net/trauma-symptom-checklist-40-tsi-40/

Briere, J., & Runtz, M. (1989). The Trauma Symptom Checklist (TSC-33): Early data on a new scale. *Journal of Interpersonal Violence, 4,* 151–163.

Briere, J., & Scott, C. (2015). *Principles of trauma therapy: A guide to symptoms, evaluation, and treatment* (2nd ed., DSM-5 update). Sage Publications.

Brodkin, E. Z. (1986). *The false promise of administrative reform: Implementing quality control in welfare.* Temple University Press.

Brown, B. (2007). *I thought it was just me (but it isn't): Telling the truth about perfectionism, inadequacy, and power.* Gotham Books.

Brown v. Maryland, 409 Md. 1 (2009).

Buckridge, M., Lowman, J., & Leon, C. S. (2022). "I'm gonna speak for me": I-poems and the situated knowledges of sex workers. *Ethics and Social Welfare, 16*(2). https://doi.org/10.1080/17496535.2022.2042039

Burns, S. L., & Peyrot, M. (2003). Tough love: Nurturing and coercing responsibility and recovery in California Drug Courts. *Social Problems, 50*(3), 416–438.

Casey, P. M., & Rottman, D. B. (2005). Problem-solving courts: Models and trends. *Justice System Journal, 26,* 35–56.

Castellano, U. (2017). The politics of benchcraft: The role of judges in mental health courts. *Law and Social Inquiry, 42,* 398–422.

Cauvin, H. E. (2009, April 3). Public defender calls Md. drug courts unconstitutional. *Washington Post.* http://www.washingtonpost.com/wp-dyn/content/article/2009/04/02/AR2009040203732.html

Charmaz, K. (2017). Constructing grounded theory: A practical guide through qualitative analysis. Sage Publications.

Cheng, S. (2013). Private lives of public women: Photos of sex workers (minus the sex) in South Korea. *Sexualities, 16*(1–2), 30–42.

Chicago Appleseed Center for Fair Courts. (2023). Improving justice for women through diversion forum on December 20th. https://www.chicagoappleseed.org/2013/12/11/improving-justice-for-women-through-diversion-forum-on-december-20th/

Cho, S. Y., Dreher, A., & Neumayer, E. (2013). Does legalized prostitution increase human trafficking? *World Development, 41,* 67–82.

Cohen, A. (2017). Trauma and the welfare state: A genealogy of prostitution courts in New York City. *Texas Law Review, 95*(5), 915–991.

Cohen, I., & Shdaimah, C. S. (under review). Beyond the micro myopia.

Collins, K., Connors, K., Davis, S., Donohue, A., Gardner, S., Goldblatt, E., Hayward, A., Kiser, L., Strieder, F., & Thompson, E. (2010). *Understanding the impact of trauma and urban poverty on family systems: Risks, resilience, and interventions.* Family Informed Trauma Treatment Center. https://www.nctsn.org/sites/default/files/resources/resource-guide/understanding_impact_trauma_urban_poverty_family_systems.pdf

Condry, R., & Minson, S. (2020). Conceptualizing the effects of imprisonment on families: Collateral consequences, secondary punishment, or symbiotic harms? *Theoretical Criminology, 25*(4). https://doi.org/10.1177/1362480619897078

Conference of the Chief Justices/Conference of State Court Administrators. (2004, July 29). Resolution 22: In support of problem-solving court principles and methods. http://cosca.ncsc.dni.us/WhitePapers/Resolution-Nat1%20Agenda-Final-Aug-04.pdf

Corrigan, R. (2013). *Up against a wall: Rape law reform and the failure of success.* New York University Press.

Corrigan, R., & Shdaimah, C. S. (2016). People with secrets: Contesting, constructing, and resisting women's claims about sexual victimization. *Catholic University Law Review*, 65(3), 429–487.

Dalla, R. L., Xia, Y., & Kennedy, H. (2003). "You just give them what they want and pray they don't kill you": Street-level sex workers' reports of victimization, personal resources, and coping strategies. *Violence Against Women*, 9(11), 1367–1394.

Dank, M., Yahner, J., Yu, L., Mogulescu, K., & White, K. B. (2017). *Consequences of policing prostitution: An analysis of individuals arrested and prosecuted for commercial sex in New York City*. Urban Institute. https://www.urban.org/research/publication/con sequences-policing-prostitution

Decker, M. R., Pearson, E., Illangasekare, S. L., Clark, E., & Sherman, S. G. (2013). Violence against women in sex work and HIV risk implications differ qualitatively by perpetrator. *BMC Public Health*, 13(1), 876–886.

Denney, A. S., Tewksbury, R., & Jones, R. S. (2014). Beyond basic needs: Social support and structure for successful offender reentry. *Journal of Quantitative Criminal Justice & Criminology*, 2(1). https://doi.org/10.21428/88de04a1.d95029f6

Dewey, S., & St. Germain, T. (2016). *Women of the street: How the criminal justice-social services alliance fails women in prostitution*. New York University Press.

Diaz, J., Strauss, E. M., Welsh, S., Effron, L., & Valiente, A. (2016, April 21). *Ex-Oklahoma City cop spending 263 years in prison for rape and his accusers share their stories*. ABC News. https://abcnews.go.com/US/oklahoma-city-cop-spending-263-years-prison-rape /story?id=38517467

Donisch, K., Bray, C., & Gewirtz, A. (2016). Child welfare, juvenile justice, mental health, and education providers' conceptualizations of trauma-informed practice. *Child maltreatment*, 21(2), 125–134.

El-Bassel, N., Witte, S. S., Wada, T., Gilbert, L., & Wallace, J. (2001). Correlates of partner violence among female street-based sex workers: Substance abuse, history of childhood abuse, and HIV risks. *AIDS Patient Care STDS*, 15(1), 41–51.

European Commission. (2022). Communication from the Commission to the European Parliament, the Council, the European Economic and Social Committee and the Committee on Regions on the EU strategy on combatting trafficking in human beings 2021–2025. Brussels, 14.4.2021 COM(2021) 171 Final. https://www.google.com/url?q=https:// eur-lex.europa.eu/legal-content/EN/TXT/PDF/?uri%3DCELEX:52021DC0171%26fr om%3DEN&sa=D&source=docs&ust=1674111994656852&usg=AOvVaw3tyjq-kScPD _84ltvwHR9r

Fairbanks, R. P, II. (2009). *How it works: Recovering citizens in post-welfare Philadelphia*. University of Chicago Press.

Farkas, M. A., & Miller, G. (2007). Reentry and reintegration: Challenges faced by the families of convicted sex offenders. *Federal Sentencing Reporter*, 20(1): 88–92.

Farole, D. J. (2009). Problem solving and the American Bench. *The Justice System Journal*, 65(1), 50–59.

Farole, D. J., Puffett, N., Rempel, M., & Byrne, F. (2004). *Collaborative justice in conventional courts: Opportunities and barriers*. Center for Court Innovation. https://www .courtinnovation.org/sites/default/files/collaborativejustice.pdf

Fassin, D., & Rechtman, R. (2009). *The empire of trauma: An inquiry into the condition of victimhood*. Princeton University Press.

First Judicial District. (2020). *2019 Annual Report*. https://www.courts.phila.gov/pdf /report/2019-FirstJudicial-District-Annual-Report.pdf

Foa, E. B., Hembree, E. A., & Rothbaum, B. O. (2007). *Prolonged exposure therapy for PTSD: Emotional processing of traumatic experiences.* Oxford University Press.

Footer, K. H. A., Silberzahn, B. E., Tormohlen, K. N., & Sherman, S. G. (2016). Policing practices as a structural determinant for HIV among sex workers: A systematic review of empirical findings. *Journal of the International AIDS Society, 19*(Suppl 3), 1–13.

Fording, R. C., Soss, J., & Schram, S. F. (2011). *Disciplining the poor: Neoliberal paternalism and the persistent power of race.* University of Chicago Press.

Foucault, M. (1995). *Discipline and punish: The birth of the prison.* Vintage.

Franke, N. D., & Shdaimah, C. S. (2022). "I have different goals than you, we can't be a team": Navigating the tensions of a courtroom workgroup in a prostitution diversion program. *Ethics and Social Welfare, 16*(2), 193–205.

Fukushima, A. I., Gonzalez-Pons, K., Gezinski, L., & Clark, L. (2020). Multiplicity of stigma: Cultural barriers in anti-trafficking response. *International Journal of Human Rights in Healthcare, 13*(2), 125–142.

Garrett, P. M. (2019). What are we talking about when we talk about 'Neoliberalism'? *European Journal of Social Work, 22*(2), 188–200.

Gesser, N. (2022). "[Peers give] you hope that you can change too": Peers' helping relationships for women exiting street-based sex trade. *Ethics and Social Welfare, 16*(2), 151–168. https://doi.org.10.1080/17496535.2022.2033292

Gesser, N., & Shdaimah, C. S. (2021). "I'm doing everything right all over again": How women manage the prostitution exiting process over time. *Journal of Qualitative Criminal Justice & Criminology, 10*(4). https://doi.org/10.21428/88de04a1.e639c1ce

Gessler, P. (2023, January 20). Baltimore State's Attorney Ivan Bates to try Gordon Staron for murdering cellmate. *CBS News.* https://www.cbsnews.com/baltimore/news/baltimore-states-attorney-ivan-bates-to-try-gordon-staron-in-murder-of-cellmate-at-central-booking/

Gilliom, J. (2001). *Overseers of the poor: Surveillance, resistance, and the limits of privacy.* University of Chicago Press.

Global Health Justice Partnership. (2018). *Diversion from justice: A rights-based analysis of local "prostitution diversion programs" and their impacts on people in the sex sector in the United States.* Yale Law School and School for Public Health in cooperation with the Sex Workers Project of the Urban Justice Center.

Global Network of Sex Work Projects. (2017). *The impact of criminalisation on sex workers' vulnerability to HIV and violence.* https://www.nswp.org/sites/nswp.org/files/impact_of_criminalisation_pb_prf01.pdf

Goffman, E. (1963). *Stigma: Notes on the management of spoiled identity.* Simon & Schuster.

Gordon, L. (1994). *Pitied but not entitled: Single mothers and the history of welfare, 1890–1935.* Free Press.

Gradus, J. D. (2013). *Epidemiology of PTSD.* National Center for PTSD, U.S. Department of Veterans Affairs. https://www.mentalhealth.va.gov/coe/cih-visn2/Documents/Provider_Education_Handouts/Epidemiology_of_PTSD_Version_3.pdf

Gruber, A., Cohen, A. J., & Mogulescu, K. (2016). Penal welfare and the new human trafficking intervention courts. *Florida Law Review, 68*(5), 1333–1402.

Hail-Jares, K., Paquette, C., & Le Neveu, M. (2017). Meeting the new neighbors: A case study on gentrification and sex work in Washington, D.C. In K. Hail-Jares, C. S. Shdaimah, & C. S. Leon (Eds.), *Challenging perspectives on street-based sex work* (pp. 51–77). Temple University Press.

Hankel, J., Brown, K., Dewey, S., & McKinnon, C. (2019). The difference a job makes: Licit and illicit work experiences and aspirations at a transitional housing facility for women leaving the sex industry. *Women & Criminal Justice, 29*(2), 98–111.

Hankel, J., Dewey, S., & Martinez, N. (2016). Women exiting street-based sex work: Correlations between ethno-racial identity, number of children, and violent experiences. *Journal of Evidence-Informed Social Work, 13*(4), 412–424.

Hartman, K. (n.d.). *Project Dawn*. Kumi & Bill Martin First Edition Initiative. People's Light Theatre.

Hasenfeld, Y. (1983). *Human service organizations*. Prentice Hall.

Hasenfeld, Y. (2000). Organizational forms as moral practices: The case of welfare departments. *Social Service Review, 74*(3), 329–351.

Haskins, P. A. (2019). *Problem-solving courts: Fighting crime by treating the offender*. National Institutes of Justice. https://www.ojp.gov/pdffiles1/nij/252735.pdf

Herman, J. L. (1992). Complex PTSD: A syndrome in survivors of prolonged and repeated trauma. *Journal of Traumatic Stress, 5*, 377–391.

Heydebrand, W., & Seron, C. (1990). *Rationalizing justice: The political economy of federal district courts*. State University of New York Press.

Hill, A. (2014). Demanding victims: The sympathetic shift in British prostitution policy. In C. R. Showden & S. Majic (Eds.), *Negotiating sex work: Unintended consequences of policy and activism* (pp. 77–98). University of Minnesota Press.

Hora, P. F., Schma, W. G., & Rosenthal, J. T. A. (1999). Therapeutic jurisprudence and the drug treatment court movement: Revolutionizing the criminal justice system's response to drug abuse and crime in America. *Notre Dame Law Review, 74*(2), 439–538.

Human Rights Watch. (2012, July 19). *Sex workers at risk: Condoms as evidence of prostitution in four U.S. cities*. https://www.hrw.org/report/2012/07/19/sex-workers-risk/condoms-evidence-prostitution-four-us-cities

Human Rights Watch. (2019, August 7). *Why sex work should be decriminalized*. https://www.hrw.org/news/2019/08/07/why-sex-work-should-be-decriminalized

Karandikar, S., Casassa, K., Knight, L., España, M., & Kagotho, N. (2022b). "I am almost a breadwinner for my family": Exploring the manifestation of agency in sex workers' personal and professional contexts. *Affilia: Journal of Women and Social Work, 37*(1), 26–41. https://journals.sagepub.com/doi/10.1177/08861099211022717

Karandikar, S., Knight, L., Casassa, K., España, M., & Kagotho, N. (2022a). Economic considerations of migrant female sex workers in India. *Sexuality & Culture, 26*, 853–877. https://doi.org/10.1007/s12119-021-09921-x

Kaufman, G. (1996). *The psychology of shame: Theory and treatment of shame-based syndromes*. Springer.

Kessler, R. C., Berglund, P., Delmer, O., Jin, R., Merikangas, K. R., & Walters, E. E. (2005). Lifetime prevalence and age-of-onset distributions of *DSM-IV* disorders in the National Comorbidity Survey Replication. *Archives of General Psychiatry, 62*(6), 593–602.

Kilmer, A. (2016). "I'm just trying to fit back in": The role of social bonds, stigma, and legal consciousness on the reentry experiences of recently incarcerated adults (Publication No. 10157850) [Doctoral dissertation, University of Delaware]. ProQuest Dissertations & Theses Global.

Kinney, E. (2017). Policing, protectionism, and prevention: Prostitution, sexual delinquency, and the politics of victimhood in Thai and American antitrafficking campaigns. In K. Hail-Jares, C. S. Shdaimah, & C. S. Leon (Eds.), *Challenging perspectives on street-based sex work* (pp. 51–77). Temple University Press.

Knesset. (2022, July 6). Bill for regulating activity of community courts in Israel passes final readings. *Knesset News*. https://main.knesset.gov.il/EN/News/PressReleases/Pages/press6722w.aspx

Koegler, E. (2014). Specialized Prostitution Diversion Program, Baltimore City, Maryland. On file with the authors.

Koegler, E., Preble K. M., Cimino, A. N., Stevens, J. E., & Diehl, S. (2020). Examining recidivism in a prostitution diversion program. *International Journal of Offender Therapy and Comparative Criminology, 64*(2–3), 232–248. https://doi.org/10.1177/0306624X19866115

Krueger, R. A. (1994). *Focus groups: A practical guide for applied research* (2nd ed.). Sage Publications.

Krüsi, A., Pacey, K., Bird, L., Taylor, C., Chettiar, J., Allan, S., Bennett, D., Montaner, J., Kerr, T., & Shannon, K. (2014). Criminalisation of clients: Reproducing vulnerabilities for violence and poor health among street-based sex workers in Canada—a qualitative study. *BMJ Open, 4*, 1–10. http://doi.org/10.1136/bmjopen-2014-005191

Kurtz, S. P., Surratt, H. L., Kiley, M. C., & Inciardi, J. A. (2005). Barriers to health and social services for street-based sex workers. *Journal of Health Care for the Poor and Underserved, 16*(2), 345–361.

Lara-Millán, A., & Van Cleve, N. G. (2017). Interorganizational utility of welfare stigma in the criminal justice system. *Criminology, 55*(1), 59–84.

Lazarus, L., Deering, K., Nabess, R., Gibson, K., Tyndall, M., & Shannon, K. (2012). Occupational stigma as a primary barrier to health care for street-based sex workers in Canada. *Culture, Health & Sexuality, 14*(2), 139–150.

LeBel, T. P. (2012). Invisible stripes? Formerly incarcerated persons' perceptions of stigma. *Deviant Behavior, 33*(2), 89–107.

Lemert, E. M. (1951). *Social pathology: A systematic approach to the theory of sociopathic behavior.* McGraw-Hill.

Lens, V. (2005). Bureaucratic disentitlement: Are fair hearings the cure? *Georgetown Journal on Poverty Law and Policy 12*, 13–54.

Lens, V. (2009). Confronting government after welfare reform: Moralists, reformers, and narratives of (ir)responsibility at administrative fair hearings. *Law & Society Review, 43*(3), 563–592.

Leon, C. S. (2011). *Sex fiends, perverts, and pedophiles: Understanding sex crime policy in America.* New York University Press.

Leon, C. S., & Kilmer, A. R. (2022). "Secondary registrants": A new conceptualization of the spread of community control. *Punishment & Society*, advance online publication. https://doi.org/10.1177/14624745221094255

Leon, C., & Shdaimah, C. S. (2012). JUSTifying scrutiny: State power in prostitution diversion programs. *Journal of Poverty, 16*(3), 250–273.

Leon, C., & Shdaimah, C. S. (2019). "We'll take the tough ones": Expertise in problem-solving justice. *New Criminal Law Review, 22*(4), 587–605.

Leon, C., & Shdaimah, C. (2021). Targeted sympathy in "whore court": Criminal justice actors' perceptions of prostitution diversion programs. *Law & Policy, 43*, 126–148.

Lewis, H. B. (1971). *Shame and guilt in neurosis.* International Universities Press.

Lewis, J. (2010). Shifting the focus: Restorative justice and sex work. *Canadian Journal of Criminology and Criminal Justice, 52*, 285–301.

Li, W., & Mahajan, I. (2021, September 1). Police say demoralized officers are quitting in droves. Labor data says no. *The Marshall Project*, published in partnership with *Time*.

https://www.themarshallproject.org/2021/09/01/police-say-demoralized-officers-are
-quitting-in-droves-labor-data-says-no

Lilley, T. G., Leon, C. S., & Bowler, A. E. (2020). The same old arguments: Tropes of race and class in the history of prostitution from the Progressive Era to the present. *Social Justice, 46*(4), 31–51.

Link, B. G., Yang, L. H., Phelan, J. C., & Collins, P. Y. (2004). Measuring mental illness stigma. *Schizophrenia Bulletin, 30*(3): 511–541.

Lipsky, M. (1971). Street-level bureaucracy and the analysis of urban reform. *Urban Affairs Quarterly, 6*(4), 391–409.

Lipsky, M. (1980). *Street-level bureaucracy: Dilemmas of the individual in public services.* Russell Sage Foundation.

Lobasz, J. K. (2018). *Constructing human trafficking: Evangelicals, feminists, and an unexpected alliance.* Springer.

Lowman, J. (2000). Violence and the outlaw status of (street) prostitution in Canada. *Violence Against Women 6*(9): 987–1011.

Lutnick, A., & Cohan, D. (2009). Criminalization, legalization or decriminalization of sex work: What female sex workers say in San Francisco, USA. *Reproductive Health Matters, 17*(34), 38–46.

Lynch, M. (2017). The situated actor and the production of punishment: Toward an empirical social psychology of criminal procedure. In *The New Criminal Justice Thinking.* NYU Press.

Lyons, T., Krüsi, A., Pierre, L., Small, W., & Shannon, K. (2017). The impact of construction and gentrification on an outdoor trans sex work environment: Violence, displacement, and policing. *Sexualities, 20*(8), 881–903.

Ma, P. H. X., Chan, Z. C. Y., & Loke, A. Y. (2018). A systematic review of the attitudes of different stakeholders towards prostitution and their implications. *Sexuality Research and Social Policy, 15*, 231–241.

Mackinem, M. B., & Higgins, P. (2007). Tell me about the test: The construction of truth and lies in drug court. *Journal of Contemporary Ethnography, 36*(3), 223–251.

MacKinnon, K. (2004). Pornography as trafficking. *Michigan Journal of International Law, 26*, 993–1012.

Majic, S. (2015). "I'm just a woman. But I've never been a victim": Re-conceptualizing prostitution policy through individual narratives. *Journal of Women, Politics & Policy, 36*(4), 365–387.

Månsson, S., & Hedin, U. (1999). Breaking the Matthew effect—On women leaving prostitution. *International Journal of Social Welfare, 8*(1), 67–77.

María-Ríos, C. E., & Morrow, J. D. (2020). Mechanisms of shared vulnerability to post-traumatic stress disorders and substance use disorders. *Frontiers in Behavioral Neuroscience, 14*(6). https://doi.org/10.3389/fnbeh.2020.00006

Maynard-Moody, S., & Musheno, M. (2003). *Cops, teachers, counselors: Stories from the front lines of public service.* University of Michigan Press.

McCaghy, C. H., & Hou, C. (1994). Family affiliation and prostitution in a cultural context: Career onsets of Taiwanese prostitutes. *Archives of Sexual Behavior, 23*(3), 251–265.

McCorkel, J. (2013). *Breaking women: Gender, race, and the new politics of imprisonment.* New York University Press.

McCoy, C. (2003). The politics of problem-solving: An overview of the origins and development of therapeutic courts. *American Criminal Law Review, 40*, 1513–1534.

McLellan, A. T., Luborsky, L., Woody, G. E., & O'Brien, C. P. (1980). An improved diagnostic evaluation instrument for substance abuse patients: The Addiction Severity Index. *Journal of Nervous and Mental Disease, 168*, 26–33.

Melrose, M. (2006). Trying to make a silk purse from a sow's ear? A comment on the government's prostitution strategy. *Safer Communities, 5*(2), 4–13.

Millan-Alanis, J. M., Carranza-Navarro, F., de León-Gutiérrez, H., Leyva-Camacho, P. C., Guerrero-Medrano, A. F., Barrera, F. J., Garza Lopez, L. E., & Saucedo-Uribe, E. (2021). Prevalence of suicidality, depression, post-traumatic stress disorder, and anxiety among female sex workers: A systematic review and meta-analysis. *Archives of Women's Mental Health, 24*(6), 867–879.

Mirchandani, R. (2005). What's so special about specialized courts? The state and social change in Salt Lake City's Domestic Violence Court. *Law & Society Review, 39*(2), 379–417.

Moses, D. J., Reed, B. G., Mazelis, R., & D'Ambrosio, B. (2003). Creating trauma services for women with co-occurring disorders: Experiences from the SAMHSA Women with Alcohol, Drug Abuse, and Mental Health Disorder who have Histories of Violence Study. https://www.researchgate.net/publication/252171592_Creating_Trauma_Services_for_Women_with_Co-Occurring_Disorders

Mueller, D. (2012). *Treatment courts and court-affiliated diversion projects for prostitution in the United States.* Chicago Coalition for the Homeless. https://www.issuelab.org/resources/14135/14135.pdf

Mueller, D. (2022, July 14). *Navigating boundaries and managing risk in police encounters among women who trade sex on the streets* [Conference presentation]. Annual Meeting of the Law & Society Association, Lisbon, Portugal.

Muldoon, K., Deering, K., Feng, C., Shoveller, J., & Shannon, K. (2015). Sexual relationship power and intimate partner violence among sex workers with non-commercial intimate partners in a Canadian setting. *AIDS Care: Psychological & Socio-Medical Aspects of AIDS/HIV, 27*(4), 512–519.

Muraresku, L. (2017). "Just to be there": A probation officer's reflection on Project Dawn Court. In K. Hail-Jares, C. Shdaimah, and C. Leon (Eds.), *Challenging perspectives on street-based sex work* (pp. 41–50). Temple University Press.

Murtha, T. (2010, August 3). A new dawn: Philly court uses compassion to fight prostitution. *Philadelphia Weekly.* http://www.philadelphiaweekly.com/news-and-opinion/cover-story/A-New-Dawn-Philly-Court-Uses-Compassion-to-Fight-Prostitution.html?utm_source=feedburner&utm_medium=feed&utm_campaign=Feed%3A+PhillyWeekly+%28PhiladelphiaWeekly.com%29

Musto, J. (2016). *Control and protect: Collaboration, carceral protection, and domestic sex trafficking in the United States.* University of California Press.

Nathanson, D. L. (1992). *Shame and pride.* W.W. Norton.

National Association of Drug Court Professionals. (2021). *Incentives and sanctions.* National Drug Court Institute. https://www.ndci.org/resource/training/incentives-and-sanctions/

National Drug Court Resource Center. (2016). Incentives and sanctions. http://www.ndcrc.org/content/list-incentives-and-sanctions

Nelson, M. S., Gabbidon, S. L., & Boisvert, D. (2015). Philadelphia area residents' views on the disproportionate representation of Blacks and Hispanics in the criminal justice system. *Journal of Crime and Justice, 38*(2), 270–290. https://doi.org/10.1080/0735648X.2014.882268

New York State Unified Court System, Office for Justice Initiatives. (n.d.). *Human traf-ficking intervention courts.* https://ww2.nycourts.gov/courts/problem_solving/htc/courts.shtml

Nolan, J. L. (2001). *Reinventing justice: The American drug court movement.* Princeton University Press.

North, A. (2019, August 2). The movement to decriminalize sex work, explained. *Vox.* https://www.vox.com/2019/8/2/20692327/sex-work-decriminalization-prostitution-new-york-dc

O'Brien, E. (2013). Ideal victims in human trafficking awareness campaigns. In K. Carrington, M. Ball, E. O'Brien, & J. Tauri (Eds.), *Crime, justice, and social democracy: International perspectives* (pp. 315–326). Palgrave Macmillan.

O'Brien, E. (2021). *Challenging the human trafficking narrative: Victims, villains and heroes.* Routledge.

O'Connell Davidson, J. (1998). *Prostitution, power, and freedom.* University of Michigan Press.

Office of the State's Attorney for Baltimore City. (2022, March 16). State's Attorney Mosby shares steps to undo racial inequities in the criminal justice system, reaffirming the office's continued commitment to racial justice [Press release]. https://www.stattorney.org/media-center/press-releases/2522-state-s-attorney-mosby-shares-steps-to-undo-systemic-racial-disparities-in-the-criminal-justice-system

O'Hear, M. M. (2009). Rethinking drug courts: Restorative justice as a response to racial injustice. *Stanford Law & Policy Review, 20*(2), 101–137.

O'Keefe, K. (2006). *The Brooklyn Mental Health Court evaluation: Planning, implementation, courtroom dynamics, and participant outcomes.* Center for Court Innovation. https://www.courtinnovation.org/publications/brooklyn-mental-health-court-evaluation-planning-implementation-courtroom-dynamics-and

Orr, C. H., Hall, J. W., Reimer, N. L., Mallett, E. A., O'Dowd, K., & Frazer, A. C. (2009). *America's problem-solving courts: The criminal costs for treatment and the case for reform.* National Association of Criminal Defense Lawyers. https://www.nacdl.org/Document/AmericasProblemSolvingCourtsCriminalCostsofTreatme

Oselin, S. S. (2014). *Leaving prostitution: Getting out and staying out of sex work.* New York University Press.

Oselin, S. S., Hail-Jares, K., & Kushida, M. (2022). Different strolls, different worlds? Gentrification and its impact on outdoor sex work. *Social Problems, 69*(1), 282–291. https://doi.org/10.1093/socpro/spaa056

Padgett, D. K. (2017). Qualitative methods in social work research. (3rd ed.) Sage Publications.

Pager, D. (2003). The mark of a criminal record. *American Journal of Sociology, 108*(5), 937–975.

Paik, L. (2006). Organizational interpretations of drug test results. *Law & Society Review, 40*(4), 931–962.

Paik, L. (2009). Maybe he's depressed: Mental illness as a mitigating factor for drug offender accountability. *Law and Social Inquiry, 34*(3), 569–602.

Parkinson, S., & Whiter, C. (2016). Exploring art therapy group practice in early intervention psychosis. *International Journal of Art Therapy, 21*(3), 116–127. https://doi.org/10.1080/17454832.2016.1175492

Parmanand, S. (2022). The many faces of care: A comparative analysis of anti-trafficking approaches to domestic work and sex work in the Philippines. *Ethics and Social Welfare, 16*(2), 129–143. https://doi.org/10.1080/17496535.2022.2070234

People's Light. (2022). *Project Dawn, 2017.* https://www.peopleslight.org/about/new-plays -projects/new-play-frontiers/project-dawn-2017/

Pfeffer, R., Ormachea, P., & Eagleman, D. (2018). Gendered outcomes in prostitution arrests in Houston, Texas. *Crime & Delinquency, 64*(12), 1538–1567.

Philadelphia District Attorney's Office. (n.d.). *Pre-trial diversion programs.* https://phl council.com/wp-content/uploads/2016/04/Pre-Trial-Diversion.Philadelphia.pdf

Philadelphia Housing Authority. (2020). *Admissions.* http://www.pha.phila.gov/housing /admissions.aspx

Philadelphia Reinvestment Fund. (2017). *Philadelphia's middle neighborhoods: Demographic and market differences by race, ethnicity and nation of origin.* https://www.re investment.com/wp-content/uploads/2017/06/ReinvestmentFund-Philadelphia-Middle -Neighborhoods-Brief.pdf

Phillipson, R. (1992). *Linguistic imperialism.* Oxford University Press.

Phoenix, J. (1999). Prostitutes, ponces and poncing: Making sense of violence. In J. Seymour & P. Bagguley (Eds.), *Relating intimacies. Explorations in sociology. British Sociological Association Conference Volume Series.* Palgrave Macmillan.

Platt, L., Grenfell, P., Meiksin, R., Elmes, J., Sherman S. G, Sanders, T., Mwangi, P., & Crago, A-L. (2018) Associations between sex work laws and sex workers' health: A systematic review and meta-analysis of quantitative and qualitative studies. *PLOS Medicine, 15*(12), e1002680.

Porter, R., Rempel, R., & Mansky, A. (2010). *What makes a court problem-solving: Universal performance indicators for problem-solving justice.* Center for Court Innovation. https://www.courtinnovation.org/sites/default/files/What_Makes_A_Court_P _S.pdf

Portillo, S., & Rudes, D. S. (2014). Construction of justice at the street level. *Annual Review of Law and Social Science, 10,* 321–334.

Powell, K. (2021, July 21). *A conversation with Catharine A. MacKinnon: Prostitution as sex work or sexual exploitation.* Council on Foreign Relations. https://www.cfr.org /blog/conversation-catharine-mackinnon-prostitution-sex-work-or-sexual-exploita tion

Quinn, M. (2000). Whose team am I on anyway? Musings of a public defender about drug treatment court practice. *New York University Law Review, 26,* 37–75. https://papers .ssrn.com/sol3/papers.cfm?abstract_id=3233861

Quinn, M. C. (2006). Revisiting Anna Moskowitz Kross's critique of New York City's Women's Court: The continued problem of solving the problem of prostitution with specialized courts. *Fordham Urban Law Journal, 33,* 675–676.

Quirouette, M., Hannah-Moffat, K., Maurutto, P. (2016). A precarious place: Housing and clients of Specialized Courts. *The British Journal of Criminology, 56* (2), 370–388. https:// doi.org/10.1093/bjc/azv050

Radhakrishnan, S., & Solari, C. (2015). Empowered women, failed patriarchs: Neoliberalism and global gender anxieties. *Sociology Compass, 9*(9), 784–802.

Rapp, L. A. (2012). Women in romantic relationships with convicted sex offenders (Publication No. 3498536) [Doctoral dissertation, University of Delaware]. ProQuest Dissertations & Theses Global.

Red Umbrella Fund. (2014). *Criminal, victim, or workers: The effect of human trafficking intervention courts on adults charged with prostitution-related offenses.* https://www .nswp.org/sites/nswp.org/files/RedUP-NYHTIC-FINALweb.pdf

Red Umbrella Fund. (n.d.). *Resources for sex workers (links).* https://www.redumbrella fund.org/sex-workers-rights/resources/

Reno, R., Karandikar, S., McCloskey, R. J., & España, M. (2020). Structural vulnerabilities and breastfeeding among female sex workers in Mumbai. *Matern Child Nutrition*, *25*(1), 66–71.

Roe-Sepowitz, D., Gallagher, J., Hickle, K. E., Pérez Loubert, M., & Tutelman, J. (2014). Project ROSE: An arrest alternative for victims of sex trafficking and prostitution. *Journal of Offender Rehabilitation*, *53*(1), 57–74.

Roe-Sepowitz, D. E., Hickle, K. E., & Cimino, A. (2012). The impact of abuse history and trauma symptoms on successful completion of a prostitution-exiting program. *Journal of Human Behavior in the Social Environment*, *22*(1), 65–77.

Rosen, E., & Venkatesh, S. A. (2008). A "perversion" of choice: Sex work offers just enough in Chicago's urban ghetto. *Journal of Contemporary Ethnography*, *37*(4), 417–441.

Rowen, J. (2020). Worthy of justice: A veterans treatment court in practice. *Law & Policy*, *42*(1), 78–100.

Saldaña, J. (2009). *The coding manual for qualitative researchers*. Sage Publications.

SAMHSA awards more than $38.2 million to help expand adult drug treatment courts. (2009, October 2). SAMHSA News Release. http://www.samhsa.gov/newsroom/advisories/0910024929.aspx

Samuel Centre for Social Connectedness. (2018, May 4). *The stigmatization behind sex work*. https://www.socialconnectedness.org/the-stigmatization-behind-sex-work/

Sandelowski, M. (2000). Whatever happened to qualitative description? *Research in Nursing and Health*, *23*, 334–340.

Sanders, T. (2004). The risks of street prostitution: Punters, police, and protesters. *Urban Studies*, *41*(9), 1703–1717.

Sanders, T. (2005). *Sex work: A risky business*. Routledge.

Sandfort, J.R., Kalil, A., & Gottschalk, J.A. (1999). The mirror has two faces: Welfare clients and front-line workers view policy reforms. *Journal of Poverty*, *3*(3), 71–91.

Sarat, A. (1990). "The law is all over": Power, resistance, and the legal consciousness of the welfare poor. *Yale Journal of Law and the Humanities*, *2*, 343–379.

Schwartzman, P. (2021, April 10). In crime-battered Baltimore, a halt to some drug and prostitution prosecutions is causing fresh anxiety. *Washington Post*. https://www.washingtonpost.com/local/md-politics/baltimore-crime-mosby-misdemeanors/2021/04/10/730a679c-9650-11eb-962b-78c1d8228819_story.html

Schwarz, C. (2022). Theorising human trafficking through slow violence. *Feminist Theory*, early online publication, 1–20. https://doi.org/10.1177/14647001211062731

Scott, J. (1985). *Weapons of the weak: Everyday forms of peasant resistance*. Yale University Press.

Scoular, J. (2010). What's law got to do with it? How and why law matters in the regulation of sex work. *Journal of Law and Society*, *37*(1), 12–39.

Shapiro, F. (2018). *Eye Movement Desensitization and Reprocessing (EMDR): Basic principles, protocols, and procedures* (3rd ed.). Guilford Press.

Shdaimah, C. S. (2010). Taking a stand in a not-so-perfect world: What's a critical supporter of problem-solving courts to do? *University of Maryland Law Journal of Race, Religion, Gender & Class*, *10*(1), 89–111.

Shdaimah, C. S. (2015). Connecting and disconnecting: Losses from leaving street-based sex work. In C. Walters & J. L. M. McCoyd (Eds.), *Loss and grief across the life span* (2nd ed., pp. 241–245). Springer.

Shdaimah, C. S. (2018). Prostitution/human trafficking courts: Policy frontline as fault line. *Texas Law Review*. Online Edition, 96, 14–22.

Shdaimah, C. (2019). Prostitution diversion programs. In F. P. Bernat, K. Frailing, L. Gelsthorpe, S. Kethenani, & L. Pasko (Eds.), *The encyclopedia of women and crime* (Vols. 1–3). Wiley-Blackwell. https://onlinelibrary.wiley.com/doi/10.1002/9781118929803.ewac0423

Shdaimah, C. (2020). *Problem-solving courts, street level bureaucrats, and clients as policy agents in a prostitution diversion program.* Qualitative Data Repository. QDR Main Collection, vol. 1. https://doi.org/10.5064/F6C8VUHP

Shdaimah, C. S., & Bailey-Kloch, M. (2014). Can you help me with that instead of putting me in jail? Participant perspectives on Baltimore City's Specialized Prostitution Diversion program. *Justice System Journal, 35*(3), 287–300.

Shdaimah, C. S., Franke, N., Becker, T., & Leon, C. (in press). Of house and home: The meanings of housing for women engaged in criminalised street-based sex work. *Anti-Trafficking Review.*

Shdaimah, C. S., Kaufman, B. R., Bright, C. L, & Flower, S. M. (2014). Neighborhood assessment of prostitution as a pressing social problem and appropriate responses: Results from a community survey. *Criminal Justice Policy Review, 25*(3), 275–297.

Shdaimah, C., & Leon, C. (2015). "First and foremost they're survivors": Selective manipulation, resilience and assertion among prostitute women. *Feminist Criminology, 10*(4), 326–347.

Shdaimah, C., & Leon, C. (2016). Relationships among stigmatized women engaged in street-level prostitution: Coping with stigma and stigma management. *Studies in Law, Politics, and Society, 71*, 43–62.

Shdaimah, C. S., & Leon, C. (2018). Whose knowledges? Moving away from damage-centred research in studies with women in street-based sex work. *Criminological Encounters 1*(1). https://criminologicalencounters.org/index.php/crimenc/article/view/CE18010103

Shdaimah, C., & McGarry, B. (2018). Social workers' use of moral entrepreneurship to enact professional ethics in the field: Case studies from the social justice profession. *British Journal of Social Work, 48*(1), 21–36.

Shdaimah, C. S., & Wiechelt, S. A. (2012a). Converging on empathy: Perspectives on Baltimore City's Specialized Prostitution Diversion Program. *Women and Criminal Justice, 22*(2), 156–173.

Shdaimah, C. S., & Wiechelt, S. A. (2012b). Crime and compassion: Women in prostitution at the intersection of criminality and victimization. *International Review of Victimology, 19*(1), 23–35.

Shdaimah, C., & Wiechelt, S. (2017). Eliciting street-based sex worker perspectives to inform prostitution policy development. *Journal of Policy Practice, 16*(4), 351–368.

Sherman, S. G., Footer, K., Illangaskare, S., Clark, E., Pearson, E., & Decker, M. R. (2015). "What makes you think you have special privileges because you are a police officer?" A qualitative exploration of police's role in the risk environment of female sex workers. *AIDS Care, 27*(4), 473–480.

Shively, M., Jalbert, S. K., Kling, R., Rhodes, W., Finn, P., Flygare, C., Tierney, L., Hunt, D., Squires, C., Dyous, C., & Wheeler, K. (2008). *Final report on the evaluation of the First Offender Prostitution Program: Report summary.* National Institute of Justice, Office of Research and Evaluation. www.ncjrs.gov/pdffiles1/nij/grants/222451.pdf

Showden, C. (2011). *Choices women make: Agency in domestic violence, assisted reproduction, and sex work.* University of Minnesota Press.

Simon, W. H. (1983). Legality, bureaucracy, and class in the welfare system. *Yale Law Journal, 92*, 1198–1269.

Singer, S. I., Fagan, J., & Liberman, A. (2000). Reproduction of juvenile justice in criminal court: A case study of New York's juvenile offender law. In J. Fagan & F. E. Zimring (Eds.), *The changing borders of juvenile justice: Transfer of adolescents to the criminal court* (pp. 353–375). University of Chicago Press.

Singh, R. (2017). "Setting a good example for the ladies": Example setting as a technique of penal reform in specialized prostitution court. *British Journal of Criminology, 58*(3), 569–587. https://doi.org/10.1093/bjc/azx037

Skilbrei, M., & Holmström, C. (2014). *Prostitution policy in the Nordic region: Ambiguous sympathies.* Routledge.

Ślęzak, I. (2015). The influence of significant others on the course of the process of leaving sex work. *Przeglad Socjologii Jakosciowej, 11*(3), 132–153.

Sloss, C. M., Harper, G. W., & Budd, K. S. (2004). Street sex work and mothering. *Journal of the Motherhood Initiative for Research and Community Involvement, 6*(2).

Smith, V. C. (2017). Substance-abusing female offenders as victims: Chronological sequencing of pathways into the criminal justice system. *Victims and Offenders, 12*(1), 113–137.

Smoyer, A. B., Keene, D. E., Oyola, M., & Hampton, A. C. (2021). Ping-pong housing: Women's post-incarceration trajectories. *Affilia: Journal of Women and Social Work, 36*(3), 336–356.

Stamm, B. H., Rudolph, J. M., Dewane, S., Gaines, N., Gorton, K., Paul, G., McNeil, F., Bowen, G., & Ercolano, M. (1996). Psychometric review of Stressful Life Experiences Screening. In B. H. Stamm (Ed.), *Measurement of stress, trauma, and adaptation.* Sidran Press.

State of Maryland Department of Public Safety and Correctional Services Division of Pretrial Detention and Services (n.d.), Specialized Prostitution Diversion Program directives. On file with the authors.

Steele, A., & Terruso, J. (2021, May 15). Kensington symbolizes the promise and peril of Philly DA Larry Krasner's policies as he seeks reelection. *Philadelphia Inquirer.* https://www.inquirer.com/politics/election/kensington-philadelphia-da-larry-krasner-reelection-20210515.html

Stolberg, S.G., & Bidgood, J. (2016). Some women won't "ever again" report a rape in Baltimore. *The New York Times.* https://www.nytimes.com/2016/08/12/us/baltimore-police-sexual-assault-gender-bias.html

Strangio, C. (2017). Project ROSE: A case study on diversion, sex work, and constitutionality. In K. Hail-Jares, C. S. Shdaimah, & C. S. Leon (Eds.), *Challenging perspectives on street-based sex work* (pp. 257–281). Temple University Press.

Swidler, A. (2013). *Talk of love: How culture matters.* University of Chicago Press.

Sykes, G. M., & Matza, D. (1957). Techniques of neutralization: A theory of delinquency. *American Sociological Review, 22*(6), 664–670.

Taxman, F. S., & Bouffard, J. (2002). Treatment inside the drug treatment court: The who, what, where, and how of treatment services. *Substance Use & Misuse, 37*(12–13), 1665–1687.

Toquinto, S. (2017). Pregnancy obscured: Street-based sex work and the experience of pregnancy. In K. Hail-Jares, C. S. Shdaimah, & C. S. Leon (Eds.), *Challenging perspectives on street-based sex work* (pp. 17–39). Temple University Press.

Tschoeke, S., Borbé, R., Steinert, T., & Bichescu-Burian, D. (2019). A systematic review of dissociation in female sex workers. *Journal of Trauma & Dissociation, 20*(2), 242–257.

TurnAround, Inc., & Specialized Prostitution Diversion Program. (n.d.). Screening women charged with prostitution for trafficking and service needs. On file with the authors.

Urban Displacement Project. (2021). *The housing precarity risk model.* https://www.ur
bandisplacement.org/maps/housing-precarity-risk-model/

U.S. Census Bureau. (n.d.a.). *Quick facts: Baltimore City, Maryland.* U.S. Department of
Commerce. https://www.census.gov/quickfacts/fact/table/baltimorecitymaryland
/INC110220

U.S. Census Bureau. (n.d.b.). *Quick facts: Philadelphia City, Pennsylvania.* U.S. Department of Commerce. https://www.census.gov/quickfacts/philadelphiacitypennsylvania

U.S. Department of Justice Civil Rights Division (2016, August 10). *Investigation of the
Baltimore City Police Department.* https://www.justice.gov/crt/file/883296/download

Valverde, M., & Mopas, M. (2004). Insecurity and the dream of targeted governance. In
W. Larner & W. Walters (Eds.), *Global governmentality: Governing international spaces*, (pp. 28, 233). Routledge.

Vance, C. S. (Ed.). (1984). *Pleasure and danger: Exploring female sexuality.* Routledge &
K. Paul.

van der Kolk, B. A. (2005). Developmental trauma disorder: Toward a rational diagnosis
for children with complex trauma histories. *Psychiatric Annals, 35,* 401–408.

Vella, V. (2022, May 23). As Philly prostitution cases dwindle to almost nothing, some
worry that sex workers won't get help. *Philadelphia Inquirer.* https://www.inquirer
.com/news/prostitution-legal-cases-philadelphia-sex-workers-programs-20220523
.html

Verona, E., Murphy, B., & Javdani, S. (2016). Gendered pathways: Violent childhood maltreatment, sex exchange, and drug use. *Psychology of Violence, 6*(1), 124–134.

Wahab, S. (2005). Navigating mixed-theory programs: Lessons learned from a prostitu-
tion-diversion project. *Affilia: Journal of Women and Social Work, 20*(2), 203–221.

Wahab, S. (2006). Evaluating the usefulness of a prostitution diversion project. *Qualitative Social Work, 5*(1), 67–92.

Wahab, S., & Panichelli, M. (2013). Ethical and human rights issues in coercive interventions with sex workers. *Affilia: Journal of Women and Social Work, 28*(4), 344–349.

Weathers, F. W., Huska, J. A., Keane, T. M. (1991). PCL-C for DSM-IV. National Center
for PTSD—Behavioral Science Division.

Weathers, F. W., Litz, B. T., Herman, D. S., Huska, J. A., & Keane, T. M. (1993). *The PTSD
Checklist (PCL): Reliability, validity, and diagnostic utility* [Conference presentation].
International Society for Traumatic Stress Studies, San Antonio, TX.

Weigel, R. (2017, September 26). We are kinda unbreakable. *Baltimore City Paper.* https://
www.baltimoresun.com/citypaper/bcpnews-we-are-kinda-unbreakable-20170926
-htmlstory.html

Weitzer, R. (2009). Sociology of sex work. *Annual Review of Sociology, 35,* 213–234.

Weitzer, R. (2010). The movement to criminalize sex work in the United States. *Journal
of Law and Society, 37*(1), 61–84.

Weitzer, R. (2013). Rethinking human trafficking. *Dialectical anthropology, 37*(2), 309–
312.

Weitzer, R. (2018). Resistance to sex work stigma. *Sexualities, 21*(5–6), 717–729.

Weitzer, R. (2021). Legal prostitution systems in Europe. In H. Nelen & D. Siegel, *Contemporary organized crime: Developments, challenges, and responses* (2nd ed., pp. 47–
66). Springer.

Westervelt, E. (2021, June 24). *Cops say low morale and department scrutiny are driving
them away from the job* [Radio broadcast]. NPR. https://www.npr.org/2021/06/24/100
9578809/cops-say-low-morale-and-department-scrutiny-are-driving-them-away
-from-the-job

White, L. (1990). Subordination, rhetorical skills, and Sunday shoes: Notes on the hearing of Mrs. G. *Buffalo Law Review, 38,* 1–58.

Whittle, T. N. (2017). *Constructing prisoner reentry service providers' roles and perceptions of law, justice and fairness* [Doctoral dissertation, Delaware State University]. https://research.paynecenter.org/desu_chess/22/

Wiechelt, S. A. (2014). Intersections between trauma and substance misuse: Implications for trauma-informed care. In S. L. Straussner (Ed.), *Clinical work with substance abusing clients* (3rd ed., pp. 179–201). Guilford Press.

Wiechelt, S. A., & Shdaimah, C. (2011). Trauma and substance abuse among women in prostitution: Implications for a specialized diversion program. *Journal of Forensic Social Work, 1*(1), 1–26.

Williams, M., Comartin, E. B., & Lytle, R. D. (2020). The politics of symbolic laws: State resistance to the allure of sex offender residence restrictions. *Law & Policy, 42*(3), 209–235.

Winick, B. J., & Wexler, D. B. (2003). *Judging in a therapeutic key: Therapeutic jurisprudence and the courts.* Carolina Academic Press.

Wolf, R. (2001). Management note: New strategies for an old profession: A court and a community combat a streetwalking epidemic. *The Justice System Journal, 22*(3), 348–359.

Wolf, R. (2007). *Principles of problem-solving justice.* Center for Court Innovation. https://www.courtinnovation.org/sites/default/files/Principles.pdf

Zeglin, R. (2014). Participation in prostitution: Associated outcomes within familial relationships. *Sexuality Research & Social Policy, 11*(1), 50–62.

Index

Corey S. Shdaimah is Daniel Thursz Distinguished Professor of Social Justice at the University of Maryland School of Social Work. She is the author of *Negotiating Justice: Progressive Lawyering, Low-Income Clients, and the Quest for Social Change*; coauthor of *Social Welfare Policy in a Changing World*, among other books; and the coeditor of *Challenging Perspectives on Street-Based Sex Work.*

Chrysanthi S. Leon is Professor of Sociology and Criminal Justice at the University of Delaware. She is the author of *Sex Fiends, Perverts, and Pedophiles: Understanding Sex Crime Policy in America* and coeditor of *Challenging Perspectives on Street-Based Sex Work.*

Shelly A. Wiechelt is Associate Professor and Associate Dean and Chair in the School of Social Work at the University of Maryland, Baltimore County. She is the coauthor of *Examining the Relationship between Trauma and Addiction.*

www.ingramcontent.com/pod-product-compliance
Lightning Source LLC
Chambersburg PA
CBHW071121280326
41935CB00010B/1084